Glossary of Generic Terms in Canada's Geographical Names

Glossaire des génériques en usage dans les noms géographiques du Canada

Terminology Bulletin 176

Bulletin de terminologie 176

Canadian Cataloguing in Publication Data

Main entry under title:

Glossary of generic terms in Canada's
geographical names = Glossaire des
génériques en usage dans les noms
géographiques du Canada.

(Bulletin de terminologie =
Terminology bulletin ; 176)
Text in English and French.
Co-published by Energy, Mines and
Resources Canada.
ISBN 0-660-53764-8

1. Toponymy—Dictionaries. 2. Names,
Geographical— Canada—Dictionaries.
3. English language— Dictionaries—
French. I. Canada. Dept. of the Secretary
of State of Canada. II. Canada. Energy,
Mines and Resources Canada.
III. Canada. Translation Bureau.
Terminology and Linguistic Services
Branch. IV. Title: Glossaire des
génériques en usage dans les noms
géographiques du Canada. V. Series:
Bulletin de terminologie (Canada.
Translation Bureau. Terminology and
Linguistic Services Branch) ; 176.

FC36.G56 1987   910.'014   C87-099400-XE
F1004.G56 1987

Données de catalogage avant publication (Canada)

Vedette principale au titre:

Glossary of generic terms in Canada's
geographical names = Glossaire des
génériques en usage dans les noms
géographiques du Canada.

(Bulletin de terminologie =
Terminology bulletin ; 176)
Texte en anglais et en français.
Publié en collab. avec Énergie, mines et
ressources Canada.
ISBN 0-660-53764-8

1. Toponymie—Dictionnaires anglais.
2. Noms géographiques—Canada—
Dictionnaires anglais. 3. Anglais
(Langue)—Dictionnaires français.
I. Canada. Secrétariat d'État du Canada.
II. Canada. Énergie, mines et ressources
Canada. III. Canada. Bureau des
traductions. Direction générale de la
terminologie et des services linguistiques.
IV. Titre: Glossaire des génériques en
usage dans les noms géographiques du
Canada. V. Collection: Bulletin de
terminologie (Canada. Bureau des
traductions. Direction générale
de la terminologie et des services
linguistiques) ; 176.

FC36.G56 1987   910.'014   C87-099400-XF
F1004.G56 1987

Table of Contents

Table des matières

Preface

It gives me considerable pleasure to endorse the *Glossary of Generic Terms in Canada's Geographical Names* as an invaluable tool for the improvement of communications within each of Canada's official languages as well as between the two.

In 1975, the Advisory Committee on Glaciological and Alpine Nomenclature recommended to the Canadian Permanent Committee on Geographical Names (CPCGN) that definitions of terminology used in geographical names should be compiled and widely distributed to promote a better understanding of the application of generics in use in Canada. The Glossary is a major step towards this goal. At the same time, it fulfils an important function of the CPCGN in furthering the coordination and consistency of geographical naming in the country. As the first authoritative publication on generics in use in Canada, the Glossary should prove most beneficial for teachers and students, as well as for cartographers and editors, both in Canada and abroad. It will also help promote a better understanding of the named landscape and cultural heritage of Canada.

Canada has played a prominent role in the standardization of geographical names at the international level. As the host of the Fifth United Nations Conference on the Standardization of Geographical Names being held in Montréal in 1987, I am recommending this glossary to the international community of toponymists, cartographers, terminologists and related specialists.

Préface

C'est avec grand plaisir que j'approuve la publication du *Glossaire des génériques en usage dans les noms géographiques du Canada;* outil de travail très précieux, il facilitera sans aucun doute la communication dans les deux langues officielles et entre les deux principaux groupes linguistiques du Canada.

En 1975, le Comité consultatif de la nomenclature glaciologique et alpine demandait au Comité permanent canadien des noms géographiques (CPCNG) d'inventorier les génériques utilisés dans les noms géographiques du Canada, de les définir et d'en circonscrire l'aire d'application, en vue d'une diffusion très large de cette information. Le présent glossaire permettra au CPCNG de coordonner et d'uniformiser l'établissement des noms géographiques au Canada. Premier ouvrage faisant autorité sur la question, il devrait être particulièrement utile aux enseignants et aux étudiants, ainsi qu'aux cartographes et aux éditeurs du Canada et d'ailleurs. Il contribuera également à faire mieux apprécier la géomorphologie et la culture du Canada.

Le Canada joue, à l'échelle internationale, un rôle de premier plan dans la normalisation des noms géographiques. À titre d'hôte de la cinquième conférence des Nations Unies sur la normalisation des noms géographiques, qui se tiendra à Montréal en 1987, j'aurai la fierté de présenter le Glossaire à des spécialistes du monde entier, en particulier à des toponymistes, à des cartographes et à des terminologues.

The members of the Advisory Committee on Glaciological and Alpine Nomenclature and those of the Translation Bureau's special terminology committee are to be congratulated on a fine piece of work.

J'ai donc tout lieu de me réjouir du travail magnifique qu'ont accompli les membres du Comité consultatif de la nomenclature glaciologique et alpine et ceux du comité de terminologie constitué spécialement par le Bureau des traductions; je tiens à féliciter chacun d'eux.

Le président du
Comité permanent canadien des noms géographiques,

Jean-Paul Drolet
Chairman
Canadian Permanent Committee on Geographical Names

Foreword

The publication of this *Glossary of Generic Terms in Canada's Geographical Names* is a joint effort of the Translation Bureau and the Canadian Permanent Committee on Geographical Names (CPCGN).

In recognition of the importance of maintaining accuracy in writing geographical names and in translating geographical terminology, the Bureau was designated a member of the reorganized CPCGN in 1961. The Bureau has continued to take an active part in the development of Canadian toponymic principles, procedures and policies over the past 25 years. It contributed extensively to this publication through the work of a multi-disciplinary committee of historians, geographers, linguists and terminologists.

This glossary of English and French generics is certain to become an important reference tool for translators, interpreters, terminologists and linguists. It draws attention to the multiple definitions that many generic terms have been given; it indicates similar terms which have acquired different meanings in English and French; and it provides some appropriate equivalents to use when translating texts from one official language to the other.

As well as publishing this glossary jointly with the CPCGN, the Bureau has entered all the material into its TERMIUM Bank, which will ensure wide dissemination of this information on geographical terminology through data bank exchanges both within Canada and abroad.

Avant-propos

Le Bureau des traductions et le Comité permanent canadien des noms géographiques (CPCNG) ont collaboré à la production du *Glossaire des génériques en usage dans les noms géographiques du Canada.*

Le Bureau est devenu membre du CPCNG en 1961; sa présence reflétait l'importance attachée à la précision dans la graphie et la traduction des noms géographiques. Au cours des 25 dernières années, il a pris une part active à l'élaboration des principes, des politiques et des méthodes de nomenclature toponymique au Canada. Il a apporté une large contribution à la rédaction du Glossaire, en participant aux travaux d'un comité multidisciplinaire regroupant des historiens, des géographes, des linguistes et des terminologues.

Ce glossaire bilingue occupera sans aucun doute une place de choix parmi les outils de travail des traducteurs, des interprètes, des terminologues et des linguistes, puisqu'il met de l'ordre dans les termes polysémiques, dénonce les faux amis et propose des équivalents à utiliser dans les traductions.

Le Glossaire, publié conjointement par le Bureau et le CPCNG, a été versé dans la banque TERMIUM, qui, par voie d'échanges de données avec les banques du Canada et celles d'autres pays, assurera une large diffusion de l'information qu'il contient.

I am personally pleased to see the publication of this glossary and highly recommend that it be consulted frequently to ensure consistent treatment of geographical terminology in English and French.

Je me réjouis personnellement de la publication de ce glossaire et je recommande vivement qu'on s'y réfère pour uniformiser la terminologie géographique en anglais et en français.

Le sous-secrétaire d'État adjoint
(Langues officielles et Traduction),

Alain Landry
Assistant Under Secretary of State
(Official Languages and Translation)

Introduction

The Advisory Committee on Glaciological and Alpine Nomenclature (ACGAN) was established in 1975 by the Canadian Permanent Committee on Geographical Names (CPCGN) to provide expert toponymic advice and technical interpretation of terrain and ice features in areas of permanent ice and mountain topography.

The Committee, which has expanded from its original six members, currently includes representatives from the CPCGN jurisdictions of British Columbia, Alberta, Yukon, Northwest Territories, Newfoundland and Environment Canada (Parks); technical experts from the Geological Survey of Canada, the Alpine Club of Canada, and the National Hydrology Research Institute; a member of the public with a long association with the Rocky Mountains; and both a member and the Secretary from the CPCGN Secretariat.

The main role of the Committee has been to advise the CPCGN members on the physical limits of glacial and alpine features. Early on, the ACGAN realized that this task could not be done properly if there was no consensus on the nature or identity of types of features, and no authoritative reference on Canadian generic terminology. Toponymists consulted British, American and French sources, such as L.D. Stamp's *A Glossary of Geographical Terms*, the American Geological Institute's *Glossary of Geology*, and P. George's *Dictionnaire de la géographie*. The ACGAN members considered it essential that generics be defined as

Introduction

En 1975, le Comité permanent canadien des noms géographiques (CPCNG) créait le Comité consultatif de la nomenclature glaciologique et alpine (CCNGA); il lui confiait le mandat de le conseiller sur des questions d'ordre toponymique et de lui fournir une interprétation des termes techniques désignant les formes du relief alpin et du modelé glaciaire.

Constitué de six membres à l'origine, le Comité comprend maintenant des représentants de provinces et d'organismes membres du CPCNG, c'est-à-dire la Colombie-Britannique, l'Alberta, le Yukon, les Territoires du Nord-Ouest, Terre-Neuve et Environnement Canada (Parcs); des experts techniques de la Commission géologique du Canada, du Club alpin du Canada et de l'Institut national de recherche en hydrologie; une citoyenne qui s'intéresse depuis longtemps aux montagnes Rocheuses, et un membre du Secrétariat du CPCNG. De plus, une personne du Secrétariat remplit les fonctions de secrétaire du Comité.

Le principal rôle du CCNGA est de conseiller les membres du CPCNG sur les limites physiques des formes du relief alpin et du modelé glaciaire. Pour mener cette tâche à bien, le Comité devait arrêter une définition des entités à partir d'une nomenclature des génériques vernaculaires qui fasse autorité. Les toponymistes n'avaient alors à leur disposition que des ouvrages britanniques, américains et français, comme le *Glossary of Geographical Terms* de L.D. Stamp, le *Glossary of Geology* de l'American Geological Institute et le *Dictionnaire de la géographie* de P. George. Les membres du CCNGA jugeaient cependant essentiel de défi-

they are used in Canada. Thus, one of the first major tasks that the ACGAN set itself was the preparation of a glossary of generics used in official Canadian geographical names.

Most geographical names contain a specific (e.g. "Kelligrews" in "Kelligrews Point") as well as a generic (e.g. "glacier" in "Tiedemann Glacier"). The generic identifies the type of feature being named.

Because the general public usually defines a geographical feature by its external appearance, the ACGAN decided that the Glossary should include descriptions of the visual characteristics of the landscape, but omit genetic information relating to the physical processes by which a feature was formed. Appropriate geomorphological generic terms are not always used in official geographical names. Therefore, the paucity of some more technical generics may not reflect the actual abundance in Canada of the features they designate. For example, the existence of few official names including the generic "esker" does not necessarily mean that there are few named eskers, but rather that some may be named using other terms descriptive of their physical form (e.g. "ridge").

At first, the ACGAN restricted itself to studying alpine and glaciological generics, but it soon became apparent that some terms, particularly those for water features, could not be properly described without reference to their use outside alpine areas.

nir les génériques tels qu'ils sont utilisés au Canada. Aussi une de ses premières tâches a-t-elle été d'établir un glossaire des génériques qui font partie des noms géographiques officiels du Canada.

La plupart des noms géographiques sont constitués d'un spécifique (comme «Orléans» dans «île d'Orléans») et d'un générique (comme «chenal» dans «chenal du Diable»). En règle générale, le générique indique le type d'entité désigné par le toponyme.

Étant donné que le profane nomme un élément géographique d'après son aspect extérieur, le CCNGA a jugé bon de décrire dans le Glossaire les formes du relief, mais d'exclure toute information relative à leur genèse. Le générique employé dans les toponymes n'est pas toujours le terme géomorphologique qui conviendrait en l'occurrence; aussi, la faible fréquence d'un terme scientifique dans les noms géographiques officiels n'est pas toujours un indice de la rareté, au Canada, de l'entité qu'il sert généralement à désigner. Par exemple, le fait qu'il y ait peu de noms officiels contenant le générique «esker» ne signifie pas nécessairement qu'il y ait peu d'eskers au Canada; certains eskers peuvent être désignés par un générique moins rigoureux sur le plan scientifique, qui en décrit l'aspect extérieur (par ex. «chaînon»).

Au début, le CCNGA limitait son étude aux génériques de la nomenclature alpine et glaciaire. Or, il s'est vite rendu compte qu'il ne pouvait définir adéquatement certains génériques, en particulier ceux qui désignent des plans d'eau, sans parler de leur emploi hors du domaine alpin. Il a donc résolu d'étendre ses

Thus, the Committee decided to consider all physical generics used in official geographical names across Canada. Later, a decision was made to include features which, although initially man-made, were subsequently perceived to be essentially natural (e.g. cutoff, dugway, reservoir and canal). Generics of undersea features have been included only where they designate near-shore phenomena; thus "shoal" is listed, but "seamount" is not.[1] Simple descriptive names (e.g. "Hens and Chickens" – the name of a group of rocks), because they contain no apparent generic, have been excluded from this compilation; so too have terms that are used with only a definite article (e.g. "The Key", "Le Repos"). In this glossary, no reference is made to the myriad of cultural generics (e.g. "road" or "barrage") used in Canada.

The purpose of this glossary is two-fold: first, to provide users with an indication of how generics of topographical features are applied in Canada and how this may vary across the country; second, to further the exchange of information between Canada's two official language groups by providing an authoritative source for possible equivalent generic terms in the other official language.

Definitions used here may differ slightly from those in federal and provincial gazetteers, particularly if they encompass significant regional variations in usage. For example, the published definitions of French generic classes ("entités") developed by the Commission de toponymie du Québec and standardized by the Office de la langue française have

recherches à tous les génériques utilisés dans les noms géographiques officiels. Par la suite, il a décidé d'y inclure des entités qui, bien qu'édifiées par l'homme, passent aujourd'hui pour des formations naturelles (par ex. certains passages, réservoirs et canaux). En ce qui concerne les noms d'entités sous-marines, le CCNGA n'a retenu que les formes du relief qui se rencontrent à proximité des côtes; ainsi, on trouvera dans le Glossaire le mot «haut-fond», mais non le terme «mont sous-marin».[1] Par ailleurs, il a exclu de son inventaire les noms descriptifs où le générique est sous-entendu (par ex. le nom «Hens and Chickens», qui désigne en fait un groupe de rochers), ainsi que les termes accompagnés uniquement d'un article défini (comme «The Key» ou «Le Repos»). Finalement, le CCNGA a écarté tous les génériques de nature culturelle (par ex. «road» ou «barrage») en usage au Canada.

Le Glossaire a deux objectifs : d'une part, circonscrire l'aire d'utilisation des génériques employés au Canada pour désigner des accidents de terrain, compte tenu des variations régionales; d'autre part, faciliter la communication entre les deux principaux groupes linguistiques du Canada, en indiquant les équivalents possibles des génériques dans l'autre langue officielle.

Les définitions que nous donnons ici peuvent différer légèrement de celles que proposent les répertoires toponymiques fédéraux et provinciaux, en particulier dans les cas où l'usage amène des variations d'une région à l'autre. Par exemple, les définitions

---

[1] A more complete listing of definitions of undersea generics is included in the "*Gazetteer of Undersea Feature Names 1983*", published by the Department of Fisheries and Oceans, Ottawa.

[1] Une liste plus complète des génériques désignant les entités sous-marines et de leurs définitions figure dans le glossaire intitulé *«Répertoire des noms d'entités sous-marines 1983»*, publié à Ottawa par le ministère des Pêches et des Océans.

sometimes been modified to include local variations of generics used by francophones in other parts of Canada. Some of the definitions listed in the English language column describe usage that differs from the standard found in British or American sources. Unconventional applications include, for example, the Canadian use of "desert", "savane" and "savannah".

Local or regional aspects of Canadian culture and heritage are illustrated by less common terms such as "blow-me-down", "buffalo jump", "pingo", "barachois" and "snye". Regional variations are seen in the preference for "brook" in the Atlantic Provinces and "creek" in the West, or for the use of "pond" in Newfoundland to designate features named "lake" elsewhere in the country. Changing times have made some usages obsolescent – "basin" for the bowl-shaped head of a valley in British Columbia, and "land" for a general area of country in the early days of Arctic exploration. Other generics (e.g. arête, mere, rivulet), although used informally, do not occur in any approved geographical names in Canada. Their omission from this list does not necessarily imply that they are considered inappropriate for use in Canada.

While the ACGAN worked primarily with the generics used in English-speaking areas of the country, a terminology committee set up by the Translation Bureau of the Department of the Secretary of State compiled and verified information for generics used in French-language geographical names. This committee, assisted by translators, provided possible equivalent generics for use in the translation of English or French texts.

des termes géographiques français établis par la Commission de toponymie du Québec et normalisées par l'Office de la langue française ont parfois été modifiées en fonction de l'usage attesté dans d'autres milieux francophones du Canada. De même, quelques-unes des descriptions figurant dans la colonne anglaise du Glossaire s'écartent des définitions relevées dans des sources britanniques ou américaines. Par exemple, les mots «desert», «savane» et «savannah» ont un sens différent de celui qu'on leur attribue d'ordinaire.

Parmi les régionalismes appartenant à l'héritage culturel du Canada, on trouvera des mots et expressions d'emploi peu courant tels que «blow-me-down», «buffalo jump», «pingo», «barachois» et «snye». Le Glossaire mentionne aussi les diverses façons de nommer une même entité suivant les régions. Ainsi, pour désigner un ruisseau, on utilise le mot «brook» dans les provinces de l'Atlantique, tandis que dans l'Ouest on parlera plus volontiers de «creek». Dans le même ordre d'idées, les Terreneuviens désignent par le mot «pond» ce qui s'appelle «lake» ailleurs au pays. Certains termes sont devenus désuets; c'est le cas du mot «basin» utilisé au sens de la partie amont d'une vallée en forme de cuvette en Colombie-Britannique, et du mot «land» qu'on utilisait au début de l'exploration des terres arctiques pour désigner une vaste région. D'autres termes (comme «arête», «mere» et «rivulet») ne se rencontrent dans aucun nom géographique approuvé. Leur absence du Glossaire ne signifie pas pour autant qu'ils sont de mauvais aloi au pays.

Pendant que le CCNGA se concentrait sur les génériques employés dans les milieux anglophones du Canada, un comité de terminologie formé par le Bureau des traductions du Secréta-

Comments and contributions are welcomed from readers, particularly if they identify applications of official Canadian names that add dimension to the descriptions provided here. Correspondence should be sent to the CPCGN Secretariat, Energy, Mines and Resources Canada, 650-615 Booth Street, Ottawa, Ontario, K1A 0E9.

I wish to thank all those past and present members of the ACGAN who have worked diligently to bring this project to fruition; the Chairman and other members of the CPCGN who have supported the work of the ACGAN; the experts who have provided valuable comments; the staff of the CPCGN Secretariat and of the Translation Bureau; and particularly Louise Baudouin-Tardif and Helen Kerfoot, without whom none of this work could have been completed.

This glossary is dedicated to Neal Carter and Alex Stevenson, members of the ACGAN who contributed to the early stages of the Committee's work, but who died before this publication was completed.

riat d'État a dressé la liste des génériques en usage dans les noms géographiques de langue française et a défini chacun d'eux. De plus, ce comité, avec la collaboration de traducteurs, a proposé des équivalents pour la traduction des textes anglais ou français.

Nous accueillerons avec plaisir toutes les observations et les suggestions de nature à enrichir la matière du présent glossaire. Elles devront être adressées au Secrétariat du CPCNG, ministère de l'Énergie, des Mines et des Ressources, 615, rue Booth, pièce 650, Ottawa (Ontario), K1A 0E9.

Je désire remercier tous les membres du CCNGA, qui se sont acquittés de leur mission avec diligence, le président et les autres membres du CPCNG qui nous ont appuyés dans notre travail, les spécialistes qui nous ont donné de précieux conseils, le personnel du Secrétariat du CPCNG et du Bureau des traductions et, en particulier, Louise Baudouin-Tardif et Helen Kerfoot, sans lesquelles tout ce travail aurait été impossible.

Nous dédions cet ouvrage à nos deux collègues décédés, Neal Carter et Alex Stevenson, qui ont contribué aux premiers travaux du Comité.

Le président du
Comité consultatif de la nomenclature glaciologique et alpine,

C. Simon L. Ommanney
Chairman
Advisory Committee on Glaciological and Alpine Nomenclature

ACGAN Members/Membres du CCNGA (1986-1987)

C. Simon L. Ommanney	Chairman Président	National Hydrology Research Institute Institut national de recherche en hydrologie
Don F. Pearson	Member Membre	British Columbia Colombie-Britannique
Marie Dorsey	Member Membre	Alberta
Dale Perry	Member Membre	Yukon Territory Yukon
Randolph Freeman	Member Membre	Northwest Territories Territoires du Nord-Ouest
Heman Whalen	Member Membre	Newfoundland Terre-Neuve
Maxwell Sutherland	Member Membre	Environment Canada, Parks Environnement Canada, Parcs
Glenn Woodsworth	Member Membre	Geological Survey of Canada Commission géologique du Canada
Edward Whalley	Member Membre	Alpine Club of Canada Club alpin du Canada
Maryalice Stewart	Member Membre	Banff, Alberta
Alan Rayburn	Member Membre	CPCGN Secretariat Secrétariat du CPCNG

* * * * * *

Helen Kerfoot	Secretary Secrétaire	CPCGN Secretariat Secrétariat du CPCNG

Guide for Users

The format of the Glossary follows the two-language column style familiar to terminologists. English and French generic entries are integrated and listed in alphabetical order.

Each entry contains a block of information in both official languages, English on the left, French on the right. The position of the boldfaced term is either in the left- or the right-hand column, depending on the language in which usage of the generic has been recorded. The subsequent text is printed in the regular upright type where it is the original entry and in italic type where it is a translation into the other official language.

Generic entries are subdivided into five parts:

DES   This is a broad and simple description covering a wide range of applications in official Canadian names.

OBS   Some general observations are provided to amplify the description, or to comment upon the application of a generic and its area of use.

"Maritime Provinces" refers to Nova Scotia, New Brunswick and Prince Edward Island, whereas "Atlantic Provinces" also includes Newfoundland. Throughout the text, the following abbreviations are used for the names of the provinces and territories:

Alta./Alb.	Alberta
B.C./C.-B.	British Columbia
Man.	Manitoba
N.B./N.-B.	New Brunswick
Nfld./T.-N.	Newfoundland

Comment utiliser le glossaire

Le Glossaire est présenté sur deux colonnes, disposition bien connue des terminologues. Les entrées anglaises et françaises sont intégrées et se suivent dans l'ordre alphabétique.

Chaque entrée, imprimée en caractères gras, est suivie d'un article dans les deux langues officielles – l'anglais à gauche et le français à droite. L'entrée se trouve dans la colonne de gauche ou la colonne de droite, selon que le générique est attesté en anglais ou en français. Le texte original est imprimé en caractères romains et la traduction, en italique.

Chaque article comprend cinq parties :

DES   Description générale et simple, qui tient compte de la polysémie de plusieurs génériques.

OBS   Observations générales, qui ajoutent à la description ou encore donnent des précisions sur l'emploi d'un générique et sur son aire d'utilisation.

Les «Maritimes» comprennent la Nouvelle-Écosse, le Nouveau-Brunswick et l'Île-du-Prince-Édouard, tandis que les «provinces de l'Atlantique» englobent également Terre-Neuve. Les noms des provinces et des territoires sont ainsi abrégés :

Alb./Alta.	Alberta
C.-B./B.C.	Colombie-Britannique
Î.-P.-É./ P.E.I.	Île-du-Prince-Édouard
Man.	Manitoba
N.-B./N.B.	Nouveau-Brunswick

N.S./N.-É.	Nova Scotia		N.-É./N.S.	Nouvelle-Écosse
N.W.T./T.N.-O.	Northwest Territories		Ont.	Ontario
Ont.	Ontario		Qué./Que.	Québec
P.E.I./Î.-P.-É.	Prince Edward Island		Sask.	Saskatchewan
Que./Qué.	Quebec		T.-N./Nfld.	Terre-Neuve
Sask.	Saskatchewan		T.N.-O./N.W.T.	Territoires du Nord-Ouest
Y.T./Yuk.	Yukon Territory		Yuk./Y.T.	Yukon

EQ — Indicates an equivalent generic term in the other official language. In most instances where a generic translation is required, this equivalent term is recommended as appropriate. However, in some cases, a locally used equivalent may be considered more suitable.

Equivalents are printed within square brackets if the suggested terms are (a) not currently used, or (b) not used in exactly the same sense in official geographical names. For example, [peat bog] is the suggested English equivalent for the French "tourbière", but there are no official geographical names containing the term "peat bog"; [bras] is given as the French equivalent of "backwater", but the bracketed form is used to show that this use of "bras" differs from that described in the alphabetical entry for "bras".

Some English terms have no listed French equivalents (e.g. back, barren, castle, deadwater, ears and ground). These generics are still being investigated for suitable equivalents in French.

EQ — Équivalent du générique dans l'autre langue officielle. C'est celui que nous jugeons le plus approprié et dont nous recommandons l'emploi. Il peut arriver, cependant, que l'usage local ait consacré un terme différent de celui que nous proposons; il sera alors préférable de s'y conformer.

L'équivalent proposé est placé entre crochets, a) s'il n'est pas utilisé dans les noms géographiques officiels, ou b) s'il figure dans la nomenclature officielle, mais dans un sens différent. Ainsi le terme [peat bog] est recommandé comme équivalent anglais du générique français «tourbière», mais il ne fait partie d'aucun nom géographique officiel. Le mot [bras], donné comme équivalent du générique anglais «backwater», est indiqué entre crochets, car son sens diffère de la définition proposée à l'entrée «bras».

Nous nous sommes abstenus de proposer un équivalent français pour certains génériques anglais (par ex. back, barren, castle, deadwater, ears et ground). Ces termes sont encore à l'étude.

REL   For most generics, there are other terms that refer to the same kind of feature; some of those more commonly used are identified as related terms.

EX   Examples are selected from various jurisdictions to show typical usage. Each official name is followed by the abbreviation of its province or territory, its latitude and longitude to the nearest minute, and a reference to the appropriate National Topographic System map (e.g. 63 G/3), Canadian Hydrographic Service chart (e.g. C.4216), or small-scale map produced by Energy, Mines and Resources (e.g. MCR 125).

REL   Termes corrélatifs. Ce sont des génériques qui servent tous à désigner le même genre d'entité.

EX   Exemples choisis dans diverses régions et caractéristiques de l'usage du mot. Le nom officiel est suivi de l'abréviation correspondant à la province ou au territoire, des coordonnées de l'entité exprimées à la minute près, ainsi que de l'indicatif de la carte du Système national de référence cartographique (par ex. 63 G/3), de la carte du Service hydrographique du Canada (par ex. C.4216) ou d'une carte à petite échelle établie par le ministère de l'Énergie, des Mines et des Ressources (par ex. MCR 125).

The following are also included in the Glossary:

• Photographic, cartographic or artistic representations of selected generics.

• A short annotated bibliography listing English- and French-language reference works on geographical terminology, providing more details, for example, on the generics of landscape features and the occurrence of these features outside Canada.

• Abbreviations of generic terms, as used by two of Canada's mapping and charting establishments, i.e. Surveys and Mapping Branch (EMR) and the Canadian Hydrographic Service.

Le Glossaire renferme en outre :

• Des photographies, cartes ou autres illustrations de certaines entités désignées par des génériques.

• Une courte bibliographie annotée mentionnant des ouvrages de référence en anglais et en français sur la terminologie géographique, lesquels donnent des précisions, entre autres, sur les génériques désignant des accidents de terrain et sur leur occurrence à l'extérieur du Canada.

• Les abréviations de génériques utilisées par deux organismes de cartographie du Canada, à savoir la Direction des levés et de la cartographie d'ÉMR et le Service hydrographique du Canada.

Note to Translators

Some English and French generics listed in this glossary cannot always be translated satisfactorily within a geographical name. For example, if a generic is preceded by a definite article or stands alone as a name, it should remain intact in its original language (e.g. "The Spout", "The Grand View", "Le Bras", "La Grande Chute", "Blow Me Down").

Various terms included in this glossary as English language generics essentially describe the shape or appearance of the feature. It is recommended that such terms (e.g. mouth, profile, chair, limb) should not be translated. However, sometimes in a translated text it is important to indicate the type of feature being identified. In such cases, a descriptive could be added in the French text to indicate the true nature of the entity; where an "equivalent" is provided in the Glossary, it is probably the most suitable one to use.

Examples:

Devils Limb	–	île Devils Limb
Duke's Profile	–	falaise Duke's Profile
Whale's Mouth	–	passage Whale's Mouth

Traduction des génériques

Certains des génériques répertoriés dans le Glossaire ne peuvent pas être traduits dans tous les cas. Ainsi, on conservera dans sa langue originale un générique qui est précédé d'un article défini (comme dans «The Grand View» et «La Grande Chute») ou une expression qui forme à elle seule le nom géographique (comme dans «Blow Me Down»).

Par ailleurs, plusieurs génériques anglais indiquent la forme ou l'aspect plutôt que la nature de l'accident géographique (par ex. mouth, profile, chair, limb). Il est recommandé de ne pas traduire ces termes. S'il est important de préciser quelle sorte d'entité le nom géographique sert à désigner, le traducteur pourra toujours faire précéder le toponyme non traduit du générique qui convient le mieux en l'occurrence; il emploiera dans la plupart des cas l'équivalent fourni dans le Glossaire.

Par exemple, on peut traduire :

Devils Limb	par île Devils Limb
Duke's Profile	par falaise Duke's Profile
Whale's Mouth	par passage Whale's Mouth

a

aboiteau

DES	Freshwater reservoir at sea level.	*Réservoir d'eau douce au niveau de la mer.*
OBS	Originally used by Acadians in N.S. and N.B. for a sluice gate to control infiltration of salt water. Now extended to the body of water impounded. Rare; N.S.	*À l'origine, terme utilisé par les Acadiens au N.-B. et en N.-É. pour désigner une vanne destinée à empêcher l'infiltration d'eau salée. Par extension, nappe d'eau retenue. Rare; N.-É.*
EQ		[**aboiteau** (m.)]
REL	reservoir, pond (1), lake, lagoon, barachois	
EX	Parrsboro Aboiteau, N.S./N.-É. 45° 24′ – 64° 19′ (21 H/8)	

alley

DES	See **channel (1)**	*Voir* **channel (1)**
OBS	Uncommon; Ont.	*Peu usité; Ont.*
EQ		**chenal** (m.)
REL	passage, narrows, strait, tickle	
EX	Wood Duck Alley, Ont. 42° 35′ – 80° 17′ (40 I/9) The Bowling Alley, Ont. 49° 38′ – 94° 25′ (52 E/9)	

anchor

DES	See **shoal**	*Voir* **shoal**
OBS	Rare; Nfld. Might be a variant of "anchorage".	*Rare; T.-N. Parfois variante de «anchorage».*
EQ		**haut-fond** (m.)
REL	bank (1), ground (1)	
EX	Offer Anchor, Nfld./T.-N. 47° 38′ – 58° 05′ (C.4638)	

anchorage

DES	Area of water in which vessels can anchor.	*Étendue d'eau où un navire peut jeter l'ancre.*
OBS	Usually sheltered water. Used in the Atlantic Provinces, Ont., B.C., and N.W.T.	*S'applique habituellement à une zone protégée. En usage dans les provinces de l'Atlantique, en Ont., en C.-B. et dans les T.N.-O.*
EQ		**mouillage** (m.)
REL	harbour, haven, bay	
EX	Battery Bluff Anchorage, Ont. 45° 53′ – 82° 48′ (41 G/15)	

anse (f.)   (Fig. 1, 7, 32)

DES	*Indentation in the line of a coast or shore, rounded in form and small in size.*	Rentrant du tracé d'un littoral ou d'une rive, de forme arrondie et de petite dimension.
OBS	*Smaller than a* baie. *Used especially in Que. and sporadically in the Atlantic Provinces and N.W.T.*	Plus petite qu'une baie. Attesté au Qué. surtout et sporadiquement dans les provinces de l'Atlantique et les T.N.-O.
EQ	**cove**	
REL		baie, crique (2), trou (1)
EX	Anse de Berthier, Qué./Que. 46° 56′ – 70° 43′ (21 L/15) Anse des Fribert, N.-É./N.S. 46° 30′ – 61° 04′ (11 K/11) Anse de Villiers, T.N.-O./N.W.T. 59° 20′ – 69° 19′ (24 N)	

arch

DES	Feature having the appearance of an arch.	*Relief en forme d'arche.*
OBS	Rare; Alta. and N.W.T.	*Rare; Alb. et T.N.-O.*
EQ		[**arche** (f.)]
REL	cliff	
EX	The Natural Arch, Alta./Alb. 53° 26′ – 118° 51′ (83 E/7) Rainbow Arch, N.W.T./T.N.-O. 65° 27′ – 128° 13′ (106 H/8)	

2

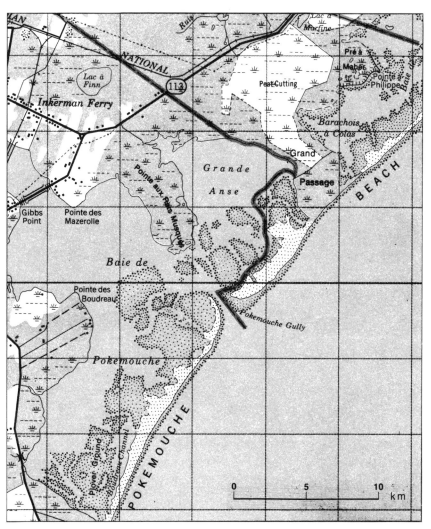

Figure 1. Coast of the Gulf of St.
Lawrence in northeastern New Brunswick,
showing Grande Anse, Baie de
Pokemouche, Barachois à Colas,
Pokemouche Beach, Pointe des Boudreau,
Pré à Maher, Plover Ground, and
Pokemouche Gully.
(National Topographic System map
21 P/10; 1977)

Figure 1. Côte du golfe du Saint-Laurent,
dans le nord-est du Nouveau-Brunswick.
Entités représentées : Grande Anse, Baie
de Pokemouche, Barachois à Colas,
Pokemouche Beach, Pointe des Boudreau,
Pré à Maher, Plover Ground et
Pokemouche Gully.
(Carte 21 P/10 du Système national de
référence cartographique; 1977)

3

archipel (m.)

DES	*Group or chain of islands.*	Groupe ou chaîne d'îles.
OBS	*Originally, the term indicated a sea strewn with islands. Used in Que.*	À l'origine, le terme désignait une mer semée d'îles. Attesté au Qué.
EQ	**archipelago**	
REL		
EX	Archipel de Blanc-Sablon, Qué./Que. 51° 25' – 57° 20' (12 P/6)	

archipelago

DES	Group or chain of islands.	*Groupe ou chaîne d'îles.*
OBS	Rare; B.C. and N.W.T.	*Rare; C.-B. et T.N.-O.*
EQ		**archipel** (m.)
REL	islands, rocks (1)	
EX	Duke of York Archipelago, N.W.T./T.N.-O. 68° 15' – 112° 45' (77 B)	

arm (1)

DES	Long narrow extension of a water body.	*Partie étroite et allongée d'une étendue d'eau.*
OBS	Widely used.	*Emploi généralisé.*
EQ		[**bras** (m.)]
REL	inlet (1), fiord, sound (2), reach, creek (2), channel (1)	
EX	Alice Arm, B.C./C.-B. 55° 27' – 129° 35' (103 P/5)	

arm (2)

DES	Long narrow extension of a land mass.	*Partie étroite et allongée d'une masse de terre.*
OBS	Rare; Sask.	*Rare; Sask.*
EQ		[**bras** (m.)]
REL	peninsula, point (1)	
EX	South Arm, Sask. 58° 16′ – 103° 40′ (64 L/5)	

arm (3)

DES	Tributary of a glacier.	*Tributaire d'un glacier.*
OBS	Rare; B.C.	*Rare; C.-B.*
EQ		[**bras** (m.)]
REL	glacier	
EX	Ross Arm, B.C./C.-B. 50° 23′ – 123° 52′ (92 J/5)	

b

back

DES	Feature having the appearance of an animal's back.	*Relief dont la forme rappelle un dos d'animal.*
OBS	Applied to hills, ridges, and shoals, particularly in Nfld. and N.B.	*S'emploie pour des collines, des chaînons et des hauts-fonds, surtout à T.-N. et au N.-B.*
EQ		
REL	ridge (1), hill, shoal	
EX	Whales Back (shoal – haut-fond), Nfld./T.-N. 47° 33′ – 57° 41′ (C.4637) Devils Back (ridge-chaînon), N.B./N.-B. 46° 36′ – 66° 10′ (21 J/9) Boars Back (hill-colline), N.B./N.-B. 45° 54′ – 64° 45′ (21 H/15) Turtles Back (hill-colline), Man. 49° 02′ – 100° 00′ (62 G/4)	

backside (Fig. 2)

DES	Water area across a narrow neck of land from the main harbour or cove.	*Étendue d'eau séparée d'un havre ou d'une anse par une langue de terre étroite.*
OBS	Particular to Nfld.	*Particulier à T.-N.*
EQ		**anse** (f.)
REL	cove, bay, hole (1)	
EX	Backside of Hell Cove, Nfld./T.-N. 52° 35′ – 55° 48′ (3 D/12)	

backwater

DES	Inland extension of a bay or bight.	*Prolongement d'une baie dans les terres.*
OBS	Rare; Nfld.	*Rare; T.-N.*
EQ		**[bras** (m.)**]**
REL	arm (1), inlet (1)	
EX	Southern Backwater, Nfld./T.-N. 52° 58′ – 56° 07′ (13 A/16)	

6

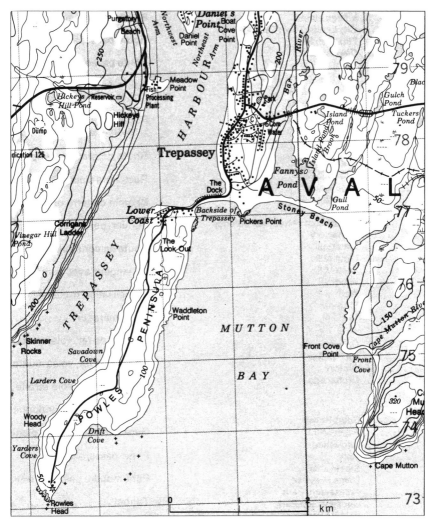

Figure 2. Trepassey Bay, Newfoundland, showing Backside of Trepassey, Stoney Beach, Cape Mutton, Drift Cove, Trepassey Harbour, Powles Head, and Powles Peninsula.
(National Topographic System map 1 K/11; 1985)

Figure 2. Baie Trepassey, à Terre-Neuve. Entités représentées : Stoney Beach, Cape Mutton, Drift Cove, Trepassey Harbour, Powles Head et Powles Peninsula.
(Carte 1 K/11 du Système national de référence cartographique; 1985)

7

bag

DES	See **cove**	*Voir* **cove**
OBS	Rare; Nfld. Perhaps originally a typographical error for "bay".	*Rare; T.-N. Ce mot résulte peut-être d'une erreur typographique dans l'écriture du mot «bay».*
EQ		**anse** (f.)
REL	bay, hole (1)	
EX	Peggys Bag, Nfld./T.-N. 47° 33' – 52° 40' (1 N/10)	

baie (f.) (Fig. 1, 24)

DES	*Deep indentation of a coastline or shore.*	Échancrure profonde d'un littoral ou d'une rive.
OBS	*Smaller than a* golfe, *but larger than an* anse. *Used across the country.*	Plus petite qu'un golfe, mais plus grande qu'une anse. Attesté à travers le pays.
EQ	**bay**	
REL		anse, crique (2), trou (1)
EX	Baie des Chaleurs, Qué. – N.-B./Que. – N.B. 47° 47' – 65° 30' (21 P) Baie Verte, T.-N./Nfld. 50° 00' – 56° 08' (12 H/16) Baie De Rozière, T.N.-O./N.W.T. 60° 30' – 69° 45' (25 C)	

baissière (f.)

DES	*Low, swampy ground.*	Terrain bas et marécageux.
OBS	*The original meaning of "baissière", also known as "baisseur", is a hollow or depression in cultivated land where rainwater collects. Used in Que.*	Dans son sens premier, une baissière, aussi appelée «baisseur», est un enfoncement ou une dépression de terrain labouré dans lequel s'amasse l'eau des pluies. Attesté au Qué.
EQ	**meadow (1)**	
REL		bogue, marais, marche, marécage, mocauque, savane, tourbière
EX	Baissière Patry, Qué./Que. 46° 09' – 75° 57' (31 J/4)	

ball

DES	See **rock (1)**	*Voir* **rock (1)**
OBS	Rare; N.S.	*Rare; N.-É.*
EQ		**rocher** (m.)
REL	reef, inlet	
EX	Robinsons Ball, N.S./N.-É. 43° 30′ − 65° 27′ (20 P/6)	
	The Ball, N.S./N.-É. 43° 30′ − 65° 46′ (20 P/12)	

banc(s) (m.) (Fig. 7)

DES	*Elevation of the seabed above which water depth is relatively shallow.*	Élévation du fond marin au-dessus de laquelle la profondeur est relativement faible.
OBS	*Banks can pose a certain hazard to general surface navigation. The term "banc" is often used for a "banc de sable" (sand bank) or for a "banc de pêche" (fishing bank), indicating the area of the sea favourable for commercial fishing. Used for underwater features recorded off the shores of Que. and Nfld.*	Le banc peut présenter un certain danger pour la navigation courante de surface. On emploie souvent le terme «banc» pour «banc de sable» et pour «banc de pêche» qui désigne la zone de la mer propice à la pêche commerciale. Entité sous-marine attestée au large des côtes du Qué. et de T.-N.
EQ	**bank (1)**	
REL		basse, fond, haut-fond
EX	Banc de Portneuf, Qué./Que. 48° 36′ − 69° 04′ (22 C/11)	
	Les Grands Bancs de Terre-Neuve, 45° 30′ − 52° 30′ (C.800A)	

bank(s) (1) (Fig. 54)

DES	Elevated portion of the seafloor or lake bottom, which is exposed at low water or over which the depth of water is shallow.	*Élévation du fond d'une mer ou d'un lac qui découvre à marée basse ou au-dessus de laquelle la profondeur d'eau est faible.*
OBS	Used off east, west, and north coasts of Canada, and in major lakes.	*S'emploie au large des côtes est, ouest et nord du Canada, et dans les lacs de grande étendue.*
EQ		**banc** (m.)
REL	shoal, ground (1)	
EX	Hecla and Griper Bank, N.W.T./T.N.-O. 71° 10′ – 69° 30′ (C.7054) Berens Bank, Man. 52° 24′ – 97° 13′ (63 A/6) Gull Banks, B.C./C.-B. 52° 07′ – 130° 58′ (C.3855)	

bank (2)

DES	Abrupt slope at the edge of a water body.	*Talus abrupt bordant une nappe d'eau.*
OBS	Few officially named examples; Ont.	*Rare dans les noms approuvés; Ont.*
EQ		[**berge** (f.)]
REL	cliff, bluff (1)	
EX	Rolling Bank, Ont. 44° 34′ – 76° 02′ (31 C/9)	

bantam

DES	See **shoal** and **bank (1)**	*Voir **shoal** et **bank (1)***
OBS	Used only off Nfld. and N.S.	*Ne s'emploie qu'au large des côtes de T.-N. et de la N.-É.*
EQ		**haut-fond** (m.)
REL	ground (1)	
EX	Renews Bantam, Nfld./T.-N. 46° 52′ – 52° 50′ (1 K/15)	

bar (Fig. 62)

DES	Ridge or succession of ridges which may obstruct water navigation.	*Haut-fond ou succession de hauts-fonds pouvant constituer un obstacle à la navigation.*
OBS	Composed of sand, gravel, or other unconsolidated material. May be offshore, across a river mouth, or in a river. Widely used.	*Accumulation de sable, de gravier ou d'autres matériaux non consolidés, au large, en travers d'une embouchure ou dans un cours d'eau. Emploi généralisé.*
EQ		**barre** (f.)
REL	shoal, spit, flat (1)	
EX	Irvings Bar, P.E.I./Î.-P.-É. 46° 10′ – 62° 57′ (11 L/2) Cassiar Bar, Y.T./Yuk. 61° 48′ – 135° 00′ (105 E/15)	

barachois

DES	Tidal pond partly obstructed by a bar.	*Étang engendré par la marée et partiellement obstrué par une barre.*
OBS	From French expressions such as "barre échouée" or "barre-à-cheoir". Formerly applied to the bar itself. Used in the Atlantic Provinces.	*Déformation de «barre échouée» ou «barre-à-cheoir». A déjà désigné la barre proprement dite. En usage dans les provinces de l'Atlantique.*
EQ		**barachois** (m.)
REL	lagoon, lake, barasway, barrisway	
EX	Big Barachois, Nfld./T.-N. 47° 03′ – 53° 47′ (1 N/4) MacLean Barachois, N.S./N.-É. 46° 00′ – 59° 58′ (11 J/4)	

barachois (m.)   (Fig. 1, 32)

DES	*Area of salt water of shallow depth, comparable in size to a pond or small bay, and partly obstructed by a bank of mud, sand, or gravel.*	Étendue d'eau salée de peu de profondeur et de dimensions comparables à celles d'un étang ou d'une petite baie et partiellement obstruée par un banc de boue, de sable ou de gravier.
OBS	*"Barachois" is sometimes used for the bar itself, formed at a river's mouth where the waves break. The term, probably of Portuguese origin ("barra" + "choa"), is derived from such expressions as "barre-à-cheois", "barre-éschué", "barre échouée", or "barre-à-échoir" – meaning "where vessels go aground". Used sporadically in Que., but more commonly in the Atlantic Provinces.*	On appelle parfois «barachois» la barre elle-même, formée à l'embouchure d'une rivière là où se brisent les vagues. Ce terme, probablement d'origine portugaise («barra» + «choa»), est dérivé d'expressions comme «barre-à-cheois», «barre-éschué», «barre échouée», «barre-à-choir» ou encore «barre-à-échoir», «là où les navires viennent choir». Attesté sporadiquement au Qué. mais plus usité dans les provinces de l'Atlantique.

EQ   **barachois**

REL   lagune, barasway

EX   Barachois à Colas, N.-B./N.B. 47° 41' – 64° 46' (21 P/10)
Barachois du Barre, T.-N./Nfld. 47° 35' – 55° 27' (1 M/11)
Barachois à Alcide, Qué./Que. 47° 15' – 61° 56' (11 N/5)

barasway   (Fig. 3)

DES	Variant of **barachois**.	*Variante de* **barachois**.
OBS	Used in Nfld.	*En usage à T.-N.*
EQ		**barasway** (m.)
REL	lagoon, lake	

EX   Big Barasway, Nfld./T.-N. 47° 48' – 55° 48' (1 M/13)

Figure 3. Southeast shore of Fortune Bay, Newfoundland, showing Frenchman's Cove Barasway and Garnish Barasway. (National Air Photo Library, A25811-10; 1981)

Figure 3. Rivage sud-est de la baie Fortune, à Terre-Neuve. La photo fait voir deux barachois, le Frenchman's Cove Barasway et le Garnish Barasway. (Photothèque nationale de l'air, A25811-10; 1981)

barasway (m.)

DES	*Variant of* **barachois**.	Variante de **barachois**.
OBS	*Used in Nfld.*	Attesté à T.-N.
EQ	**barasway**	
REL		lagune
EX	Barasway de Cerf, T.-N./Nfld. 47° 46′ – 55° 49′ (1 M/13)	

barre (f.)

DES	*Ridge or succession of ridges that can constitute an obstacle to navigation.*	Rides ou succession de rides qui peuvent constituer un obstacle à la navigation.
OBS	*Made up of sand, mud, gravel, or pebbles; forms at the mouth of a stream, the entrance to a port, or parallel to a coastline. Underwater feature; used in Que. and N.S.*	Cette masse est composée de sable, de boue, de gravier ou de galets et se forme à l'embouchure d'un cours d'eau, à l'entrée d'un port ou encore parallèlement au littoral. Entité sous-marine attestée au Qué. et en N.-É.
EQ	**bar**	
REL		
EX	Barre à Boulard, Qué./Que. 46° 38′ – 71° 56′ (21 L/12) Barre au Chat, N.-É./N.S. 45° 29′ – 60° 55′ (11 F/7)	

barren(s) (Fig. 44)

DES	Expanse of sparsely vegetated land, generally treeless.	*Terre occupée par une végétation clairsemée, généralement sans arbres.*
OBS	Usually unproductive area, either rugged upland or flat wet terrain. Used in Nfld., N.B., and N.S.	*Désigne habituellement une terre stérile, qui est haute et accidentée ou plate et humide. En usage à T.-N., au N.-B. et en N.-É.*
EQ		
REL	bog, heath, meadow (1)	
EX	Freeman Barren, N.B./N.-B. 45° 21′ – 66° 53′ (21 G/7) Bateau Barrens, Nfld./T.-N. 50° 25′ – 57° 29′ (12 I/6)	

barrisway

DES	Variant of **barachois**.	*Variante de* **barachois**.
OBS	Rare; Nfld.	*Rare; T.-N.*
EQ		**barachois** (m.)
REL	lagoon, lake	
EX	Ryle Barrisway, Nfld./T.-N. 47° 39′ – 54° 46′ (1 M/10)	

basin (1)

DES	Seafloor or lake-bottom depression, more or less equidimensional in plan and of variable extent.	*Dépression d'un fond marin ou lacustre, de forme plus ou moins circulaire et d'étendue variable.*
OBS	Used off the east, west, and north coasts of Canada.	*S'emploie au large des côtes est, ouest et nord du Canada.*
EQ		**bassin** (m.) **(1)**
REL	deeps, valley (2)	
EX	Frobisher Basin, 62° 45′ – 66° 40′ (C.1399A)	

basin (2)

DES	Body of water, usually equidimensional in plan, connected to a larger body of water by one or more passages.	*Étendue d'eau de forme généralement circulaire et reliée à une plus vaste étendue d'eau par un ou plusieurs passages.*
OBS	Widely used.	*Emploi généralisé.*
EQ		**bassin** (m.) **(2)**
REL	bay, inlet (1), sound (1), cove, lagoon	
EX	Foxe Basin, N.W.T./T.N.-O. 68° 25′ – 77° 00′ (MCR 4032) Bedford Basin, N.S./N.-É. 44° 42′ – 63° 38′ (11 D/12)	

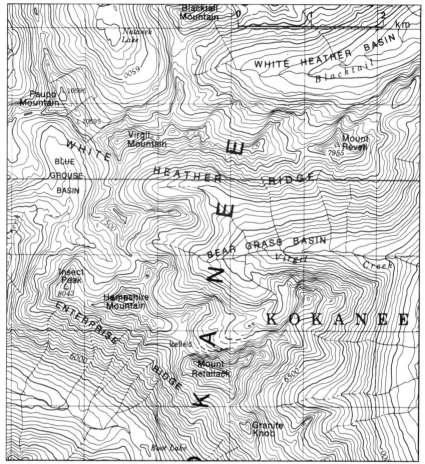

Figure 4. Part of the Columbia Mountains, west of Kootenay Lake, British Columbia, showing Bear Grass Basin, Virgil Creek, Granite Knob, Hampshire Mountain, and Enterprise Ridge.
(National Topographic System map 82 F/14; 1981)

Figure 4. Partie des monts Columbia, à l'ouest du lac Kootenay, en Colombie-Britannique. Entités représentées : Bear Grass Basin, Virgil Creek, Granite Knob, Hampshire Mountain et Enterprise Ridge.
(Carte 82 F/14 du Système national de référence cartographique; 1981)

basin (3) (Fig. 4)

DES	Bowl-shaped head of a valley in foothills or mountains.	*Partie amont d'une vallée, en forme de cuvette, dans le piémont ou la montagne.*
OBS	Few officially named examples; Alta., B.C., and N.W.T.	*Rare dans les noms approuvés; Alb., C.-B. et T.N.-O.*
EQ		**[bassin** (m.)]
REL	valley (1), cirque	
EX	Horseshoe Basin, Alta./Alb. 49° 08' – 113° 55' (82 H/4)	

basse (f.)

DES	*Isolated elevation of the sea floor, made up of loose material and posing a hazard to navigation.*	Élévation isolée du fond de la mer, formée de matériaux meubles et constituant un danger pour la navigation.
OBS	*Underwater feature; generic of Celtic origin.*	Entité sous-marine; terme d'origine celte.
EQ	**shoal**	
REL		banc, fond, haut-fond
EX	Basse du Bélier, 46° 45' – 56° 14' (C.4625)	

bassin (m.) (1)

DES	*Depression in the seabed, more or less rounded in general form and variable in extent.*	Dépression du fond marin de forme générale plus ou moins arrondie et d'étendue variable.
OBS	*Underwater feature found off Canadian shores.*	Entité sous-marine attestée au large des côtes du Canada.
EQ	**basin (1)**	
REL		
EX	Bassin Canada, T.N.-O./N.W.T. 78° 00' – 144° 00' (C.800A)	

bassin (m.) (2)

DES	*Body of water giving shelter to vessels and often joined to another water area by a narrow entrance.*	Plan d'eau abritant les navires et souvent relié à une nappe d'eau par une entrée étroite.
OBS	*Used in Que.*	Attesté au Qué.
EQ	**basin (2)**	
REL		
EX	Bassin Bickerdike, Qué./Que. 45° 30′ – 73° 33′ (31 H/5)	

battery

DES	See **head (1)**	*Voir* **head (1)**
OBS	Rare; Nfld.	*Rare; T.-N.*
EQ		**cap** (m.)
REL	cape, peninsula, point (1)	
EX	Gull Battery, Nfld./T.-N. 55° 12′ – 58° 46′ (13 O/2)	

batture(s) (f.)

DES	*Flat portion of a shore or shoal of sand or rock affected by the fluctuation of water in a stream or along the shore.*	Portion plate d'un rivage ou haut-fond de sable ou de roche affectés par la fluctuation des eaux dans un cours d'eau ou le long de la côte.
OBS	*A very old term, which apparently comes from the verb "battre"; used mainly in the plural and almost exclusive to Canada. In seventeenth-century Que., this term referred mainly to the banks along the shores of the St. Lawrence River. International French uses the word "estran". Used in Que. and the Atlantic Provinces.*	Terme très ancien, employé surtout au pluriel et presque exclusivement au Canada, et qui viendrait du verbe «battre». Au XVIIe siècle, au Qué., ce terme désignait surtout les bancs le long des rives du Saint-Laurent. En français international, on emploie «estran». Attesté au Qué. et dans les provinces de l'Atlantique.
EQ	**flat (1)**	
REL		platin
EX	Grande Batture, N.-B./N.B. 47° 53′ – 64° 42′ (21 P/15) Batture de Foin, T.-N./Nfld. 52° 44′ – 66° 10′ (23 B/9) Battures de Beauport, Qué./Que. 46° 51′ – 71° 11′ (21 L/14)	

bay(s) (Fig. 41, 49)

DES	Water area in an indentation of the shoreline of seas, lakes, or large rivers.	*Partie d'une mer, d'un lac ou d'un grand cours d'eau occupant une échancrure du littoral.*
OBS	Usually smaller than a gulf and larger than a cove. Widely used.	*«Bay» désigne généralement une échancrure plus petite que «gulf» mais plus grande que «cove». Emploi généralisé.*
EQ		**baie** (f.)
REL	cove, bight, gulf, basin (2), inlet (1)	
EX	James Bay, N.W.T./T.N.-O. 53° 30′ – 80° 30′ (MCR 4032) Twin Bays, B.C./C.-B. 49° 20′ – 116° 43′ (82 F/7)	

beach(es) (Fig. 1, 2, 44)

DES	Gently sloping shore of unconsolidated material along the margins of a sea, lake, or river.	*Partie du rivage d'un lac, d'une mer ou d'un cours d'eau, de faible pente et constituée de matériaux non consolidés.*
OBS	Widely used.	*Emploi généralisé.*
EQ		**plage** (f.)
REL	shore	
EX	Cavendish Beach, P.E.I./Î.-P.-É. 46° 30′ – 63° 26′ (11 L/6) Devonshire Beach, Alta./Alb. 55° 20′ – 114° 45′ (83 O/7) Sherkston Beaches, Ont. 42° 52′ – 79° 08′ (30 L/14)	

beak

DES	See **peak (1)**	*Voir* **peak (1)**
OBS	Rare; N.W.T.	*Rare; T.N.-O.*
EQ		**pic** (m.)
REL	summit, mountain, needle, pinnacle (1), spire	
EX	Eagles Beak, N.W.T./T.N.-O. 66° 35′ – 62° 30′ (16 L)	

bed

DES	See **bank (1)**	*Voir* **bank (1)**
OBS	Used in Nfld. and N.S.	*En usage à T.-N. et en N.-É.*
EQ		**banc** (m.)
REL	shoal, ground (1)	
EX	Mussel Bed, N.S./N.-É. 44° 55′ – 62° 31′ (11 D/15)	
	Feather Bed, Nfld./T.-N. 48° 02′ – 52° 59′ (2 C/2)	

beinn

DES	Variant of **ben**.	*Variante de* **ben**.
OBS	Rare; N.S.	*Rare; N.-É.*
EQ		**colline** (f.)
REL	hill, mountain	
EX	Beinn Bhreagh, N.S./N.-É. 46° 06′ – 60° 42′ (11 K/2)	

bell(s)

DES	See **rock (1)**	*Voir* **rock (1)**
OBS	Rare; Nfld.	*Rare; T.-N.*
EQ		**rocher** (m.)
REL	reef, islet	
EX	The Bell, Nfld./T.-N. 47° 37′ – 53° 01′ (1 N/11)	
	The Bells of Chance Cove, Nfld./T.-N. 46° 45′ – 52° 59′ (1 K/15)	

ben

DES	See **mountain** and **hill**	*Voir* **mountain** *et* **hill**
OBS	Gaelic term, usually in a transfer name from Scotland, as in "Ben Lomond"; N.B. and B.C.	*Mot gaélique faisant généralement partie d'un nom emprunté à l'Écosse, comme «Ben Lomond». Relevé au N.-B. et en C.-B.*
EQ		**colline** (f.) (dans les provinces de l'Atlantique) **montagne** (f.) (en C.-B.)
REL	hill, mountain, beinn	
EX	Ben Lomond, N.B./N.-B. 45° 21′ – 65° 54′ (21 H/5)	

bench

DES	Level strip of land, bounded above and below by steeper slopes.	*Bande de terre plane, bordée de part et d'autre par des talus.*
OBS	Few officially named examples; B.C.	*Rare dans les noms approuvés; C.-B.*
EQ		[**terrasse** (f.)]
REL	terrace	
EX	Larsons Bench, B.C./C.-B. 49° 05′ – 121° 40′ (92 H/4)	

bend(s)   (Fig. 35)

DES	Distinct curve in a water body.	*Inflexion dans le tracé d'une étendue d'eau.*
OBS	Widely used.	*Emploi généralisé.*
EQ		**courbe** (f.)
REL	elbow, oxbow	
EX	Camsell Bend, N.W.T./T.N.-O. 62° 17′ – 123° 22′ (95 J) Bearpaw Bend, Sask. 50° 38′ – 107° 32′ (72 J/12) Horseshoe Bends, N.B./N.-B. 46° 33′ – 65° 49′ (21 I/12)	

berth

DES	See **anchorage**	*Voir* **anchorage**
OBS	Rare; N.S.	*Rare; N.-É.*
EQ		**mouillage** (m.)
REL	harbour, haven	
EX	The Seine Berth, N.S./N.-É. 44° 35′ – 64° 10′ (21 A/9)	

bight   (Fig. 5, 60)

DES	Water area in a broad indentation of the shoreline.	*Étendue d'eau occupant une large échancrure du littoral.*
OBS	Used on east, west, and north coasts. In Nfld., a bight may be similar in size to, or smaller than, a bay.	*En usage sur les côtes est, ouest et nord. À T.-N., «bight» désigne une échancrure de dimension comparable ou inférieure à «bay».*
EQ		**baie** (f.)
REL	bay, cove, gulf, bite (1)	
EX	Robinson Bight, Nfld./T.-N. 48° 06′ – 53° 48′ (2 C/4) Babbage Bight, Y.T./Yuk. 69° 10′ – 138° 10′ (117 D)	

bill

DES	Long narrow promontory or small point.	*Promontoire étroit et allongé, ou pointe de petite dimension.*
OBS	Rare; Nfld.	*Rare; T.-N.*
EQ		**pointe** (f.)
REL	point (1), peninsula, spit, head (1)	
EX	Middle Bill, Nfld./T.-N. 49° 16′ – 53° 29′ (2 F/6)	

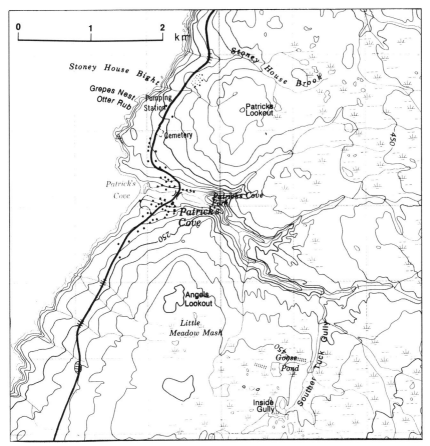

Figure 5. Placentia Bay, Newfoundland, showing Stoney House Bight, Stoney House Brook, Patricks Cove Fork, Inside Gully and Souther Tuck Gully, Patricks Lookout and Angels Lookout, Little Meadow Mash, Grepes Nest, Goose Pond, and Otter Rub.
(National Topographic System map 1 M/1; 1985 with added information)

Figure 5. Baie Placentia, à Terre-Neuve. Entités représentées : Stoney House Bight, Stoney House Brook, Patricks Cove Fork, Inside Gully et Souther Tuck Gully, Patricks Lookout et Angels Lookout, Little Meadow Mash, Grepes Nest, Goose Pond et Otter Rub.
(Carte 1 M/1 du Système national de référence cartographique; 1985 avec renseignements supplémentaires)

23

bite (1)

DES	Variant of **bight**.	*Variante de* **bight**.
OBS	Rare; Nfld.	*Rare; T.-N.*
EQ		**baie** (f.)
REL	bay, cove, gulf	
EX	Buckets Bite, Nfld./T.-N. 57° 12′ – 61° 29′ (14 F/3)	

bite (2)

DES	See **gap (1)**	*Voir* **gap (1)**
OBS	Rare; Alta.	*Rare; Alb.*
EQ		[**col** (m.)]
REL	col, pass (1), notch	
EX	Devil's Bite, Alta./Alb. 50° 19′ – 114° 26′ (82 J/8)	

block

DES	See **rock (1)**	*Voir* **rock (1)**
OBS	Rare; Nfld. and N.S.	*Rare; T.-N. et N.-É.*
EQ		**rocher** (m.)
REL	reef, islet	
EX	Coopers Block, Nfld./T.-N. 52° 54′ – 55° 47′ (3 D/13)	

blow me down, blow-me-down

DES	Abrupt or isolated hill or headland rising steeply from the water and subject to sudden down-drafts of wind.	*Colline abrupte ou isolée, ou cap escarpé qui se dresse dans un plan d'eau et qui donne souvent naissance à des rafales descendantes.*
OBS	Common in Nfld., usually simply as "Blow Me Down".	*Ce générique, d'emploi fréquent à T.-N., se présente habituellement tel quel, sans autre spécifique («Blow Me Down»).*
EQ		**promontoire** (m.)
REL	hill, head (1), cape, cliff, bluff (1)	
EX	Bay of Islands Blow-Me-Down, Nfld./T.-N. 49° 04′ – 58° 17′ (12 G/1) Blow Me Down, Nfld./T.-N. 49° 31′ – 55° 09′ (2 E/11)	

bluff(s) (1) (Fig. 6)

DES	Headland, cliff, or river bank with a steep face.	*Cap, falaise ou rive présentant une face abrupte.*
OBS	Widely used.	*Emploi généralisé.*
EQ		**falaise** (f.)
REL	cliff, head (1), bank (2), wall, ramparts, cape	
EX	Uluksartok Bluff, N.W.T./T.N.-O. 70° 44′ – 117° 48′ (87 F) Hoia Bluff, B.C./C.-B. 57° 39′ – 130° 50′ (104 G/10) Scarborough Bluffs, Ont. 43° 42′ – 79° 14′ (30 M/11)	

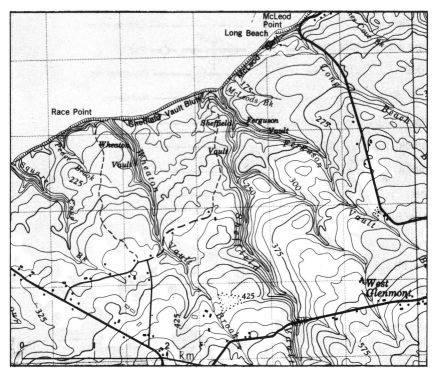

Figure 6. Southeast coast of the Bay of Fundy, Nova Scotia, showing Sheffield Vault Bluff and McLeod Bluff, Ferguson Vault, Sheffield Vault, Wheaton Vault, and their associated brooks (e.g. Wheaton Vault Brook).
(National Topographic System map 21 H/2; 1984)

Figure 6. Côte sud-est de la baie de Fundy, en Nouvelle-Écosse. Entités représentées : Sheffield Vault Bluff et McLeod Bluff, Ferguson Vault, Sheffield Vault et Wheaton Vault, ainsi que leurs ruisseaux respectifs (dont le Wheaton Vault Brook).
(Carte 21 H/2 du Système national de référence cartographique; 1984)

bluff (2)

DES	Isolated clump of trees.	*Groupe d'arbres isolé.*
OBS	Particularly in Manitoba.	*En usage surtout au Manitoba.*
EQ		**bosquet** (m.)
REL	woods, tuck, grove	
EX	Campbells Bluff, Man. 51° 47′ – 99° 43′ (62 O/13)	

bog(s)

DES	Wet spongy land area, containing abundant organic matter.	*Terrain spongieux, riche en matières organiques.*
OBS	Widely used.	*Emploi généralisé.*
EQ		**marais** (m.)
REL	marsh, swamp, fen, muskeg, barren, heath	
EX	Alfred Bog, Ont. 45° 29′ – 74° 50′ (31 G/7) Molson Bog, Man. 50° 00′ – 96° 20′ (62 I/1) Moosebone Bogs, N.S./N.-É. 44° 21′ – 65° 11′ (21 A/6)	

bogan

DES	Narrow backwater inlet of a flowing watercourse.	*Partie resserrée d'un cours d'eau qui s'avance dans les terres.*
OBS	Derived from Maliseet language. Only in N.B.	*Mot dérivé du maliseet. On ne le trouve qu'au N.-B.*
EQ		**[bras** (m.)]
REL	inlet (1), cove	
EX	Blackmore Bogan, N.B./N.-B. 46° 57′ – 65° 52′ (21 I/13)	

27

bogue (f.)

DES	*See* **marais**	Voir **marais**
OBS	*Regionalism used in Que.*	Régionalisme attesté au Qué.
EQ	**bog**	
REL		baissière, marche, marécage, mocauque, savane, tourbière
EX	Bogue à Bédard, Qué./Que. 46° 28′ – 70° 23′ (21 L/8)	

bois (m.)

DES	*Area of land covered by trees.*	Étendue de terrain peuplée d'arbres.
OBS	*Used in Que.*	Attesté au Qué.
EQ	**woods**	
REL		bosquet, forêt
EX	Bois de Verchères, Qué./Que. 45° 42′ – 73° 18′ (31 H/11)	

bonnet (m.)

DES	*See* **mont**	Voir **mont**
OBS	*Descriptive term used in Que.*	Descriptif attesté au Qué.
EQ	**mount**	
REL		montagne
EX	Bonnet à Amédée, Qué./Que. 46° 40′ – 70° 13′ (21 L/9)	

boots

DES	See **rock (1)**	*Voir* **rock (1)**
OBS	Rare; Nfld. and Ont.	*Rare; T.-N. et Ont.*
EQ		**rochers** (m.)
REL	reef, islet	
EX	Sly Boots, Ont. 45° 56′ – 81° 15′ (41 H/14) Sly Boots, Nfld./T.-N. 47° 38′ – 53° 58′ (1 N/12)	

bosquet (m.)

DES	*Small woods or group of trees often set aside for practical or decorative purposes.*	Petit bois ou groupe d'arbres souvent réservés à des fins utilitaires ou décoratives.
OBS	*Used in Que.*	Attesté au Qué.
EQ	**grove**	
REL		bois, forêt
EX	Bosquet Poirier, Qué./Que. 46° 55′ – 71° 30′ (21 L/13)	

bosse (f.)

DES	*See* **colline**	Voir **colline**
OBS	*Descriptive term used in N.S.*	Descriptif attesté en N.-É.
EQ	**hill**	
REL		butte, buttereau, dôme, morne
EX	Bosse à Christine, N.-É./N.S. 44° 11′ – 66° 12′ (21 B/1)	

bottom (1)

DES	Level land of a valley floor.	*Fond plat d'une vallée.*
OBS	Uncommon; Nfld. and Alta.	*Peu fréquent; T.-N. et Alb.*
EQ		[**fond** (m.)]
REL	flat (2), valley (1), ground (2), meadow (1), intervale	
EX	Gull Pond Bottom, Nfld./T.-N. 46° 51′ – 53° 16′ (1 K/14) Jerry the Bird's Bottom, Alta./Alb. 49° 38′ – 112° 56′ (82 H/10)	

bottom (2)

DES	Head of a cove or bay.	*Fond d'une anse ou d'une baie.*
OBS	Used in Nfld.	*En usage à T.-N.*
EQ		[**fond** (m.)]
REL	cove, bay, creek (2)	
EX	Colliers Bay Bottom, Nfld./T.-N. 47° 34′ – 53° 43′ (1 N/12)	

boulder

DES	See **rock (1)**	*Voir* **rock (1)**
OBS	Rare; B.C.	*Rare; C.-B.*
EQ		**rocher** (m.)
REL	reef, islet	
EX	Datum Boulder, B.C./C.-B. 50° 28′ – 126° 01′ (92 L/8)	

branch

DES	Tributary or distributary of a watercourse.	*Tributaire ou défluent d'un cours d'eau.*
OBS	Widely used.	*Emploi généralisé.*
EQ		**bras** (m.)
REL	creek (1), brook, stream, fork (2), channel (2)	
EX	Farlinger Branch, Ont. 45° 04′ – 74° 40′ (31 G/2) Fishing Branch, Y.T./Yuk. 66° 27′ – 138° 35′ (116 J & K) West Branch Little Southwest Miramichi River, N.B./N.-B. 46° 59′ – 66° 39′ (21 J/15) Right Hand Branch Three Brooks, N.B./N.-B. 46° 59′ – 67° 26′ (21 J/14)	

branche (f.)

DES	*See* **bras**	Voir **bras**
OBS	*Still used today in Que., this term was very common in the nineteenth century. In N.B., among other places, "branche" is used for a main watercourse as well as for a tributary. Used in Que. and N.B.*	Encore présent aujourd'hui au Qué., ce terme était très usité au XIXe siècle. Au N.-B., entre autres, ce générique désigne aussi la rivière ou le ruisseau, aussi bien que la ramification. Attesté au Qué. et au N.-B.
EQ	**branch**	
REL		embranchement, fourche (2)
EX	Branche Chartier, Qué./Que. 46° 07′ – 72° 21′ (31 I/1) Branche à Charles, N.-B./N.B. 47° 29′ – 68° 04′ (21 N/8)	

brandies

DES	Partly submerged rocks; a reef.	*Rochers partiellement submergés; récif.*
OBS	Originated from "brandise", an iron tripod used for cooking (Ireland); probably originally used to refer to a group of three rocks. Usually "The Brandies". Used only in Nfld.	*Mot dérivé de «brandise», qui désigne un genre de trépied en fer utilisé pour faire cuire les aliments (Irlande). Ce générique désignait probablement, à l'origine, un groupe de trois rochers. On le rencontre habituellement sous la forme «The Brandies». On ne le trouve qu'à T.-N.*
EQ		**rochers** (m.)
REL	rock (1), reef	
EX	Change Brandies, Nfld./T.-N. 49° 42′ – 54° 24′ (2 E/9)	

bras (m.)

DES	*Each of the branches of a main watercourse.*	Chacune des ramifications d'un cours d'eau principal.
OBS	*When the branch no longer serves as a channel for water flow, the water becomes stagnant; it is then referred to as a "bras mort". Used in Que.*	Lorsque le bras ne sert plus de chenal pour laisser les eaux s'écouler, celles-ci deviennent dormantes ou stagnantes; on parle alors d'un «bras mort». Attesté au Qué.
EQ	**branch**	
REL		branche, embranchement, fourche (2)
EX	Bras des Angers, Qué./Que. 48° 07′ – 71° 29′ (22 D/3)	

break

DES	Opening or clearing in a woodland.	*Percée ou clairière dans un bois.*
OBS	Used in Nfld.	*S'emploie à T.-N.*
EQ		[**clairière** (f.)]
REL	trail	
EX	Little Juniper Break, Nfld./T.-N. 46° 54′ – 53° 16′ (1 K/14)	

breaker(s)

DES	Seafloor elevation causing the breaking of waves.	*Élévation du fond marin sur laquelle les vagues se brisent.*
OBS	Used in the Atlantic Provinces.	*En usage dans les provinces de l'Atlantique.*
EQ		**brisants** (m.)
REL	shoal, reef, ledge (1)	
EX	Broad Breaker, N.S./N.-É. 44° 43′ – 62° 41′ (C.4353) Battery Island Breakers, N.S./N.-É. 45° 54′ – 59° 57′ (11 G/13)	

brisants (m.)   (Fig. 7)

DES	*Reef, close to a shore, on which the waves break.*	Écueil proche d'une côte sur lequel les vagues se brisent et déferlent.
OBS	*Generally used in the plural. Used in Que.*	Habituellement utilisé au pluriel. Attesté au Qué.
EQ	**breakers**	
REL		
EX	Brisants Aguanus, Qué./Que. 50° 12' – 62° 05' (12 L/1)	
	Brisants Landry, Qué./Que. 50° 03' – 61° 52' (12 K/4)	

broad

DES	See **beach**	*Voir* **beach**
OBS	Rare; Nfld.	*Rare; T.-N.*
EQ		**plage** (f.)
REL	shore	
EX	Broad of the Island, Nfld./T.-N. 47° 14' – 52° 47' (1 N/2)	

brook(s)   (Fig. 5, 6, 37)

DES	Small watercourse, often tributary to a river, stream, or creek.	*Petit cours d'eau qui, souvent, se jette dans un autre cours d'eau.*
OBS	Widely used, but most common in the Atlantic Provinces.	*S'emploie partout, mais particulièrement dans les provinces de l'Atlantique.*
EQ		**ruisseau** (m.)
REL	creek (1), stream, river (1)	
EX	Nevers Brook, N.B./N.-B. 46° 05' – 65° 19' (21 I/3)	
	Bain Brook, B.C./C.-B. 51° 06' – 117° 36' (82 N/4)	
	Wester Brooks, Nfld./T.-N. 47° 36' – 53° 46' (1 N/12)	

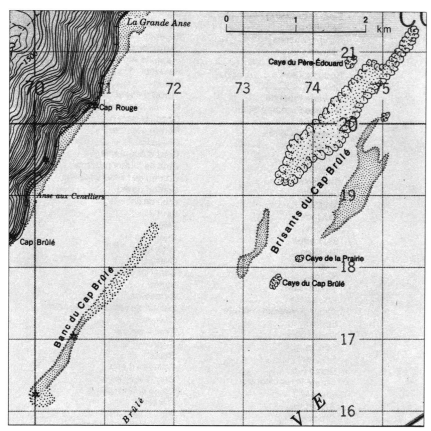

Figure 7. A section of the St. Lawrence River, downstream from Québec, showing Brisants du Cap Brûlé, La Grande Anse, Banc du Cap Brûlé, and Caye de la Prairie.
(National Topographic System map 21 M/2; 1983)

Figure 7. Section du fleuve Saint-Laurent, en aval de Québec. Entités représentées : Brisants du Cap Brûlé, La Grande Anse, Banc du Cap Brûlé et Caye de la Prairie.
(Carte 21 M/2 du Système national de référence cartographique; 1983)

brow

DES	Top of a steep slope.	*Sommet d'un talus abrupt.*
OBS	Used in N.B.	*En usage au N.-B.*
EQ		**sommet** (m.)
REL	summit	
EX	Mast Brow, N.B./N.-B. 45° 30′ – 65° 23′ (21 H/11)	

buffalo jump (Fig. 8)

DES	Vertical side of a coulee, hill, or river bank.	*Versant vertical d'une coulée, d'une colline ou d'une rive.*
OBS	Place where Plains Indians killed herds of bison by driving them over steep cliffs. Rare; Alta.	*Lieu où les amérindiens des Plaines tuaient des troupeaux de bisons en les faisant sauter à bas de falaises escarpées. Rare; Alb.*
EQ		**escarpement** (m.)
REL	bank (2), cliff, bluff (2), escarpment	
EX	Head-Smashed-In Buffalo Jump, Alta./Alb. 49° 43′ – 113° 39′ (82 H/12)	

bull(s)

DES	See **rock (1)**	*Voir* **rock (1)**
OBS	Rare; Nfld., N.S., and N.B.	*Rare; T.-N., N.-É. et N.-B.*
EQ		**rocher** (m.)
REL	reef, islet	
EX	Passage Bull, N.S./N.-É. 44° 41′ – 62° 52′ (C.4352) Five Eyed Bulls, N.S./N.-É. 44° 43′ – 62° 45′ (C.4352)	

Figure 8. Head-Smashed-In Buffalo Jump, west of Fort Macleod, Alberta. (Alberta Culture – Historic Sites Service, G&D 27)

Figure 8. Head-Smashed-In Buffalo Jump, escarpement situé à l'ouest de Fort Macleod, en Alberta. (Alberta Culture – Historic Sites Service, G&D 27)

burn

DES	Small watercourse.	*Petit cours d'eau.*
OBS	Rare; Ont. and B.C.	*Rare; Ont. et C.-B.*
EQ		**[ruisselet** (m.)]
REL	brook, creek (1), stream	
EX	Leys Burn, Ont. 44° 20′ – 80° 09′ (41 A/8) Bannock Burn, B.C./C.-B. 49° 41′ – 117° 37′ (82 F/12)	

burr

DES	See **rock (1)**	*Voir* **rock (1)**
OBS	Rare; Nfld.	*Rare; T.-N.*
EQ		**rocher** (m.)
REL	reef, islet	
EX	Uncle Dickies Burr, Nfld./T.-N. 47° 01′ – 55° 08′ (C.4616)	

buse

DES	See **hill**	*Voir* **hill**
OBS	Rare; Nfld.	*Rare; T.-N.*
EQ		**colline** (f.)
REL	knoll (1), tolt, knob	
EX	Great Buse, Nfld./T.-N. 51° 08′ – 55° 45′ (2 M/4)	

butte(s)   (Fig. 9)

DES	Conspicuous isolated hill with steep sides and a flat top.	*Colline isolée aux versants raides et au sommet plat.*
OBS	Widely used in the western provinces and the territories.	*Largement utilisé dans les provinces de l'Ouest et les territoires.*
EQ		**butte** (f.)
REL	hill, tolt, tower, knoll (1), lump	
EX	Castle Butte, Sask. 49° 13′ – 105° 13′ (72 H/3) Twin Buttes, B.C./C.-B. 49° 04′ – 120° 07′ (92 H/1)	

Figure 9. Antelope Butte, northeast of Blairmore, Alberta. (Alberta Culture – Historic Sites Service, RG81-6-35)

Figure 9. Antelope Butte, au nord-est de Blairmore, en Alberta. (Alberta Culture – Historic Sites Service, RG81-6-35)

butte (f.) (Fig. 32)

DES	*Steep and isolated elevation of terrain; isolated small hill.*	Élévation abrupte et isolée de terrain; petite colline isolée.
OBS	*Term formerly used by French-speaking explorers, voyageurs, and pioneers. Used in Que., N.B., and B.C.*	Terme autrefois employé par les explorateurs, les voyageurs et les pionniers d'expression française. Attesté au Qué., au N.-B. et en C.-B.
EQ	**butte**	
REL		bosse, buttereau, colline, dôme, morne
EX	Butte à Cailla, Qué./Que. 47° 23′ – 70° 25′ (21 M/8) Grosse Butte, N.-B./N.B. 47° 51′ – 64° 31′ (21 P/15) La Jolie Butte, C.-B./B.C. 59° 41′ – 123° 55′ (94 O/12)	

buttereau (m.)

DES	*Rounded hill.*	Colline arrondie.
OBS	*This generic has variations in meaning; in the Îles-de-la-Madeleine region, the term "buttereau" is sometimes used for sand dunes. In the Maritimes, it describes a quite high ground elevation; elsewhere in French Canada, it designates a low ground elevation. Only in Que. is the generic used in official names.*	Ce générique n'est pas défini clairement; en effet, aux Îles-de-la-Madeleine, le terme «buttereau» est utilisé parfois pour les dunes de sable. Dans les Maritimes, il décrit une assez haute élévation de terrain; et ailleurs au Canada français, il représente une faible élévation de terrain. Attesté officiellement au Qué. seulement.
EQ	**knoll (1)**	
REL		bosse, butte, colline, dôme, morne
EX	Buttereau du Nègre, Qué./Que. 47° 30′ – 61° 44′ (11 N/12)	

butterpot, butter pot

DES	Feature having the shape of a butter pot.	*Relief en forme de pot de beurre.*
OBS	Applied to hills and ponds. Used in Nfld.	*S'emploie pour des collines et des étangs. Relevé à T.-N.*
EQ		
REL	pot	
EX	Big Butterpot (pond-étang), Nfld./T.-N. 46° 58′ – 53° 02′ (1 K/14) Butter Pot (hill-colline), Nfld./T.-N. 46° 58′ – 53° 03′ (1 K/14)	

C

cairn

DES	Conspicuous hill or mountain.	Colline ou montagne détachée du relief environnant.
OBS	May resemble a man-made cairn; sometimes used in surveying or navigation. Rare; Nfld. and Alta.	Peut ressembler à un cairn édifié par l'homme. Terme parfois utilisé en arpentage ou en navigation. Rare; T.-N. et Alb.
EQ		[cairn (m.)]
REL	hill, mountain, man, lookout	
EX	Captain Orlebars Cairn, Nfld./T.-N. 47° 19′ – 52° 48′ (1 N/7) Southesk Cairn, Alta./Alb. 52° 43′ – 117° 08′ (83 C/11)	

canal (1)

DES	Narrow natural channel or long, narrow, saltwater inlet.	Chenal naturel resserré, ou bras de mer étroit et allongé.
OBS	Used in N.B. and B.C.	En usage au N.-B. et en C.-B.
EQ		chenal (m.)
REL	inlet (1), channel (1), arm (1), reach	
EX	Gardner Canal, B.C./C.-B. 53° 27′ – 128° 25′ (103 H)	

canal (2)

DES	Artificial waterway.	Voie d'eau artificielle.
OBS	Widely used.	Emploi généralisé.
EQ		canal (m.)
REL	cut, drain	
EX	St. Peters Canal, N.S./N.-É. 45° 39′ – 60° 52′ (11 F/10) Rideau Canal, Ont. 44° 53′ – 76° 00′ (31 G/12) Brazeau Canal, Alta./Alb. 52° 54′ – 115° 25′ (83 B/14)	

canal (m.)

DES	*Artificial waterway.*	Voie d'eau artificielle.
OBS	*Used in Que.*	Attesté au Qué.
EQ	**canal (2)**	
REL		
EX	Canal de Lachine, Qué./Que. 45° 26′ – 73° 40′ (31 H/5)	

canyon (Fig. 10)

DES	Deep narrow valley with precipitous walls.	*Vallée profonde et étroite aux versants escarpés.*
OBS	Widely used. Western examples are mainly gorge-like with fast-flowing watercourses. In early days canyon was used in the Spanish form "cañon".	*Emploi généralisé. Dans l'Ouest, ce générique désigne principalement des gorges traversées par des cours d'eau rapides. Autrefois, le mot s'écrivait à l'espagnole «cañon».*
EQ		**canyon** (m.)
REL	valley (1), ravine, gorge, trench, coulee	
EX	Bowdoin Canyon, Nfld./T.-N. 53° 34′ – 64° 16′ (23 H/9)	
	Roaring River Canyon, Man. 51° 52′ – 101° 13′ (62 N/14)	
	Maligne Canyon, Alta./Alb. 52° 55′ – 118° 00′ (83 D/16)	
	Grand Canyon of the Stikine, B.C./C.-B. 58° 07′ – 130° 38′ (104 J)	

Figure 10. Ouimet Canyon, northeast of Thunder Bay, Ontario. (H. Kerfoot)

Figure 10. Ouimet Canyon, au nord-est de Thunder Bay, en Ontario. (H. Kerfoot)

canyon (m.)

DES	*Deep, narrow and tortuous depression with rocky, steep sides.*	Dépression profonde, étroite et sinueuse, aux versants rocheux et abrupts.
OBS	*Term of Spanish origin. The related terms listed all indicate an elongated depression usually with a stream flowing through. Used in Que.*	Terme d'origine espagnole. Les termes semblables retenus désignent tous une dépression allongée permettant le passage d'un cours d'eau. Attesté au Qué.
EQ	**canyon**	
REL		coulée (1), gorge, ravin, ravine, rigwash, vallée
EX	Canyon Eaton, Qué./Que. 55° 33′ – 68° 12′ (23 N/9)	

cap (1)

DES	Feature with a rounded cap-like top.	*Relief au sommet en forme de bonnet.*
OBS	Applied to islands, rocks, hills, and mountains. Widely used.	*S'emploie pour des îles, des rochers, des collines et des montagnes. Emploi généralisé.*
EQ		
REL	hat	
EX	Chockle Cap (islet-îlot), N.S./N.-É. 44° 24′ – 64° 13′ (21 A/8) Frenchman Cap (mountain – montagne), B.C./C.-B. 51° 19′ – 118° 28′ (82 M/8)	

cap (2)

DES	Variant of **cape**.	*Variante de **cape**.*
OBS	Anglicized version of French "cap". Rare; Ont.	*Emprunt au français «cap». Rare; Ont.*
EQ		**cap** (m.)
REL	head (1), point (1), bluff (1)	
EX	North Gros Cap, Ont. 46° 34′ – 84° 36′ (41 K/10)	

cap (m.) (Fig. 32)

DES	*Projection of land, usually high and massive, jutting into a body of water.*	Saillie de terre habituellement élevée et massive, qui s'avance dans une étendue d'eau.
OBS	A cap *is customarily smaller than a* promontoire, *but larger than a* pointe. *Formerly, "cap" and "promontoire" were synonyms. Now "promontoire" indicates a high land mass, whereas "cap" may apply to high or low projecting land. Used mainly in Que., but sporadically in the Atlantic Provinces.*	Le cap est habituellement plus petit que le promontoire, mais plus gros que la pointe. Anciennement, le cap et le promontoire étaient synonymes. Aujourd'hui, le promontoire indique une masse de terre élevée tandis que le cap désigne tout ce qui s'avance de façon élevée ou non. Attesté au Qué. surtout et sporadiquement dans les provinces de l'Atlantique.
EQ	**cape**	
REL		tête (1), nez, pointe, promontoire
EX	Cap Tourmente, Qué./Que. 47° 05′ – 70° 45′ (21 M/2) Cap Pelé, N.-B./N.B. 47° 49′ – 65° 09′ (21 P/14)	

cape(s) (Fig. 2)

DES	Prominent elevated projection of land extending into a body of water.	*Saillie de terre élevée qui s'avance dans une étendue d'eau.*
OBS	Widely used. Some capes do not have a pronounced elevation. The generic term may precede or follow the specific.	*Emploi généralisé. Dans certains cas, le relief n'est pas très élevé. Le générique peut précéder ou suivre le spécifique.*
EQ		**cap** (m.)
REL	head (1), point (1), bluff (1), cap (2), kap	
EX	Cape Scott, B.C./C.-B. 50° 47′ – 128° 26′ (102 I/16) Abells Cape, P.E.I./Î.-P.-É. 46° 20′ – 62° 21′ (11 L/8) Kildare Capes, P.E.I./Î.-P.-É. 46° 54′ – 63° 59′ (21 I/16)	

carriers

DES	See **hill**	*Voir* **hill**
OBS	Rare; Nfld.	*Rare; T.-N.*
EQ		**collines** (f.)
REL	knoll (1), tolt, knob	
EX	Sand Carriers, Nfld./T.-N. 46° 38′ – 53° 35′ (1 K/12)	

carry

DES	See **portage**	*Voir* **portage**
OBS	Rare; N.S.	*Rare; N.-É.*
EQ		**portage** (m.)
REL	trail	
EX	Coade Carry, N.S./N.-É. 44° 25′ – 65° 18′ (21 A/6)	

cascade

DES	Series of stepped waterfalls.	*Chute d'eau comportant plusieurs paliers.*
OBS	Varying in steepness. Widely used, but uncommon.	*Pente variable. Emploi généralisé mais peu fréquent.*
EQ		**cascades** (f.)
REL	fall	
EX	Cascade of the Thirteen Steps, N.W.T./T.N.-O. 61° 26′ – 126° 36′ (95 E/7)	

cascades (f.)

DES	*Part of a stream with a small flow descending over several levels.*	Partie d'un cours d'eau de faible débit comportant ordinairement plusieurs paliers.
OBS	*A* cascade *differs from a* chute *in its smaller flow and its levels, and from a* rapide *in its broken descent. Used in the plural; noted in Que.*	La cascade se distingue de la chute par son débit d'eau plus faible et par ses paliers, et du rapide par sa rupture de pente. Utilisé au pluriel et attesté au Qué.
EQ	**cascade**	
REL		chute, rapide, sault
EX	Cascades du Batardeau, Qué./Que. 46° 47′ – 77° 15′ (31 K/14)	

castle

DES	Feature having the appearance of a castle.	*Relief dont la forme rappelle un château.*
OBS	Applied to rocks, islands, hills, and mountains. Widely used.	*S'emploie pour des roches, des îles, des collines et des montagnes. Emploi généralisé.*
EQ		
REL	tower, ramparts, fortress	
EX	Caribou Castle (rock-roche), Nfld./T.-N. 53° 43′ – 57° 02′ (13 H/11) Labrador Castle (hill-colline), N.S./N.-É. 44° 37′ – 64° 11′ (21 A/9)	

cataract

DES	Series of major unnavigable rapids.	*Succession de rapides importants et impropres à la navigation.*
OBS	Rare; B.C.	*Rare; C.-B.*
EQ		[**cataracte** (f.)]
REL	rapid (1), chute	
EX	Kodak Cataract, B.C./C.-B. 57° 35′ – 126° 31′ (94 E/10)	

cave(s)

DES	Natural subterranean chamber open to the surface.	*Cavité naturelle souterraine et ouverte sur l'extérieur.*
OBS	May be either inland or in coastal cliffs. Widely used.	*Peut être creusée dans les terres ou dans des falaises côtières. Emploi généralisé.*
EQ		**caverne** (f.)
REL		
EX	Arctomys Cave, B.C./C.-B. 53° 04′ – 118° 54′ (83 E/2) Bonnechere Caves, Ont. 45° 30′ – 77° 00′ (31 F/11)	

caverne (f.)   (Fig. 11)

DES	*Natural underground cavity hollowed in rock, and closed on all sides except for a narrow opening.*	Cavité naturelle souterraine, fermée de tous côtés à l'exception d'une étroite ouverture et creusée dans une roche.
OBS	*A* caverne *can be made up of a number of rooms, also called "grottes". Used in Que.*	La caverne peut être formée de plusieurs salles aussi appelées «grottes». Attesté au Qué.
EQ	**cave**	
REL		grotte
EX	Caverne Laflèche, Qué./Que. 45° 39′ – 75° 48′ (31 G/12)	

Figure 11. Caverne à la Patate, Île
d'Anticosti, Quebec.
(Jean-Marie Dubois)

Figure 11. Caverne à la Patate, île
d'Anticosti, au Québec.
(Jean-Marie Dubois)

cay(s)

DES	See **rock (1)**	*Voir* **rock (1)**
OBS	Used only in Nfld.	*Ne s'emploie qu'à T.-N.*
EQ		**caye** (f.)
REL	reef, islet	
EX	False Cay, Nfld./T.-N. 46° 45′ – 54° 12′ (C.4622) St. Mary's Cays, Nfld./T.-N. 46° 43′ – 54° 13′ (C.4622)	

caye(s) (f.)   (Fig. 7)

DES	*Rock exposed at low tide.*	Roche qui émerge à marée basse.
OBS	*This term seems to be borrowed from the Spanish "cayo", itself drawn from the Arawak language of the Caribbean. "Caye" is pronounced "kye" (as in "caille", the French word for quail). Used in Que., although uncommon.*	Ce terme semble être emprunté à l'espagnol «cayo», lui-même inspiré du parler arawak des Antilles. «Caye» se prononce «caille», comme pour l'oiseau. Utilisé au Qué. mais peu commun.
EQ	**cay**	
REL		récif, roche (1), rocher
EX	Caye de la Baie des Plongeurs, Qué./Que. 48° 46′ – 68° 59′ (22 C/15) Cayes de l'Anse à David, Qué./Que. 48° 09′ – 69° 50′ (22 C/4)	

chair

DES	Rocks, fancifully shaped like a chair.	*Rocher dont la forme rappelle vaguement un banc.*
OBS	Rare; Nfld. and Ont.	*Rare; T.-N. et Ont.*
EQ		**rocher** (m.)
REL	couch, seat	
EX	Devils Chair, Ont. 47° 36′ – 85° 03′ (41 N/10) The Chair, Nfld./T.-N. 53° 29′ – 55° 58′ (3 E/5)	

champ (m.)

DES	*Flat and open area.*	Espace ouvert et plat.
OBS	*Used in Que.*	Attesté au Qué.
EQ	**[field]**	
REL		plée, pré
EX	Champ du Bilbo, Qué./Que. 48° 30′ – 64° 10′ (22 A/9)	

channel (1)   (Fig. 26, 30, 54)

DES	Narrow stretch of water, either an inlet or a connection between two bodies of water.	*Bande d'eau étroite et allongée, qui prolonge une étendue d'eau ou qui met en communication deux étendues d'eau.*
OBS	Widely used.	*Emploi généralisé.*
EQ		**chenal** (m.)
REL	passage, narrows, inlet (1), sound (1), canal (1), pass (2), strait, tickle	
EX	Inman Channel, Sask. 55° 25′ – 104° 06′ (73 P/8) Dean Channel, B.C./C.-B. 52° 19′ – 127° 31′ (93 D/5)	

channel (2)

DES	Alternative course in a flowing water body, or a distributary within a delta.	*Ramification d'un cours d'eau principal ou défluent dans un delta.*
OBS	Widely used.	*Emploi généralisé.*
EQ		**branche** (f.)
REL	river (1), snye, branch	
EX	Ministicoog Channel, Y.T./Yuk. 68° 53′ – 136° 34′ (117 A) East Neebish Channel, Ont. 46° 21′ – 84° 08′ (41 K/8)	

chenal (m.)

DES	*Natural or man-made navigable waterway between land or shoals.*	Voie navigable naturelle ou aménagée entre des terres ou des hauts-fonds.
OBS	*The term «chenail» is also heard for "chenal" in Que. and French-speaking areas of the Maritime Provinces. Used in several provinces.*	On entend également le terme "chenail" pour chenal au Qué. et dans les régions d'expression française des Maritimes. Attesté dans plusieurs provinces.
EQ	**channel (1)**	
REL		détroit, goulet, passage, passe
EX	Chenal des Quatre Fourches, Alb./Alta. 58° 45′ – 111° 25′ (74 L/11) Chenal du Diable, Ont. 47° 34′ – 79° 31′ (31 M/12) Chenal des Grands Voiliers, Qué./Que. 46° 52′ – 70° 58′ (21 L/15)	

chokey

DES	Narrow channel between islands in a river.	*Passage étroit entre des îles dans une rivière.*
OBS	Rare; N.B.	*Rare; N.-B.*
EQ		**passe (f.)**
REL	channel (1), passage, tickle, pass (2), thoroughfare	
EX	Little Chokey, N.B./N.-B. 45° 59′ – 66° 45′ (21 G/15)	

chops (1)

DES	See **rip (2)**	*Voir **rip (2)***
OBS	Rare; N.S. and N.B.	*Rare; N.-É. et N.-B.*
EQ		[**rides (f.)**]
REL	rapids (2), eddy, chute	
EX	Eastern Chops, N.B./N.-B. 45° 02′ – 66° 49′ (21 G/2) The Chops, N.S./N.-É. 44° 28′ – 64° 09′ (21 A/8)	

chops (2)

DES	Feature shaped like the jaws of a horse.	*Relief dont la forme rappelle les mâchoires d'un cheval.*
OBS	Applied to hills and heads. Uncommon; Nfld.	*S'applique à des collines et à des caps. Emploi peu fréquent; T.-N.*
EQ		
REL	jaw	
EX	Horse Chops, Nfld./T.-N. 47° 30′ – 55° 28′ (1 M/6)	

chuckle

DES	Rocks at the entrance of a cove, where the water is turbulent.	*Rochers à l'entrée d'une anse, où l'eau est turbulente.*
OBS	Rare; N.S.	*Rare; N.-É.*
EQ		**rocher** (m.)
REL	rock (1), breaker, shoal, reef, ledge (1)	
EX	Whale Cove Chuckle, N.S./N.-É. 44° 28′ – 63° 42′ (11 D/5)	

chute(s)   (Fig. 12)

DES	Narrow and fast-flowing descent of a watercourse confined within steep banks.	*Partie d'un cours d'eau étroite et enserrée entre des berges abruptes, où l'eau tombe brusquement.*
OBS	Used in Ont., Man., Alta., and B.C.	*Relevé en Ont., au Man., en Alb. et en C.-B.*
EQ		**rapide** (m.)
REL	rapid (1), cataract, run (2), fall	
EX	Portage Chute, Man. 57° 49' – 95° 18' (54 E/14) Dutchman Chutes, Ont. 45° 52' – 79° 56' (31 E/13)	

Figure 12. Oblique aerial view of Vermilion Chutes on the Peace River, Alberta.
(Alberta Culture – Historic Sites Service)

Figure 12. Photographie aérienne oblique des Vermilion Chutes, sur la rivière de la Paix, en Alberta.
(Alberta Culture – Historic Sites Service)

chute(s) (f.) (Fig. 13)

DES	*Mass of water falling abruptly, at a break in descent of a watercourse.*	Masse d'eau tombant brusquement à l'emplacement d'une rupture de pente.
OBS	*A* chute *differs from a* cascade *in its greater flow and lack of levels, and from a* rapide *by having a break in descent. Used in Que. and also in the N.W.T.*	La chute se distingue de la cascade par son plus grand débit d'eau et par son absence de paliers, et du rapide par sa rupture de pente. Attesté au Qué. et aussi dans les T.N.-O.
EQ	**falls**	
REL		cascades, rapide, sault
EX	Chute Montmorency, Qué./Que. 46° 53′ – 71° 09′ (21 L/14)	
	Chutes la Martre, T.N.-O./N.W.T. 63° 08′ – 116° 54′ (85 N)	

circle (Fig. 36)

DES	Rounded bowl-shaped depression in the mountains.	*Dépression en forme de cuvette dans les montagnes.*
OBS	Rare; B.C.	*Rare; C.-B.*
EQ		[**bassin** (m.)]
REL	basin (3), cirque	
EX	Glacier Circle, B.C./C.-B. 51° 10′ – 117° 24′ (82 N/3)	

Figure 13. Chute Ouiatchouane, south of Lac Saint-Jean, Quebec.
(Jean-René Tremblay, Commission de toponymie du Québec)

Figure 13. Chute Ouiatchouane, au sud du lac Saint-Jean, au Québec.
(Jean-René Tremblay, Commission de toponymie du Québec)

cirque

DES	Deep, steep-walled, bowl-shaped indentation in a mountain side.	*Échancrure profonde, en forme de cuvette et aux parois raides dans le flanc d'une montagne.*
OBS	Formed and shaped by movement of snow and ice; may contain remnants of glacial ice, small lakes, or streams. Used in B.C. and Nfld.	*Formé et façonné par le mouvement de la neige et de la glace, le cirque peut renfermer des vestiges de glace de glacier, de petits lacs, ou des cours d'eau. Relevé en C.-B. et à T.-N.*
EQ		[**cirque** (m.)]
REL	basin (3)	
EX	Robson Cirque, B.C./C.-B. 53° 07' – 119° 08' (83 E/3) Antler Cirque, Nfld./T.-N. 53° 44' – 58° 43' (13 G/10)	

claw

DES	Feature having the appearance of a claw.	*Relief en forme de griffe d'animal ou de pince de crustacé.*
OBS	Applied to shoals and rocks. Rare; Nfld. and N.S.	*S'emploie pour des hauts-fonds et des rochers. Rare; T.-N. et N.-É.*
EQ		
REL		
EX	Eastern Lobster Claw (shoal – haut-fond), N.S./N.-É. 44° 32' – 64° 13' (21 A/9) Cats Claw (rock-rocher), Nfld./T.-N. 47° 33' – 55° 37' (C.4645)	

cliff(s)

DES	High steep face of rock and/or unconsolidated material.	*Paroi abrupte et élevée, constituée de roc ou de matériaux non consolidés, ou des deux.*
OBS	Used for sea cliffs, mountain cliffs, and river banks. Widely used.	*S'emploie pour des reliefs côtiers, des reliefs montagneux et des rives. Emploi généralisé.*
EQ		**falaise** (f.)
REL	bluff (1), head (1), bank (2), wall, ramparts	
EX	Amuchewaspimewin Cliff, Sask. 55° 26' – 104° 33' (73 P/7) Bald Cliff, N.S./N.-É. 44° 52' – 62° 46' (11 D/15) Corwin Cliffs, Y.T./Yuk. 60° 18' – 140° 17' (115 B & C)	

Figure 14. Eve Cone rising above the Big Raven Plateau, Mount Edziza area, southeast of Telegraph Creek, British Columbia.
(National Air Photo Library, A12788-421; 1950)

Figure 14. Eve Cone, colline s'élevant au-dessus du Big Raven Plateau, dans la région du mont Edziza, au sud-est de Telegraph Creek, en Colombie-Britannique.
(Photothèque nationale de l'air, A12788-421; 1950)

col

DES	Low point on a ridge joining two summits.	*Sur une crête, dépression entre deux sommets.*
OBS	Generally above timber line. Used in B.C., N.W.T., and Y.T.	*Se trouve généralement au-dessus de la ligne supérieure de la forêt. En usage en C.-B., dans les T.N.-O. et au Yukon.*
EQ		[**col** (m.)]
REL	gap (1), pass (1)	
EX	Fria Col, B.C./C.-B. 51° 44′ – 117° 51′ (82 N/12)	

colline(s) (f.)

DES	*Moderate elevation, usually with gently sloping sides.*	Élévation modérée aux versants généralement en pente douce.
OBS	*Smaller than a* montagne, *but larger than a* butte. *Used in Que.*	Plus petite que la montagne, mais plus considérable que la butte. Attesté au Qué.
EQ	**hill**	
REL		bosse, butte, buttereau, dôme, morne
EX	Colline de la Tortue, Qué./Que. 48° 37′ – 67° 15′ (22 B/11) Collines Abijévis, Qué./Que. 48° 29′ – 78° 46′ (32 O/7)	

cone (Fig. 14, 21, 45)

DES	Cone-shaped hill.	*Colline de forme conique.*
OBS	Used in Nfld. and B.C. A few in B.C. (e.g. Cinder Cone) are young volcanic vents.	*Relevé à T.-N. et en C.-B. En C.-B., désigne parfois, comme dans «Cinder Cone», des évents volcaniques de formation récente.*
EQ		**colline** (f.)
REL	hill, sugarloaf, tolt, pingo	
EX	Vargas Cone, B.C./C.-B. 49° 05′ – 125° 52′ (92 F/4) Hayes Cone, Nfld./T.-N. 56° 41′ – 61° 10′ (14 C/11)	

confluent (m.)

DES	*Junction of two watercourses.*	Point de jonction de deux cours d'eau.
OBS	*Used in Que.*	Attesté au Qué.
EQ	**fork (1)**	
REL		
EX	Confluent Kannilirqiq, Qué./Que. 57° 35′ – 69° 52′ (24 F/12)	

corner

DES	See **point (1)**	*Voir* **point (1)**
OBS	Rare; N.S. and N.W.T.	*Rare; N.-É. et T.N.-O.*
EQ		**pointe** (f.)
REL	peninsula, spit, cape, head (1)	
EX	Bear Corner, N.W.T./T.N.-O. 78° 08′ – 87° 32′ (49 F) Chimney Corner, N.S./N.-É. 46° 23′ – 61° 10′ (11 K/6)	

corniche (f.)

DES	*Natural projection overhanging a steep slope.*	Saillie naturelle surplombant une pente raide.
OBS	*Used in Que.*	Attesté au Qué.
EQ	**ledge (2)**	
REL		
EX	Corniche aux Goélands, Qué./Que. 48° 29′ – 64° 09′ (22 A/8)	

côte (f.) (1)

DES	*Slope forming one side of a hill.*	Pente qui forme l'un des versants d'une colline.
OBS	*Used in Que. and Man.*	Attesté au Qué. et au Man.
EQ	**hill**	
REL		coteau
EX	Côte Bédard, Qué./Que. 46° 55′ – 71° 19′ (21 L/14) Côte Beaulieu, Man. 49° 22′ – 98° 32′ (62 G/7)	

côte (f.) (2)

DES	*Zone of contact between land and sea.*	Zone de contact entre la terre et la mer.
OBS	*In modern French, the term "côte" applies only to the seashore, whereas the terms "rivage" and "rive" have more general meanings. Used in Que.*	En français moderne, le terme «côte» ne s'applique qu'à la mer, tandis que les ermes «rivage» et «rive» ont un sens plus général. Attesté au Qué.
EQ	**shore**	
REL		rivage
EX	Côte de la Découverte, Qué./Que. 49° 05′ – 62° 40′ (12 E/10)	

coteau

DES	Elevated plateau having the appearance of a range of hills when viewed from the adjacent prairie.	*Plateau élevé qui, de la prairie adjacente, a l'aspect d'une chaîne de collines.*
OBS	Rare; Sask.	*Rare; Sask.*
EQ		[**coteau** (m.)]
REL	plateau, hill, lookout, bank (2), escarpment	
EX	The Missouri Coteau, Sask. 50° 00′ – 105° 00′ (72 H)	

coteau (m.)

DES	*Side of a hill or of a terrace.*	Versant d'une colline ou d'une terrasse.
OBS	*"Coteau" sometimes acquires the meaning of a minor elevation; a small hill. Used mainly in Que., but also in Man.*	Le coteau prend parfois le sens d'une petite élévation peu élevée, d'une petite colline. Attesté au Qué. surtout, mais aussi au Man.
EQ	**hill**	
REL		côte (1)
EX	Coteau Vire-Crêpe, Qué./Que. 46° 41′ – 71° 22′ (21 L/11) Coteau Lambert, Man. 49° 18′ – 96° 34′ (62 H/7)	

couch

DES	Mountain, fancifully shaped like a sofa.	*Montagne dont la forme rappelle vaguement un sofa.*
OBS	Rare; B.C.	*Rare; C.-B.*
EQ		**mont** (m.)
REL	chair, seat, mountain	
EX	Devils Couch, B.C./C.-B. 49° 50′ – 117° 39′ (82 F/13)	

coude (m.)

DES	*Prominent angle in a watercourse at an abrupt change of stream direction.*	Angle saillant dans le tracé d'un cours d'eau suite à un changement brusque de direction.
OBS	*"Coude" designates a more pronounced feature than "courbe" or "détour". Used in Que.*	Le coude est plus accentué que la courbe ou le détour. Attesté au Qué.
EQ	**elbow**	
REL		détour, courbe
EX	Coude Mistinshuk, Qué./Que. 57° 41′ – 65° 27′ (24 H/11)	

coulee (Fig. 15)

DES	Usually steep-sided valley or ravine.	*Vallée ou ravin aux versants haituellement raides.*
OBS	Widely used in the prairies of Man., Sask., Alta., and B.C. Some have flat bottoms, and contain streams and lakes.	*Largement utilisé dans les prairies du Man., de la Sask., de l'Alb., et de la C.-B. Certaines coulées ont un fond plat et renferment des cours d'eau et des lacs.*
EQ		**coulée** (f.) (**1**)
REL	valley (1), ravine, canyon, trench	
EX	Thornhill Coulee, Man. 49° 17′ – 98° 01′ (62 G/8) Baker Coulee, Sask. 49° 37′ – 108° 46′ (72 F/10) Etzikom Coulee, Alta./Alb. 49° 28′ – 112° 08′ (72 E/5)	

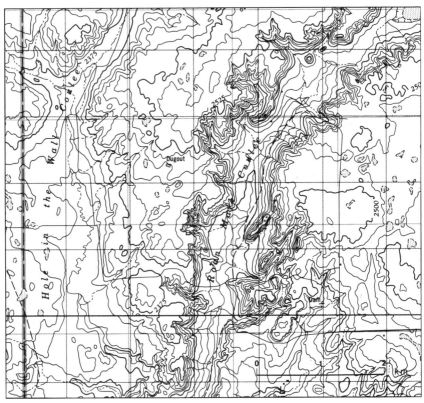

Figure 15. Roan Mare Coulee and Hole in the Wall Coulee, southeast of Bengough, Saskatchewan.
(National Topographic System map 72 H/2; 1974)

Figure 15. Roan Mare Coulee et Hole in the Wall Coulee, au sud-est de Bengough, en Saskatchewan.
(Carte 72 H/2 du Système national de référence cartographique; 1974)

coulée (f.) (1)

DES	*Considerable terrain depression, often with a stream flowing in the bottom.*	Dépression plus ou moins considérable du terrain, au fond de laquelle coule souvent un cours d'eau.
OBS	*The related terms listed all indicate an elongated depression, usually with a stream flowing through. Used in Que. and N.B.*	Les termes semblables retenus désignent tous une dépression allongée permettant le passage d'un cours d'eau. Attesté au Qué. et au N.-B.
EQ	**ravine**	
REL		canyon, gorge, ravin, ravine, rigwash, vallée
EX	Coulée à Albert, Qué./Que. 49° 14′ – 65° 36′ (22 H/4) Coulée à Siméon, N.-B./N.B. 47° 46′ – 67° 23′ (21 O/14)	

coulée (f.) (2)

DES	*The stream flowing at the bottom of a depression.*	Le cours d'eau au fond d'une dépression.
OBS	*Term used in Que.; especially widespread in the Beauce region.*	Attesté partout au Qué. et très répandu dans la Beauce.
EQ	**brook**	
REL		crique (1), ruisseau
EX	Coulée Abe-Coffin, Qué./Que. 48° 38′ – 65° 08′ (22 A/11)	

country

DES	Tract of terrain, inland from coastal settlements.	*Étendue de terrain en arrière des communautés côtières.*
OBS	Rare; Nfld.	*Rare; T.-N.*
EQ		**[arrière-pays** (m.)]
REL	barren, bog, heath	
EX	St. Shotts Country, Nfld./T.-N. 46° 42′ – 53° 35′ (1 K/12)	

courant (m.)

DES	Part of a watercourse with swifter flow.	Portion d'un cours d'eau qui se caractérise par une vitesse plus prononcée.
OBS	Used in Que.	Attesté au Qué.
EQ	**current**	
REL		
EX	Courant Sainte-Marie, Qué./Que. 45° 31′ – 73° 33′ (31 H/12)	

courbe (f.)

DES	Bend in a watercourse.	Inflexion dans le tracé d'un cours d'eau.
OBS	"Courbe" and "détour" designate less pronounced features than "coude". Used in Que.	La courbe et le détour sont moins accentués que le coude. Attesté au Qué.
EQ	**bend**	
REL		détour, coude
EX	Courbe du Sault, Qué./Que. 50° 19′ – 64° 54′ (22 I/7)	

cours d'eau (m.)

DES	Natural flowing watercourse (river, stream, etc.).	Chenal naturel (fleuve, rivière, ruisseau, etc.).
OBS	A very general term assigned to various types of natural watercourses. Used in Que., especially in the Lotbinière region.	Terme très général attribué aux différents chenaux naturels. Attesté au Qué., dans la région de Lotbinière.
EQ	**[stream]**	
REL		
EX	Le Grand Cours d'Eau, Qué./Que. 45° 14′ – 74° 22′ (31 G/1)	

66

cove (Fig. 2, 20)

DES	Water area in small indentation of the shoreline of seas, lakes, or rivers.	*Prtie d'une mer, d'un lac ou d'une rivière occupant une petite échancrure du littoral.*
OBS	Widely used for a sheltered water feature smaller than a bay.	*«Cove» désigne généralement une échancrure plus petite que "bay".*
EQ		**anse** (f.)
REL	bay, hole (1), inlet (1)	
EX	Peggys Cove, N.S./N.-É. 44° 29′ – 63° 55′ (11 D/5) Pauline Cove, Y.T./Yuk. 69° 34′ – 138° 55′ (117 D) The Cove Jim Got Paddy, Nfld./T.-N. 46° ▪○′ – 53° 36′ (1 K/12) Porter Cove, N.B./N.-B. 46° 29′ – 66° 22′ (21 J/8)	

crab

DES	See **islet**	*Voir* **islet**
OBS	Rare; Ont.	*Rare; Ont.*
EQ		**îlot** (m.)
REL	island, rock (1)	
EX	Fraser Crab, Ont. 45° 05′ – 74° 31′ (31 G/2)	

crag(s)

DES	Steep jagged prominence.	*Sommet dentelé aux flancs escarpés.*
OBS	Rare; Alta., B.C., and N.W.T.	*Rare; Alb., C.-B. et T.N.-O.*
EQ		**pic** (m.)
REL	peak (1), head (2), tower, cliff, bluff (1)	
EX	Phantom Crag, Alta./Alb. 51° 18′ – 115° 11′ (82 O/6) Cathedral Crags, B.C./C.-B. 51° 24′ – 116° 23′ (82 N/8) Leffingwell Crags, N.W.T./T.N.-O. 77° 45′ – 112° 10′ (89 D)	

cran (m.)

DES	*Rock rising above the general level of the ground.*	Rocher sortant à fleur de terre.
OBS	*Used in Que.*	Attesté au Qué.
EQ	**rock (2)**	
REL		roche (2)
EX	Cran Carré, Qué./Que. 50° 17′ – 65° 56′ (22 I/5)	

crater(s) (Fig. 16)

DES	Bowl-shaped depression.	*Dépression en forme de cuvette.*
OBS	Used for impact craters (e.g. Holleford Crater, Ont.) and depressions in the top of volcanic cones (e.g. Cocoa Crater, B.C.) Rare; Ont., B.C., and N.W.T.	*S'emploie pour des cratères météoriques (comme le Holleford Crater, Ont.) et des dépressions creusées dans le sommet de cones volcaniques (comme le Cocoa Crater, C.-B.). Rare; Ont., C.-B. et T.N.-O.*
EQ		**cratère** (m.)
REL	volcanoes	
EX	Holleford Crater, Ont. 44° 27′ – 76° 38′ (31 C/7) Cocoa Crater, B.C./C.-B. 57° 40′ – 130° 42′ (104 G/10) The Two Craters, N.W.T./T.N.-O 78° 17′ – 92° 11′ (59 F)	

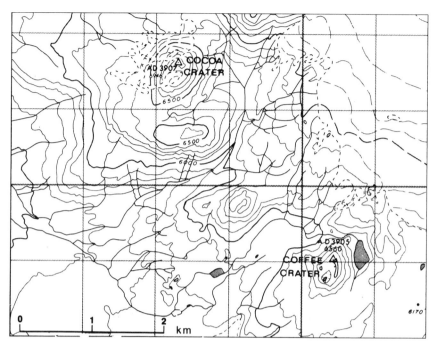

Figure 16. Cocoa Crater and Coffee Crater, Mount Edziza area, southeast of Telegraph Creek, British Columbia. (National Topographic System map 104 G/10; 1974)

Figure 16. Cocoa Crater et Coffee Crater, dans la région du mont Edziza, au sud-est de Telegraph Creek, en Colombie-Britannique. (Carte 104 G/10 du Système national de référence cartographique; 1974)

cratère (m.)   (Fig. 17)

DES	*More or less rounded, bowl-shaped depression.*	Enfoncement plus ou moins arrondi en forme de cuvette.
OBS	A cratère *can be either volcanic or meteoric in origin. Used in Que.*	Le cratère est soit d'origine volcanique, soit d'origine météorique. Attesté au Qué.
EQ	**crater**	
REL		
EX	Cratère du Nouveau-Québec, Qué./Que. 61° 17′ – 73° 40′ (35 H/5)	

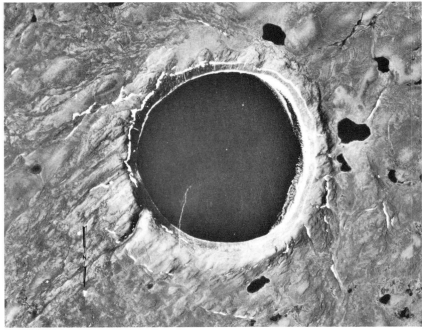

Figure 17. Lac du Cratère inside the Cratère du Nouveau-Québec, southwest of Kangiqsujuaq, Quebec.
(National Air Photo Library, A16116-110; 1958)

Figure 17. Lac du Cratère à l'intérieur du cratère du Nouveau-Québec, au sud-ouest de Kangiqsujuaq, au Québec.
(Photothèque nationale de l'air, A16116-110; 1958)

creek(s) (1) (Fig. 4, 19, 35)

DES	Watercourse, usually smaller than a river.	*Cours d'eau généralement plus petit qu'une rivière.*
OBS	Widely used except in the Atlantic Provinces where "brook" is more common.	*Emploi généralisé, sauf dans les provinces de l'Atlantique, où «brook» est plus fréquent.*
EQ		**crique** (m.) **(1)**
REL	brook, stream, river (1)	
EX	Lynn Creek, B.C./C.-B. 49° 19′ – 123° 02′ (92 G/6) Herriot Creek, Man. 58° 33′ – 94° 18′ (54 L/9) East Two Creeks, Ont. 42° 05′ – 82° 27′ (40 J/1)	

creek (2)

DES	Narrow tidal inlet, usually with a watercourse flowing in at its head.	*Étroit chenal de marée, à la source duquel se déverse généralement un cours d'eau.*
OBS	Common in the Atlantic Provinces; unusual elsewhere.	*Emploi fréquent dans les provinces de l'Atlantique; peu usité ailleurs.*
EQ		**crique** (f.) **(2)**
REL	inlet (1), cove, bay	
EX	Hornes Creek, P.E.I./Î.-P.-É. 46° 17′ – 63° 04′ (11 L/6) False Creek, B.C./C.-B. 49° 17′ – 123′ 08′ (92 G/6)	

crest (Fig. 37)

DES	See **ridge (1)**	*Voir **ridge (1)***
OBS	Rare; B.C.	*Rare; C.-B.*
EQ		[**chaînon** (m.)]
REL	back, edge	
EX	Avalanche Crest, B.C./C.-B. 51° 17′ – 117° 29′ (82 N/6)	

crête (f.)

DES	*Crest line of a mountain or mountain group.*	Ligne de faîte d'une montagne ou d'un ensemble montagneux.
OBS	*Used in Que.*	Attesté au Qué.
EQ	[**ridge**]	
REL		
EX	Crête de la Palissade, Qué./Que. 49° 15′ – 78° 51′ (32 E/7)	

crib

DES	See **shoal**	*Voir* **shoal**
OBS	Rare; Ont.	*Rare; Ont.*
EQ		**haut-fond** (m.)
REL	bank (1), ground (1)	
EX	Calf Pasture Crib, Ont. 44° 01′ – 77° 42′ (31 C/4)	

crique (m.) (1)

DES	*Small or very small watercourse.*	Petit ou très petit cours d'eau.
OBS	*"Crique" has masculine gender in this meaning. Used in Que.*	«Crique» est bien du genre masculin dans ce sens. Attesté au Qué.
EQ	**creek (1)**	
REL		coulée (2), ruisseau
EX	Crique Akerson, Qué./Que. 46° 36′ – 74° 48′ (31 J/10)	

crique (f.) (2)

DES	*Small, narrow, and elongated indentation in a shoreline.*	Petit rentrant du rivage de forme étroite et allongée.
OBS	*Term, of Scandinavian origin (kriki), having feminine gender in this meaning. On a rocky shore, the usually deep, salty water offers natural shelter for boats. Used in Que. and N.S.*	Terme d'origine scandinave (kriki) dont le genre est bien féminin dans ce sens. Sur une côte rocheuse, la crique, dont les eaux sont habituellement profondes et salées, offre un abri naturel aux embarcations. Attesté au Qué. et en N.-É.
EQ	**creek (2)**	
REL		anse, baie, trou (1)
EX	Crique de la Chaloupe, Qué./Que. 49° 08′ – 62° 32′ (12 E/2)	
	Crique des Grosses Coques, N.-É./N.S. 44° 22′ – 66° 06′ (21 B/8)	

crook

DES	See **bend**	*Voir* **bend**
OBS	Rare; N.S.	*Rare; N.-É.*
EQ		**courbe** (f.)
REL	elbow, oxbow	
EX	Basil Gates Crook, N.S./N.-É. 44° 34′ – 63° 47′ (11 D/12)	

crossing

DES	Water or ice traverse of a water body, joining land routes.	*Section d'une étendue d'eau courante ou gelée qui relie des voies de communication terrestres.*
OBS	Rare; Sask. and Y.T.	*Rare; Sask. et Yukon.*
EQ		[**traverse** (f.)]
REL	ferry, landing, ford	
EX	Sioux Crossing, Sask. 50° 48′ – 103° 54′ (62 L/13)	
	New Crossing, Y.T./Yuk. 63° 30′ – 137° 09′ (115 P)	

current

DES	Narrow channel with strong water currents.	*Chenal étroit dans lequel le courant est fort.*
OBS	Rare; Nfld. and Ont.	*Rare; T.-N. et Ont.*
EQ		**courant** (m.)
REL	channel (1), passage, pass (2)	
EX	Swift Current, Nfld./T.-N. 47° 54′ – 54° 15′ (1 M/16) Little Current, Ont. 45° 59′ – 81° 55′ (41 H/13)	

cut

DES	Artificial channel through marsh and other low-lying land.	*Chenal artificiel traversant une marche ou une autre terre basse.*
OBS	Common in Ont.; also used in Nfld. and Man.	*Emploi fréquent en Ont.; également relevé à T.-N. et au Man.*
EQ		[**passage** (m.)]
REL	canal (2), drain, cutoff	
EX	Poonamalie Cut, Ont. 44° 53′ – 76° 04′ (31 C/16) Niemis Cut, Man. 50° 21′ – 95° 27′ (52 L/6)	

cutoff, cut-off

DES	Natural or artificial channel shortening the route of a watercourse.	*Passage naturel ou artificiel servant de raccourci à un cours d'eau.*
OBS	Rare; Ont., Man., and Sask.	*Rare; Ont., Man. et Sask.*
EQ		[**passage** (m.)]
REL	cut, canal (2), drain	
EX	St. Clair Cutoff, Ont. 42° 32′ – 82° 38′ (40 J/10) Bigstone Cutoff, Sask. 53° 56′ – 102° 22′ (63 E/16) Middle Cut-off, Man. 53° 56′ – 101° 23′ (63 F/14)	

d

dalles

DES	Rocky narrows.	*Passage rocheux.*
OBS	Rare; Ont.	*Rare; Ont.*
EQ		**passage** (m.)
REL	narrows, passage, gap (2), pass (2)	
EX	The Little Dalles, Ont. 49° 52′ – 94° 34′ (52 E/15)	

dam

DES	See **pool (1)**	*Voir* **pool (1)**
OBS	Rare; N.S.	*Rare; N.-É.*
EQ		**fosse** (f.)
REL	hole (3)	
EX	Dickies Dam, N.S./N.-É. 45° 10′ – 63° 16′ (11 E/3)	

deadwater(s)

DES	Stretch of a watercourse where the surface appears motionless.	*Partie allongée d'un cours d'eau, dont la surface paraît immobile.*
OBS	Used in the Atlantic Provinces.	*En usage dans les provinces de l'Atlantique.*
EQ		
REL	steady	
EX	Nelson Deadwater, N.B./N.-B. 45° 18′ – 66° 16′ (21 G/8) Black Brook Deadwaters, N.S./N.-É. 44° 47′ – 64° 01′ (21 A/16)	

débouche (f.)

DES	See **décharge**	*Voir* **décharge**
OBS	Used in the feminine gender; a term of rare and local usage recorded in Que.	*Au féminin, terme d'usage rare et local attesté au Qué.*
EQ	**outlet (1)**	
REL		déversant
EX	Débouche Lente, Qué./Que. 45° 56′ – 73° 25′ (31 H/14)	

décharge (f.)

DES	*Outlet or small watercourse draining from a lake, pond, or basin.*	Exutoire ou petit cours d'eau qui donne issue aux eaux d'un lac, d'un étang ou d'un bassin.
OBS	*Used in Que.*	Attesté au Qué.
EQ	**outlet (1)**	
REL		débouche, déversant
EX	Décharge des Acadiens, Qué./Que. 46° 19′ – 72° 52′ (31 I/7)	

deeps

DES	Area of deep water between banks, ledges, and grounds.	*Zone d'eau profonde entre des bancs, des hauts-fonds et des chaussées.*
OBS	Used off Nfld.	*Relevé au large de T.-N.*
EQ		**[bas-fond (m.)]**
REL	basin (1), valley (2), trough	
EX	Cordelia Deeps, 47° 43′ – 52° 35′ (C.4574)	

défilé (m.)

DES	*Narrow natural channel in a watercourse.*	Passage naturel étroit dans un cours d'eau.
OBS	*Used in Que.*	Attesté au Qué.
EQ	**narrows**	
REL		
EX	Défilé Woolsey, Qué./Que. 45° 31' – 76° 12' (31 F/9)	

delta (Fig. 18)

DES	Fan-shaped alluvial land at the mouth of a river, usually with distributaries, channels, and small lakes.	*Zone d'accumulation alluviale en éventail à l'embouchure d'une rivière, qui comporte habituellement des défluents, des chenaux et de petits lacs.*
OBS	Few named examples; Man. and N.W.T.	*Rare dans les noms approuvés; Man. et T.N.-O.*
EQ		**[delta (m.)]**
REL		
EX	Mackenzie Delta, N.W.T./T.N.-O. 68° 50' – 136° 25' (107 B) Knife Delta, Man. 58° 54' – 94° 43' (54 L/15)	

den

DES	Almost enclosed area of land or water.	*Étendue de terre ou d'eau presque fermée.*
OBS	Rare; Nfld. and Ont.	*Rare; T.-N. et Ont.*
EQ		
REL	basin (2), basin (3), lair	
EX	Lions Den (bay-baie), Nfld./T.-N. 48° 33' – 53° 47' (2 C/12) Devils Den (ravine-ravin), Ont. 43° 56' – 78° 59' (30 M/15)	

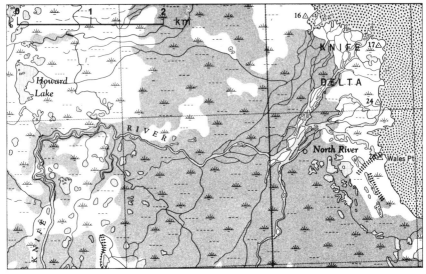

Figure 18. Knife Delta, on the west shore of Hudson Bay, Manitoba. (National Topographic System map 54 L; 1966)

Figure 18. Knife Delta, sur la côte ouest de la baie d'Hudson, au Manitoba. (Carte 54 L du Système national de référence cartographique; 1966)

depression

DES	Low-lying land surrounded by higher land.	*Creux dans la surface d'un terrain.*
OBS	Rare; Alta.	*Rare; Alb.*
EQ		**[dépression (f.)]**
REL	basin (3), valley (1), hollow	
EX	Ross Depression, Alta./Alb. 50° 35′ – 110° 33′ (72 L/10)	

descente (f.)

DES	*Very small watercourse on a steep slope.*	Très petit cours d'eau dans une pente.
OBS	*Descriptive term used in Que.*	Descriptif attesté au Qué.
EQ	**stream**	
REL		
EX	Descente Legault-Daigneault, Qué./Que. 45° 12' – 74° 06' (31 G/1)	

desert

DES	Wooded area with sandy soil.	*Terrain boisé au sol sablonneux.*
OBS	Rare; N.S. Not a desert in the conventional sense.	*Rare; N.-É. À ne pas confondre avec l'acception habituelle de ce mot.*
EQ		
REL	plain	
EX	Sandy Desert, N.S./N.-É. 45° 04' – 63° 32' (11 E/4)	

detour

DES	Horseshoe-shaped bend in a watercourse.	*Inflexion en fer à cheval dans le tracé d'un cours d'eau.*
OBS	Rare; N.W.T.	*Rare; T.N.-O.*
EQ		**détour** (m.)
REL	bend, elbow, oxbow	
EX	Grand Detour, N.W.T./T.N.-O. 60° 22' – 112° 42' (85 A)	

détour (m.)

DES	*See* **courbe**	Voir **courbe**
OBS	*"Détour" and "courbe" designate less pronounced features than a "coude". Used in Que.*	Le détour et la courbe sont moins accentués que le coude. Attesté au Qué.
EQ	**bend**	
REL		coude
EX	Le Grand Détour, Qué./Que. 52° 03′ – 76° 02′ (33 C/1)	

detroit

DES	See **narrows**	*Voir* **narrows**
OBS	Rare; Ont.	*Rare; Ont.*
EQ		**passage** (m.)
REL	passage, gap (2), pass (2)	
EX	Little Detroit, Ont. 46° 09′ – 82° 22′ (41 J/1)	

détroit (m.)

DES	*Natural sea passage between two shores and connecting two bodies of water.*	Passage maritime naturel resserré entre deux côtes et faisant communiquer deux étendues d'eau.
OBS	*In practice, "détroit" and "passage" were interchangeable. Used in Que.*	Dans la pratique, «détroit» et «passage» peuvent avoir été employés indifféremment l'un pour l'autre. Attesté au Qué.
EQ	**strait**	
REL		chenal, goulet, passage, passe
EX	Détroit de l'Entrée, Qué./Que. 50° 29′ – 59° 27′ (12 J/6) Détroit de Jacques-Cartier, Qué./Que. 50° 00′ – 63° 30′ (12 L/4)	

déversant (m.)

DES	*See* **décharge**	Voir **décharge**
OBS	*Term of rare and local usage, used in Que.*	Terme d'usage rare et local, attesté au Qué.
EQ	**outlet (1)**	
REL		débouche
EX	Déversant du Lac, Qué./Que. 45° 25′ – 73° 00′ (31 H/7)	

digue (f.)

DES	*Natural or artificial barrier made of earth, stones, etc., to block movement of water.*	Obstacle naturel ou artificiel, constitué par de la terre, des pierres, etc., et destiné à s'opposer à des mouvements d'eau.
OBS	*Used in Que.*	Attesté au Qué.
EQ	**[dike]**	
REL		
EX	Digue Campion, Qué./Que. 46° 07′ – 75° 38′ (31 J/4)	

ditch (1)

DES	Small watercourse.	*Petit cours d'eau.*
OBS	Rare; Man. and Sask.	*Rare; Man. et Sask.*
EQ		**ruisseau** (m.)
REL	creek (1), brook, stream	
EX	Yellow Grass Ditch, Sask. 49° 52′ – 104° 07′ (72 H/16) Whiskey Ditch, Man. 50° 16′ – 96° 53′ (62 I/7)	

ditch (2)

DES	See **gap (2)**	*Voir* **gap (2)**
OBS	Rare; N.S.	*Rare; N.-É.*
EQ		**passage** (m.)
REL	narrows, passage, gap (2), pass (2)	
EX	Goodwins Ditch, N.S./N.-É. 43° 31′ – 65° 46′ (20 P/12)	

dome(s)   (Fig. 19, 45)

DES	Mass of rock or ice with rounded top, elevated above the surrounding terrain.	*Masse de roche ou de glace au sommet arrondi, qui domine le terrain environnant.*
OBS	Used in Nfld., Alta., B.C., N.W.T., and Y.T.	*Relevé à T.-N., en Alb., en C.-B., dans les T.N.-O. et au Yukon.*
EQ		**dôme** (m.)
REL	summit, hill, mountain	
EX	Snow Dome, Alta./Alb. 52° 11′ – 117° 20′ (83 C/3)	
	The Domes, Nfld./T.-N. 58° 28′ – 62° 43′ (14 L/7)	
	Midnight Dome, Y.T./Yuk. 64° 04′ – 139° 23′ (116 B & C)	
	Malloch Dome, N.W.T./T.N.-O. 78° 12′ – 101° 15′ (69 F)	

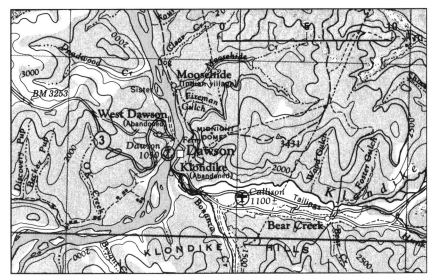

Figure 19. Various gulches (e.g. Wood Gulch), pups (e.g. Discovery Pup), creeks (e.g. Moosehide Creek), and Midnight Dome near the confluence of the Klondike River and the Yukon River at Dawson, Yukon Territory.
(National Topographic System map 116 B & 116 C (E 1/2); 1974)

Figure 19. Ravines (dont le Wood Gulch), ruisselets (dont le Discovery Pup), ruisseaux (dont le Moosehide Creek) et Midnight Dome, près du confluent de la rivière Klondike et du fleuve Yukon, à Dawson, au Yukon.
(Cartes 116 B et 116 C (E 1/2) du Système national de référence cartographique; 1974)

dôme (m.)

DES	*Elevation with little local relief, generally rounded in shape.*	Relief peu élevé et de forme plutôt arrondie.
OBS	*Used in Que.*	Attesté au Qué.
EQ	**dome**	
REL		bosse, butte, buttereau, colline, morne
EX	Dôme Pluton, Qué./Que. 49° 52′ – 75° 29′ (32 G/14)	

drain

DES	Small watercourse, tributary to a river or creek, and usually modified by ditching through relatively flat terrain.	*Petit cours d'eau qui se jette dans une rivière ou un ruisseau et dont on modifie habituellement le parcours par creusage dans un terrain relativement plat.*
OBS	Common in Ont. and Man.	*Fréquent en Ont. et au Man.*
EQ		**rigolet** (m.)
REL	cut, canal (2)	
EX	Dillabough-Ouderkirk Drain, Ont. 45° 06′ – 75° 16′ (31 G/3) Community Pasture Drain, Man. 52° 22′ – 100° 54′ (63 C/7)	

draw

DES	The upper part of a stream valley or coulee, providing access to higher ground.	*Partie amont d'une vallée fluviale ou d'une coulée, qui s'ouvre sur un terrain plus élevé.*
OBS	Rare; Alta.	*Rare; Alb.*
EQ		**ravine** (f.)
REL	gulch (1), gully (1), ravine, valley (1)	
EX	Scandia Draw, Alta./Alb. 50° 23′ – 111° 58′ (72 L/5)	

dribble

DES	Very small watercourse.	*Très petit cours d'eau.*
OBS	A trickling, barely continuous stream. Rare; Nfld.	*Ruisselet réduit à un filet d'eau à peine continu. Rare; T.-N.*
EQ		[**ruisselet** (m.)]
REL	creek (1), brook, stream	
EX	Fischells Dribble, Nfld./T.-N. 48° 18′ – 58° 38′ (12 B/7)	

droke

DES	Clump of trees.	*Bouquet d'arbres.*
OBS	Particular to Nfld.	*Propre à T.-N.*
EQ		**bosquet** (m.)
REL	woods, tuck, bluff (2), grove	
EX	Ben Droke, Nfld./T.-N. 47° 46′ – 53° 52′ (1 N/13)	

drook

DES	Narrow, steep-sided valley.	*Vallée étroite aux parois raides.*
OBS	Usually wooded and containing a stream. Particular to Nfld.	*Habituellement boisée et au fond de laquelle coule un cours d'eau. Propre à T.-N.*
EQ		**ravine** (f.)
REL	gulch (1), ravine, valley	
EX	Jobs Cove Drook, Nfld./T.-N. 47° 58′ – 53° 01′ (1 N/14)	

drop

DES	See **cliff**	*Voir* **cliff**
OBS	Uncommon; Nfld.	*Emploi peu fréquent; T.-N.*
EQ		**falaise** (f.)
REL	bank (2)	
EX	Upper Drop, Nfld./T.-N. 46° 52′ – 53° 26′ (1 K/14)	

dugway (Fig. 35)

DES	See **channel** (**1**)	*Voir* **channel** (**1**)
OBS	Rare; N.B.	*Rare; N.-B.*
EQ		**passage** (m.)
REL	passage, ditch (1), creek (1)	
EX	Morrow Dugway, N.B./N.-B. 45° 46′ – 66° 33′ (21 G/15)	

dump (1) (Fig. 59)

DES	Small waterfall and pool below it.	*Ensemble formé par une petite chute d'eau et la nappe sous-jacente.*
OBS	Rare; N.S.	*Rare; N.-É.*
EQ		**chute** (f.)
REL	fall, cascade	
EX	Hogans Dump, N.S./N.-É. 44° 40′ – 64° 45′ (21 A/10)	

dump (2)

DES	See **bluff** (**1**)	*Voir* **bluff** (**1**)
OBS	Rare; Ont.	*Rare; Ont.*
EQ		**falaise** (f.)
REL	cliff, bank (2)	
EX	High Dump, Ont. 46° 35′ – 84° 05′ (41 K/9)	

dune (Fig. 24)

DES	Stretch of coastal sand hills.	*Succession de collines de sable sur une côte.*
OBS	Uncommon in official names; N.B.	*Peu fréquent dans les noms officiels; N.-B.*
EQ		**dune** (f.)
REL	sand hills, hills, beach	
EX	South Kouchibouguac Dune, N.B./N.-B. 46° 49′ – 64° 54′ (21 I/15)	

dune (f.)   (Fig. 32)

DES	*Elevation of sand.*	Relief de sable.
OBS	*Features created by wind; usually located on the coast. Used in Que. and N.B.*	Relief édifié par le vent et habituellement situé sur le littoral de la mer. Attesté au Qué. et au N.-B.
EQ	**dune**	
REL		
EX	Dune du Havre aux Basques, Qué./Que. 47° 16′ – 61° 55′ (11 N/5) Dune de Buctouche, N.-B./N.B. 46° 29′ – 64° 38′ (21 I/7)	

dyke

DES	Small watercourse.	*Petit cours d'eau.*
OBS	Rare; N.S.	*Rare; N.-É.*
EQ		**[ruisselet** (m.)]
REL	creek (1), brook, stream	
EX	Beau Dyke, N.S./N.-É. 45° 07′ – 64° 27′ (21 H/1)	

e

ears (Fig. 20, 45)

DES	Feature having the appearance of pointed ears.	*Accident géographique en forme d'oreilles pointues.*
OBS	Applied to rocks, islands, and peaks in Nfld. and B.C.	*S'emploie pour des rochers, des îles, et des pics à T.-N. et en C.-B.*
EQ		
REL	hazers	
EX	Hares Ears (island-île), Nfld./T.-N. 46° 52′ – 55° 25′ (1 L/14) Golden Ears (peaks-pics), B.C./C.-B. 49° 22′ – 122° 30′ (92 G/7) Cats Ears (rocks-roches), Nfld./T.-N. 48° 10′ – 52° 57′ (2 C/2)	

échouerie (f.)

DES	*Blocks of flat rock extending into the sea.*	Blocs de pierres plates qui s'étendent jusqu'à la mer.
OBS	*In Canadian French, the term "échouerie" means a place where herds of seals and walruses rest, whereas in international French it refers to a place where vessels go aground. Descriptive term used in Que.*	En français d'ici, le terme «échouerie» a le sens d'un lieu pour l'échouement de troupeaux de phoques et de morses, tandis qu'en français international, il correspond à un endroit propre à l'échouement des navires. Descriptif attesté au Qué.
EQ	**ledge (1)**	
REL		
EX	La Grande Échouerie, Qué./Que. 47° 22′ – 61° 52′ (11 N/5)	

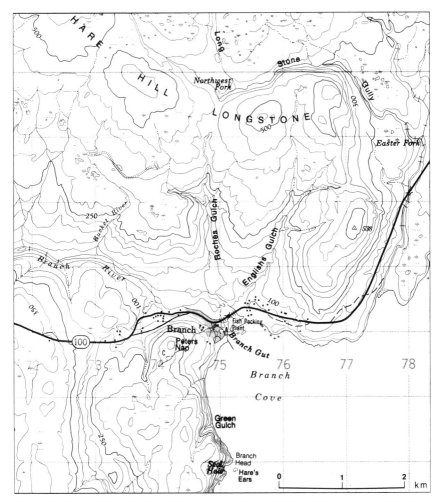

Figure 20. Branch Cove, St. Mary's Bay, Newfoundland, showing Hare's Ears, Easter Fork and Northwest Fork, Green Gulch and Roches Gulch, Long Stone Gully, Branch Gut, Seal Hole, and Peters Nap.
(National Topographic System map 1 K/13; 1984 with added information)

Figure 20. Branch Cove, dans la baie St. Mary's, à Terre-Neuve. Entités représentées : Hare's Ears, Easter Fork et Northwest Fork, Green Gulch et Roches Gulch, Long Stone Gully, Branch Gut, Seal Hole et Peters Nap.
(Carte 1 K/13 du Système national de référence cartographique; 1984 avec renseignements supplémentaires)

eddy

DES	Small whirlpool in a watercourse or in the sea, running contrary to the direction of current or tide.	*Petit tourbillon dans un cours d'eau ou dans la mer, qui se déplace dans le sens contraire à celui du courant ou de la marée.*
OBS	Widely used, but uncommon.	*Emploi généralisé mais peu fréquent.*
EQ		**remous** (m.)
REL	rip (2), pool (2), hole (4)	
EX	Three Islands Eddy, N.B./N.-B. 44° 33' – 66° 48' (21 B/10) Big Eddy, B.C./C.-B. 51° 00' – 118° 14' (82 M/1)	

edge

DES	Sharp-edged ridge.	*Élévation de terrain à arête tranchante.*
OBS	Rare; B.C.	*Rare; C.-B.*
EQ		[**chaînon** (m.)]
REL	ridge (1), back	
EX	Razors Edge, B.C./C.-B. 50° 40' – 117° 11' (82 K/11)	

elbow

DES	Sharp turn in watercourse.	*Inflexion raide dans le tracé d'un cours d'eau.*
OBS	Widely used.	*Emploi généralisé.*
EQ		**coude** (m.)
REL	bend, oxbow, hook	
EX	Assiniboine Elbow, Sask. 51° 46' – 102° 01' (62 M/16)	

embranchement (m.)

DES	*See* **bras**	Voir **bras**
OBS	*Descriptive term used in Que.*	Descriptif attesté au Qué.
EQ	**branch**	
REL		branche, fourche
EX	Embranchement chez Bergeron, Qué./Que. 45° 49′ – 72° 35′ (31 H/15)	

end

DES	See **point (1)**	*Voir* **point (1)**
OBS	Used in the Atlantic Provinces and N.W.T., usually as «Land's End».	*S'emploie dans les provinces de l'Atlantique et dans les T.N.-O., habituellement dans le toponyme "Land's End".*
EQ		**pointe** (f.)
REL	cape, head (1), peninsula, point (1)	
EX	West End, N.S./N.-É. 65° 48′ – 62° 36′ (11 E/15) Lands End, N.W.T./T.N.-O. 76° 22′ – 122° 37′ (99 A) Lands End, N.B./N.-B. 45° 20′ – 66° 10′ (21 G/8)	

entrance

DES	Outer end of a channel, harbour, or other water feature; usually allowing access to the waters within.	*Extrémité extérieure d'un chenal, d'un havre ou d'une autre étendue d'eau, par laquelle les bateaux peuvent habituellement entrer.*
OBS	Widely used. Dixon Entrance (B.C.) is an unusually large example.	*Emploi généralisé. La* Dixon Entrance *(C.-B.) est exceptionnellement large.*
EQ		[**entrée** (f.)]
REL	strait, pass (2), sound (1)	
EX	Browning Entrance, B.C./C.-B. 53° 40′ – 130° 31′ (103 G) Big Caribou Entrance, N.S./N.-É. 45° 45′ – 62° 41′ (11 E/10)	

éperon (m.)

DES	*Projecting portion of a larger geographical feature, such as a continental slope, sill, or undersea ridge.*	Partie en saillie d'un ensemble morphologique plus important comme une pente continentale, un seuil ou une dorsale océanique.
OBS	*Underwater feature noted off the shores of Que.*	Entité sous-marine attestée au Qué.
EQ	**spur (2)**	
REL		
EX	Éperon de la Pointe Loizeau, Qué./Que. 50° 16′ – 62° 48′ (C.4452)	

escarpement (m.)

DES	*Steep slope separating two distinct land areas.*	Pente raide qui délimite deux reliefs importants.
OBS	*Used in Que.*	Attesté au Qué.
EQ	**escarpment**	
REL		falaise
EX	Escarpement d'Eardley, Qué./Que. 45° 33′ – 76° 01′ (31 F/9)	

escarpment

DES	Long laterally continuous, steep slope, often cliff-like.	*Abrupt, long et latéralement continu, souvent assimilé à une falaise.*
OBS	Rare; Ont., Sask., B.C., and N.W.T.	*Rare; Ont., Sask., C.-B. et T.N.-O.*
EQ		**escarpement** (m.)
REL	bank (2), cliff, hill, ridge (1), coteau, scarp	
EX	Niagara Escarpment, Ont. 43° 50′ – 80° 00′ (30 M/3) Cape Hotham Escarpment, N.W.T./T.N.-O. 74° 52′ – 93° 27′ (58 F)	

esker

DES	Long, narrow, usually sinuous, steep-sided ridge of unconsolidated material.	*Accumulation de matériaux non consolidés en forme de chaussée longue, étroite, généralement sinueuse, et à bords raides.*
OBS	Few eskers are officially named; Man. and N.W.T.	*Peu d'eskers ont un nom officiel; Man. et T.N.-O.*
EQ		[**esker** (m.)]
REL	ridge (1), back	
EX	Christmas Lake Esker, Man. 58° 44′ – 93° 44′ (54 K/12) Siqquqtijjutitalik Esker, N.W.T./T.N.-O. 65° 57′ – 86° 42′ (46 E)	

estuaire (m.)

DES	*The widening of the mouth of a watercourse, where marine phenomena predominate over river phenomena.*	Embouchure plus ou moins évasée d'un cours d'eau, caractérisée par la prédominance des phénomènes marins sur les phénomènes fluviaux.
OBS	*Used in Que.*	Attesté au Qué.
EQ	[**estuary**]	
REL		
EX	Estuaire de la Rivière Saint-Charles, Qué./Que. 46° 49′ – 71° 12′ (21 L/14)	

étang(s) (m.)

DES	*Body of water of shallow depth and limited size.*	Nappe d'eau de faible profondeur et de dimension restreinte.

OBS	*An* étang, *often colonized by vegetation, is generally deeper and larger than a* mare, *but shallower and smaller than a* lac. *Used in Que., N.B., and N.S.*	Les étangs, souvent colonisés par la végétation, sont habituellement plus profonds et plus grands que les mares, mais moins profonds et moins vastes que les lacs. Attesté au Qué., au N.-B. et en N.-É.

EQ	**pond (1)**

REL	lac, mare

EX	Étang aux Goélands, Qué./Que. 49° 41′ – 63° 35′ (12 E/12)
	Étang Bourgeois, N.-É./N.S. 43° 38′ – 65° 48′ (20 P/12)
	Étangs Morin, N.-B./N.B. 47° 41′ – 67° 19′ (21 O/11)

eye (1)

DES	See **island**	*Voir* **island**

OBS	Use transferred from "Ireland's Eye", Ireland. Rare; Nfld. and N.W.T.	*Adaptation du toponyme «Ireland's Eye», Irlande. Rare; T.-N. et T.N.-O.*

EQ		**île** (f.)

REL	islet, rock (1)

EX	Ireland's Eye, N.W.T./T.N.-O. 77° 51′ – 115° 31′ (89 D)

eye (2)

DES	Feature bearing a resemblance to a human eye or the eye of a needle.	*Relief dont la forme rappelle l'oeil humain ou le chas d'une aiguille.*
OBS	Applied to a variety of features, including coves, runs, and caves. Widely used, but uncommon.	*S'emploie pour divers types d'accidents géographiques, notamment des anses, des rapides et des cavernes. Emploi généralisé, mais peu usité.*
EQ		
REL		
EX	Goat's Eye (cave-caverne), Alta./Alb. 51° 07' – 115° 44' (82 O/4) Needles Eye (run-rapide), N.S./N.-É. 44° 35' – 65° 20' (21 A/11) Facheux Eye (cove-anse), Nfld./T.-N. 47° 37' – 56° 18' (11 P/9)	

f

face

DES	See **cliff**	*Voir* **cliff**
OBS	Rare; N.B.	*Rare; N.-B.*
EQ		**falaise** (f.)
REL	wall, bluff (1)	
EX	Ministers Face, N.B./N.-B. 45° 24′ – 66° 02′ (21 G/8)	

falaise (f.)

DES	*Steep slope, generally at the shore.*	Abrupt souvent situé près de la mer.
OBS	*Used in Que. and N.S.*	Attesté au Qué. et en N.-É.
EQ	**cliff**	
REL		escarpement
EX	Falaise aux Goélands, Qué./Que. 49° 09′ – 61° 42′ (12 F/4) Grande Falaise, N.-É./N.S. 46° 40′ – 60° 57′ (11 K/10)	

fall(s)

DES	Perpendicular or steep descent of water.	*Rupture de pente perpendiculaire ou brusque d'où tombe une masse d'eau.*
OBS	Widely used.	*Emploi généralisé.*
EQ		**chute** (f.)
REL	cascade, chute, waterfall	
EX	Fall of the Waves, B.C./C.-B. 51° 35′ – 116° 31′ (82 N/10) Takakkaw Falls, B.C./C.-B. 51° 30′ – 116° 28′ (82 N/8) Niagara Falls, Ont. 43° 05′ – 79° 04′ (30 M/3)	

fang

DES	Isolated sharp peak.	*Pic isolé aux flancs escarpés.*
OBS	Rare; B.C.	*Rare; C.-B.*
EQ		**pic** (m.)
REL	peak (1), spire, crag, tusk, needle	
EX	Black Fang, B.C./C.-B. 50° 37′ – 116° 34′ (82 K/10)	

fare

DES	See **passage**	*Voir* **passage**
OBS	Rare; Nfld.	*Rare; T.-N.*
EQ		**passage** (m.)
REL	narrows, gap (2), thoroughfare	
EX	Souther Fare, Nfld./T.-N. 47° 44′ – 53° 10′ (1 N/11) Dully Fare, Nfld./T.-N. 47° 37′ – 53° 11′ (1 N/11)	

faux chenal (m.)

DES	*Narrow, deep and elongated body of water, secondary or tributary to a larger watercourse.*	Étendue d'eau étroite, profonde et allongée, secondaire ou tributaire d'un cours d'eau plus important.
OBS	*Used in Que.*	Attesté au Qué.
EQ	**snye**	
REL		
EX	Faux chenal Yamaska, Qué./Que. 46° 05′ – 72° 57′ (31 I/2)	

feeder

DES	Small watercourse, tributary to larger watercourse.	*Affluent d'un cours d'eau plus important.*
OBS	Rare; Nfld.	*Rare; T.-N.*
EQ		**ruisseau** (m.)
REL	creek (1), brook, stream, branch	
EX	Crooked Feeder, Nfld./T.-N. 49° 15′ – 57° 21′ (12 H/3)	

fen

DES	Waterlogged ground.	*Terrain détrempé.*
OBS	Usually smaller than a marsh or bog. Rare; Alta.	*Marais généralement plus petit que le terrain désigné par «marsh» ou «bog». Rare; Alb.*
EQ		**marais** (m.)
REL	marsh, swamp, bog	
EX	Elkwoods Fen, Alta./Alb. 50° 39′ – 115° 07′ (82 J/11)	

ferry

DES	Place for crossing a river, bay, etc., by boat.	*Endroit prévu pour traverser un cours d'eau, une baie, etc., par bateau.*
OBS	Uncommon in official names; Man.	*Peu fréquent parmi les noms approuvés; Man.*
EQ		[**traverse** (f.)]
REL	landing, crossing, ford	
EX	Stockton Ferry, Man. 49° 36′ – 99° 26′ (62 G/11)	

finger

DES	Feature having the appearance of a human finger.	*Accident géographique en forme de doigt humain.*
OBS	Rare; Nfld. and B.C. for various features including mountain, hill, and point.	*Rare. S'emploie à T.-N. et en C.-B. pour désigner diverses entités comme des montagnes, des collines et des pointes.*
EQ		
REL	thumb, peak (1)	
EX	Unuk Finger (mountain-montagne), B.C./C.-B. 56° 26′ – 130° 23′ (104 B/8) Peters Finger (point-pointe), Nfld./T.-N. 47° 42′ – 53° 30′ (1 N/11)	

fiord

DES	Long, narrow, deep, and steep-sided inlet of the sea, along a mountainous coast.	*Bras de mer long, étroit et profond, enserré par des versants montagneux à pente raide.*
OBS	Glacially eroded valley inundated by the sea. Used in Nfld. and N.W.T.	*Il s'agit en fait d'une vallée glaciaire envahie par la mer. Relevé à T.-N. et dans les T.N.-O.*
EQ		**fjord** (m.)
REL	inlet (1), arm (1), canal (1), reach	
EX	Pangnirtung Fiord, N.W.T./T.N.-O. 66° 07′ – 65° 38′ (26 I) Nachvak Fiord, Nfld./T.-N. 59° 03′ – 63° 45′ (14 M)	

fjord (m.)

DES	*Steep-walled glacial valley occupied by the sea.*	Vallée glaciaire aux parois escarpées, envahie par la mer.
OBS	*Norwegian term used in Que.*	Terme norvégien attesté au Qué.
EQ	**fiord**	
REL		
EX	Fjord du Saguenay, Qué./Que. 48° 08′ – 69° 44′ (22 C/4)	

flat(s) (1)

DES	Level area of land usually composed of fine material, extending from the shore.	*Prolongement plat d'un rivage généralement constitué de matériaux fins.*
OBS	Widely used. Coastal flats are usually covered by seawater at high tide.	*Emploi généralisé. Les battures appelées «coastal flats» sont généralement inondées à marée haute.*
EQ		**batture** (f.)
REL	beach, shore, bar	
EX	Base Flat, B.C./C.-B. 49° 31′ – 124° 50′ (92 F/10) Winter Flat, Nfld./T.-N. 51° 13′ – 56° 47′ (12 P/2) West Flat, Ont. 45° 34′ – 81° 42′ (C.2286) Tinittuktuq Flats, N.W.T./T.N.-O. 65° 52′ – 89° 25′ (56 H)	

flat(s) (2)   (Fig. 21, 25)

DES	Almost level land, usually found along a valley.	*Terre presque horizontale qui longe habituellement une vallée.*
OBS	Widely used.	*Emploi généralisé.*
EQ		**plaine** (f.) **(1)**
REL	bottom (1), bench, terrace, intervale, meadow (1)	
EX	Dead Man Flat, Alta./Alb. 51° 02′ – 115° 16′ (82 O/3) Forgan Flats, Sask. 51° 15′ – 107° 46′ (72 O/4) Northey Flats, Man. 49° 42′ – 98° 58′ (62 G/10)	

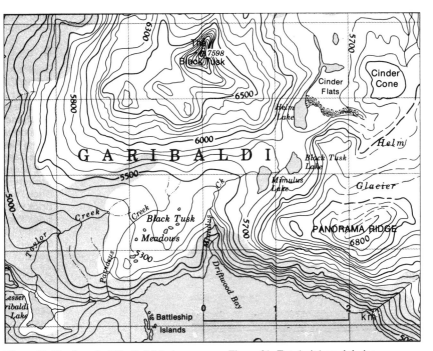

Figure 21. North end of Garibaldi Lake, north of Vancouver, British Columbia, showing Cinder Flats, Cinder Cone, Parnasus Creek, Helm Glacier, Black Tusk Meadows, Panorama Ridge, and The Black Tusk.
(National Topographic System map 92 G/14; 1980)

Figure 21. Extrémité nord du lac Garibaldi, au nord de Vancouver, en Colombie-Britannique. Entités représentées : Cinder Flats, Cinder Cone, Parnasus Creek, Helm Glacier, Black Tusk Meadows, Panorama Ridge et The Black Tusk.
(Carte 92 G/14 du Système national de référence cartographique; 1980)

flèche (f.)

DES	Long, narrow neck of sand extending from a shore.	Langue de sable longue et étroite qui s'avance dans l'eau à partir de la côte.
OBS	A flèche *resembles a* péninsule *when it emerges above sea level enough to develop vegetation; it then poses less hazard to navigation. When slightly submerged or at water level, it can resemble an* haut-fond, *and be a threat to small craft. Used in Que.*	La flèche ressemble à une péninsule lorsqu'elle émerge suffisamment pour que la végétation s'y installe, et présente alors moins de danger pour la navigation. Elle prend aussi l'allure d'un haut-fond lorsqu'elle est légèrement submergée ou est située à fleur d'eau, et constitue alors une menace pour les petites embarcations. Attesté au Qué.
EQ	**spit**	
REL		
EX	Flèche du Nord-Ouest, Qué./Que. 47° 17' – 61° 43' (11 N/5)	

fleuve (m.)

DES	Large watercourse flowing into the sea.	Cours d'eau important qui se jette dans la mer.
OBS	*Until the sixteenth century, "fleuve" and "rivière" both indicated watercourses of variable importance. From 1650, however, usage has reserved "fleuve" for the very large rivers that flow to the sea. Used in Que. and N.W.T.*	Jusqu'au XVIe siècle, «fleuve» et «rivière» signifiaient tous deux des cours d'eau d'importance variable. Mais, à partir de 1650, l'usage réserve «fleuve» aux rivières plus grandes qui transportent leurs eaux jusqu'à la mer. Attesté au Qué. et dans les T.N.-O.
EQ	**river (1)**	
REL		rivière
EX	Fleuve Saint-Laurent, Qué./Que. 49° 40' – 64° 34' (22 H/10) Fleuve Mackenzie, T.N.-O./N.W.T. 69° 21' – 133° 54' (107 C)	

flow

DES	Arm of a lake.	*Bras d'un lac.*
OBS	Rare; Ont.	*Rare; Ont.*
EQ		[**bras** (m.)]
REL	arm (1), inlet (1)	
EX	Pierces Flow, Ont. 44° 30′ – 76° 13′ (31 C/9)	

flowage

DES	Shallow area of water, usually formed by the damming of a watercourse.	*Nappe d'eau peu profonde, généralement formée par l'endiguement d'un cours d'eau.*
OBS	Rare; N.S. and N.B.	*Rare; N.-É. et N.-B.*
EQ		**réservoir** (m.)
REL	reservoir, lake, pond (1)	
EX	Anti Dam Flowage, N.S./N.-É. 45° 07′ – 62° 30′ (11 E/2)	

flumes

DES	Narrow fast-flowing section of a watercourse.	*Partie resserrée d'un cours d'eau où le courant est rapide.*
OBS	Rare; N.S.	*Rare; N.-É.*
EQ		**rapide** (m.)
REL	chute, rapid (1), race, run (2)	
EX	Third Lake Flumes, N.S./N.-É. 44° 23′ – 65° 44′ (21 A/5)	

fond (m.)

DES	*See* **haut-fond**	Voir **haut-fond**
OBS	*Underwater feature noted especially off the coasts of N.S. and Nfld.*	Entité sous-marine attestée surtout au large des côtes de la N.-É. et de T.-N.
EQ	**shoal**	
REL		banc, basse
EX	Fond de Belliveau, N.-É./N.S. 44° 04′ – 66° 13′ (21 B/1) Fond de Landry, T.-N./Nfld. 47° 03′ – 56° 12′ (C.4625)	

foothills

DES	Hilly transition zone between a mountain range and a plain.	*Région au relief ondulé qui marque la transition entre une plaine et un ensemble montagneux.*
OBS	Rare; Alta. and B.C.	*Rare; Alb. et C.-B.*
EQ		**piémont** (m.)
REL	hills	
EX	Rocky Mountain Foothills, Alta. – B.C./Alb. – C.-B. 52° 00′ – 116° 30′ (83 B)	

ford

DES	Shallow part of a watercourse that may be crossed on foot, on horseback, or by land vehicle.	*Partie peu profonde d'un cours d'eau qui peut être traversée à pied, à cheval ou au moyen d'un véhicule à moteur.*
OBS	Rare; Man. and Alta.	*Rare; Man. et Alb.*
EQ		[**gué** (m.)]
REL	ferry, crossing	
EX	Drowning Ford, Alta./Alb. 50° 27′ – 110° 35′ (72 L/7)	

forebay

DES	See **reservoir**	*Voir* **reservoir**
OBS	Uncommon; Nfld.	*Emploi peu fréquent; T.-N.*
EQ		**réservoir** (m.)
REL	lake, pond (1), flowage	
EX	Mobile Forebay, Nfld./T.-N. 47° 14′ – 52° 52′ (1 N/2)	

foreland

DES	See **point (1)**	*Voir* **point (1)**
OBS	Rare; N.W.T.	*Rare; T.N.-O.*
EQ		**pointe** (f.)
REL	peninsula, spit, cape, head (1)	
EX	Queen Elizabeth Foreland, N.W.T./T.N.-O. 62° 23′ – 64° 28′ (25 I)	

forêt (f.)

DES	*Vast expanse of tree-covered terrain.*	Vaste étendue de terrain peuplée d'arbres.
OBS	*Used in Que.*	Attesté au Qué.
EQ	[**forest**]	
REL		bois, bosquet
EX	Forêt Saint-Augustin, Qué./Que. 46° 44′ – 71° 25′ (21 L/11)	

fork(s) (1)   (Fig. 5, 20)

DES	Junction of two streams; a confluence.	*Jonction de deux cours d'eau; confluence.*
OBS	Widely used.	*Emploi généralisé.*
EQ		**confluent** (m.)
REL		
EX	Red Deer Forks, Sask. 50° 55′ – 109° 54′ (72 K/13) Becaguimec Forks, N.B./N.-B. 46° 17′ – 67° 22′ (21 J/6)	

fork (2)

DES	Branch of a stream.	*Ramification d'un cours d'eau.*
OBS	Often small headwater tributary. Used in N.B., B.C., and Y.T.	*S'emploie souvent pour un petit tributaire d'amont. Relevé au N.-B., en C.-B. et au Yukon.*
EQ		**fourche** (f.)
REL	branch, feeder, creek (1)	
EX	Mack Fork, Y.T./Yuk. 63° 49′ – 139° 03′ (115 O) Cathedral Fork, B.C./C.-B. 49° 03′ – 120° 18′ (92 H/1)	

fortress

DES	Feature having the appearance of a fortress.	*Relief ayant l'aspect d'une forteresse.*
OBS	Rare; N.W.T.	*Rare; T.N.-O.*
EQ		
REL	castle, tower, ramparts	
EX	Scott's Fortress (island-île), N.W.T./T.N.-O. 62° 37′ – 64° 55′ (25 I)	

fosse (f.)

DES	*Part of a stream that is deeper and less fast-flowing than the surrounding waters.*	Partie d'un cours d'eau généralement plus profonde et moins rapide que les eaux adjacentes.
OBS	A fosse *often serves as a rest area for salmon in their ascent to the spawning grounds; it is then known as a "fosse à saumon". Used in Que.*	La fosse sert souvent d'aire de repos au saumon dans sa montaison vers les frayères et est alors appelée «fosse à saumon». Attesté au Qué.
EQ	**pool (1)**	
REL		
EX	Fosse Adam, Qué./Que. 48° 55' – 69° 05' (32 C/14)	

fossé (m.)

DES	*Trench used for collecting or distributing water.*	Tranchée servant à la réception ou à l'écoulement des eaux.
OBS	*Used in Que.*	Attesté au Qué.
EQ	**[ditch]**	
REL		
EX	Fossé Allard, Qué./Que. 46° 05' – 72° 54' (31 I/2)	

fount

DES	See **lake**	*Voir* **lake**
OBS	Rare; N.W.T.	*Rare; T.N.-O.*
EQ		**lac** (m.)
REL	pond (1), lagoon, reservoir	
EX	Frog Creek Fount, N.W.T./T.N.-O. 67° 13' – 133° 48' (106 N)	

fourche (f.)

DES	*Small stream, tributary to a larger one.*	Petit cours d'eau tributaire d'un plus gros.
OBS	*Used in Que. and N.B.*	Attesté au Qué. et au N.-B.
EQ	**fork (2)**	
REL		branche, bras, embranchement
EX	Fourche à Clark, N.-B./N.B. 47° 20' – 67° 56' (21 O/5) Fourche des Sarcelles, Qué./Que. 47° 05' – 70° 31' (21 M/2)	

g

gables

DES	See **peaks (1)**	*Voir* **peaks (1)**
OBS	Rare; N.W.T.	*Rare; T.N.-O.*
EQ		**pics** (m.)
REL	summits, mountains	
EX	The Castle Gables, N.W.T./T.N.-O. 72° 58' – 77° 48' (38 B)	

gallery   (Fig. 22)

DES	Elongated recessed corridor in a rock face.	*Niche allongée dans une paroi rocheuse.*
OBS	Rare; B.C. and N.W.T. Galiano Gallery (B.C.) is a wave-cut platform with an overhanging roof.	*Rare; C.-B. et T.N.-O. La* Galiano Gallery *(C.-B.) est une plate-forme façonnée par les vagues et surmontée d'un toit suspendu.*
EQ		[**galerie** (f.)]
REL		
EX	Galiano Gallery, B.C./C.-B. 49° 11' – 123° 52' (92 G/4) The Gallery, N.W.T./T.N.-O. 72° 32' – 86° 25' (48 B)	

Figure 22. The wave-cut overhangs of
Galiano Gallery, Galiano Island, British
Columbia.
(Glenn Woodsworth)

Figure 22. Surplombs de la Galiano
Gallery, île Galiano, en Colombie-
Britannique.
(Glenn Woodsworth)

gap (1)

DES	Narrow opening through a ridge or mountain chain.	*Ouverture étroite dans une élévation de terrain ou une chaîne de montagnes.*
OBS	Rare; Alta. and B.C.	*Rare; Alb. et C.-B.*
EQ		[**col** (m.)]
REL	col, pass (1), notch	
EX	Blackstone Gap, Alta./Alb. 52° 36′ – 116° 35′ (83 C/10) Fury Gap, B.C./C.-B. 51° 23′ – 125° 20′ (92 N/6)	

gap (2)

DES	Narrow water passage between two bodies of land.	*Étroit passage d'eau entre deux masses de terre.*
OBS	Widely used.	*Emploi généralisé.*
EQ		**passage** (m.)
REL	passage, narrows, pass (2)	
EX	Devils Gap, Man. 54° 39′ – 100° 28′ (63 K/9) Tesseni Gap, Sask. 59° 55′ – 109° 50′ (74 N/13)	

gate

DES	Restricted passage.	*Passage resserré.*
OBS	Rare. Usually "Hell Gate" or "Hells Gate"; N.B., B.C., and N.W.T. Often marked by turbulent water.	*Rare. S'emploie habituellement dans le toponyme «Hell Gate» ou «Hells Gate»; N.-B., C.-B. et T.N.-O. Souvent caractérisé par des eaux turbulentes.*
EQ		
REL	narrows, chute, rapid (1), cataract, canyon	
EX	Hell Gate (canyon-canyon), B.C./C.-B. 59° 17′ – 125° 15′ (94 N/6) Hell Gate (strait-détroit), N.W.T./T.N.-O. 76° 42′ – 89° 44′ (59 A)	

gaze

DES	See **lookout**	*Voir* **lookout**
OBS	Rare; Nfld.	*Rare; T.-N.*
EQ		[**belvédère** (m.)]
REL	summit, brow, cairn	
EX	Fillys Gaze, Nfld./T.-N. 47° 45′ – 54° 00′ (1 N/13)	

girdle

DES	See **shoal**	*Voir* **shoal**
OBS	Rare; Nfld.	*Rare; T.-N.*
EQ		**haut-fond** (m.)
REL	bank (1), ground (1)	
EX	False Girdle, Nfld./T.-N. 47° 08′ – 54° 06′ (C.4622)	

glacier(s) (Fig. 23, 36, 37)

DES	Mass of permanent snow and ice flowing from an area of snow accumulation on higher ground.	*Masse de neige et de glace éternelles s'écoulant d'une zone d'accumulation de neige située dans une région élevée.*
OBS	Used in the mountains of Labrador (Nfld.), and western and northern Canada.	*En usage dans les montagnes du Labrador (T.-N.) ainsi que dans l'Ouest et dans le Nord du Canada.*
EQ		**glacier** (m.)
REL	ice cap, icefield, arm (3), ice shelf	
EX	Kaskawulsh Glacier, Y.T./Yuk. 60° 45′ – 139° 06′ (115 B & C) John Hill Glacier, Nfld./T.-N. 58° 54′ – 63° 43′ (14 L/13) Franklin Glacier, B.C./C.-B. 51° 16′ – 125° 23′ (92 N/6) Twin Glaciers, B.C./C.-B. 51° 33′ – 117° 53′ (82 N/12)	

glacier (m.)

DES	*Accumulation of ice resulting from the transformation of snow on higher ground.*	Accumulation de glace issue de la transformation de la neige sur un terrain plus élevé.
OBS	*Used in mountain areas of B.C. and N.W.T.*	Attesté dans les régions montagneuses de la C.-B. et des T.N.-O.
EQ	**glacier**	
REL		
EX	Glacier de Fleur des Neiges, C.-B./B.C. 49° 51′ – 122° 36′ (92 G/15) Glacier du Lièvre, T.N.-O./N.W.T. 66° 35′ – 62° 22′ (16 L & K)	

VAN ROYEN GLACIER

- N -

Nukapingwa Glacier

Arklio Glacier

Okpuddyshao Glacier

Figure 23. Nukapingwa Glacier, Arklio Glacier, Okpuddyshao Glacier, and part of Van Royen Glacier, northern Ellesmere Island, Northwest Territories. (National Air Photo Library, A16785-24; 1959)

Figure 23. Photo aérienne prise dans le nord de l'île d'Ellesmere, dans les Territoires du Nord-Ouest. Entités représentées : Nukapingwa Glacier, Arklio Glacier, Okpuddyshao Glacier et, en partie, Van Royen Glacier. (Photothèque nationale de l'air, A16785-24; 1959)

glade

DES	Wet low-lying area with sparse vegetation.	*Terre basse et mouillée, occupée par une végétation clairsemée.*
OBS	Rare; N.S.	*Rare; N.-É.*
EQ		**baissière** (f.)
REL	meadow (1), ground (2), fen	
EX	Bakeapple Glade, N.S./N.-É. 45° 14′ – 61° 54′ (11 F/4)	

glen

DES	Steep narrow valley in hills or mountains.	*Vallée étroite et abrupte dans des collines ou en terrain montagneux.*
OBS	Rare; Ont.	*Rare; Ont.*
EQ		**vallée** (f.)
REL	valley (1), gorge, ravine, canyon	
EX	Devils Glen, Ont. 44° 21′ – 80° 12′ (41 A/8)	

golfe (m.)

DES	*Large indentation in the coastline.*	Très vaste rentrant du littoral.
OBS	*A* golfe *is normally larger than a* baie. *Used in Que.*	Le golfe est habituellement plus grand que la baie. Attesté au Qué.
EQ	**gulf**	
REL		
EX	Golfe du Saint-Laurent, Qué./Que. 48° 00′ – 62° 00′ (MCR 125 F)	

gorge(s) (Fig. 61)

DES	Deep, narrow, steep-sided valley, usually containing a watercourse.	*Vallée profonde et étroite aux versants escarpés, généralement parcourue par un cours d'eau.*
OBS	Widely used, but few named examples.	*Emploi généralisé, mais rare dans les noms approuvés.*
EQ		**gorge** (f.)
REL	valley (1), ravine, canyon	
EX	Niagara Gorge, Ont. 43° 08′ – 79° 03′ (30 M/3) Isortoq Gorge, N.W.T./T.N.-O. 70° 29′ – 75° 04′ (37 E) Twin Gorges, N.W.T./T.N.-O. 60° 25′ – 111° 24′ (75 D)	

gorge(s) (f.)

DES	*Deep and narrow depression.*	Étroite et profonde dépression de terrain.
OBS	*The related terms listed all indicate an elongated depression usually with a stream flowing through. Used in Que.*	Les termes semblables retenus désignent tous une dépression allongée permettant le passage d'un cours d'eau. Attesté au Qué.
EQ	**gorge**	
REL		canyon, coulée (1), ravin, ravine, vallée
EX	Gorge d'en Bas, Qué./Que. 55° 31′ – 68° 20′ (23 N/9) Gorges de Coaticook, Qué./Que. 45° 09′ – 71° 49′ (21 E/4)	

goulet (m.)   (Fig. 24)

DES	*Restricted passage linking a coastal body of water and the sea.*	Passage resserré reliant une étendue d'eau littorale et la mer.
OBS	*Used in Que., N.B., and N.S.*	Attesté au Qué., au N.-B. et en N.-É.
EQ	**gully (2)**	
REL		chenal, détroit, passage, passe
EX	Goulet Qurngualuk, Qué./Que. 60° 55′ – 73° 38′ (35 A/13) Goulet de Terre-noire, N.-B./N.B. 46° 47′ – 64° 52′ (21 I/15) Grand Goulet, N.-É./N.S. 45° 38′ – 60° 55′ (11 F/10)	

grass

DES	See **meadow (1)**	*Voir* **meadow (1)**
OBS	Rare; Nfld. and Man.	*Rare; T.-N. et Man.*
EQ		**baissière** (f.)
REL	ground (2), intervale, glade	
EX	Big Grass, Man. 51° 00′ – 100° 19′ (62 K/16) The Grass, Nfld./T.-N. 48° 10′ – 58° 19′ (12 B/1)	

grassy

DES	See **meadow (1)**	*Voir* **meadow (1)**
OBS	Rare; N.S.	*Rare; N.-É.*
EQ		**baissière** (f.)
REL	ground (2), intervale, glade	
EX	The Big Grassy, N.S./N.-É. 43° 34′ – 65° 41′ (20 P/12)	

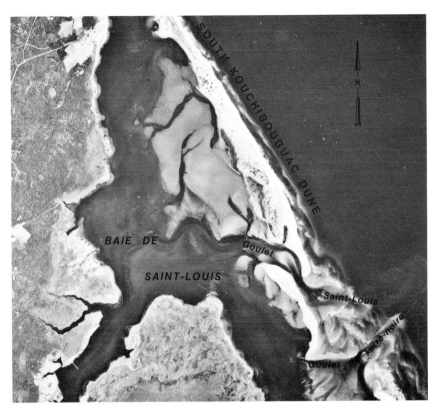

Figure 24. Coast of the Gulf of St. Lawrence, eastern New Brunswick, showing Goulet de Saint-Louis and Goulet de Terre-noire, Baie de Saint-Louis and South Kouchibouguac Dune. (National Air Photo Library, A12919-111; 1950)

Figure 24. Côte du golfe du Saint-Laurent, dans l'est du Nouveau-Brunswick. Entités représentées : Goulet de Saint-Louis et Goulet de Terre-noire, Baie de Saint-Louis et South Kouchibouguac Dune. (Photothèque nationale de l'air, A12919-111; 1950)

grève (f.)

DES	*Open section of a shore, with slight gradient and composed of pebbles or coarse material.*	Portion dégagée d'un rivage, de faible pente, constituée de galets ou de matériaux grossiers.
OBS	*A* grève *is normally made up of coarser material than a* plage. *The Nfld. fishermen use, in French, the word "grave" to indicate the seashore covered with large pebbles on which they dry their codfish. In Gaspésie, as in N.B., the term «grave» also belongs to the language of the fishermen. Used in Que.*	La grève est habituellement constituée de matériaux plus grossiers que ceux de la plage. Les pêcheurs de T.-N. emploient, en français, «grave» pour désigner le rivage de la mer, couvert de gros cailloux sur lesquels ils font sécher la morue. En Gaspésie comme au N.-B., le terme "grave" appartient aussi au langage des pêcheurs. Attesté au Qué.
EQ	**beach**	
REL		plage
EX	Grève la Baleine, Qué./Que. 47° 23′ – 70° 22′ (21 M/8)	

grotte (f.)

DES	*Natural underground hollow, of variable depth.*	Cavité naturelle souterraine, plus ou moins profonde.
OBS	*Used interchangeably for quite open depressions as well as those with more difficult access. Used in Que.*	Employé indifféremment pour les cavités nettement ouvertes sur l'extérieur et pour celles auxquelles on accède plus difficilement. Attesté au Qué.
EQ	**grotto**	
REL		caverne
EX	Grotte Maranda, Qué./Que. 46° 51′ – 71° 05′ (21 L/14)	

grotto

DES	See **cave**	*Voir* **cave**
OBS	Rare; Nfld.	*Rare; T.-N.*
EQ		**grotte** (f.)
REL	oven	
EX	Whale Grotto, Nfld./T.-N. 51° 20′ – 53° 36′ (2 M/5)	

ground (1)   (Fig. 60)

DES	Area of a sea or lake bed.	*Partie du lit d'une mer ou d'un lac.*
OBS	Generally used to describe fishing areas, which may be in either shallow or deep water; Nfld., N.B., Ont., and B.C.	*Désigne généralement des zones de pêche profondes ou non; T.-N., N.-B., Ont. et C.-B.*
EQ		
REL	bank (1), shoal, patch	
EX	Middle Ground, B.C./C.-B. 48° 22′ – 123° 42′ (92 B/5) Kerry Ground, Nfld./T.-N. 52° 14′ – 55° 35′ (C.4701)	

ground(s) (2)   (Fig. 1)

DES	Relatively flat terrain, covered with vegetation and subject to periodic flooding.	*Terrain relativement plat, couvert de végétation et inondé périodiquement.*
OBS	Used in the Atlantic Provinces.	*En usage dans les provinces de l'Atlantique.*
EQ		**baissière** (f.)
REL	meadow (1), intervale, flat (2), marsh, barren	
EX	Alder Ground, N.S./N.-É. 45° 09′ – 62° 16′ (11 E/1) Alder Grounds, N.B./N.-B. 46° 35′ – 67° 10′ (21 J/11)	

group

DES	Collective term for a cluster of similar topographic features (e.g. islands, peaks).	*Collectif désignant une réunion d'accidents géographiques de même nature (par ex. des îles ou des pics).*
OBS	Widely used.	*Emploi généralisé.*
EQ		[**groupe** (m.)]
REL		
EX	Barnard Dent Group (mountains-montagnes), B.C. – Alta./C.-B. – Alb. 51° 44′ – 116° 56′ (82 N/10) Broken Group (islands-îles), B.C./C.-B. 48° 54′ – 125° 20′ (92 C/14)	

grove

DES	Small wooded area.	*Petit terrain boisé.*
OBS	Rare; Ont. and Alta.	*Rare; Ont. et Alb.*
EQ		**bosquet** (m.)
REL	woods, bluff (2), tuck	
EX	Cottonwood Grove, Alta./Alb. 50° 20′ – 110° 41′ (72 L/7) Wolves Grove, Ont. 45° 11′ – 76° 15′ (31 F/1)	

gulch (1)   (Fig. 19, 20, 25)

DES	Deep, steeply graded, V-shaped declivity, sometimes containing a stream.	*Entaille profonde, à pente raide et en forme de V, parfois traversée par un cours d'eau.*
OBS	Widely used. Generally smaller than a ravine but larger than a gully. Yukon use is in gold mining areas of the late 1890s.	*Emploi généralisé. «Gulch» désigne généralement une dépression plus petite que «ravine» mais plus grande que «gully». Au Yukon, ce générique s'emploie dans les régions associées aux exploitations d'or de la fin du XIXᵉ siècle.*
EQ		**ravine** (f.)
REL	ravine, gully (1), valley (1), gorge, pup	
EX	Grub Gulch, B.C./C.-B. 53° 02' – 121° 42' (93 H/4) Gold Bottom Gulch, Y.T./Yuk. 63° 54' – 138° 59' (115 N & O) Bears Paw Gulch, Man. 49° 39' – 98° 53' (62 G/10) Arch Gulch, N.S./N.-É. 45° 21' – 64° 52' (21 H/7)	

gulch (2)   (Fig. 20)

DES	Narrow cove with steep shoreline.	*Anse étroite et bordée de versants raides.*
OBS	Used in Nfld.	*En usage à T.-N.*
EQ		**anse** (f.)
REL	cove, bay, hole (1)	
EX	Guys Gulch, Nfld./T.-N. 49° 33' – 53° 49' (2 F/12) Bear Gulch, Nfld./T.-N. 49° 44' – 56° 48' (12 H/10)	

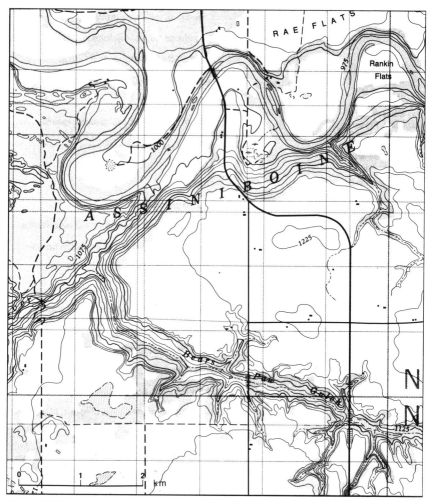

Figure 25. Bears Paw Gulch above the Cypress River valley, and Rae Flats and Rankin Flats beside the Assiniboine River, Manitoba.
(National Topographic System map 62 G/10; 1985)

Figure 25. Bears Paw Gulch, ravine au-dessus de la vallée de la rivière Cypress; Rae Flats et Rankin Flats, plaines bordant la rivière Assiniboine, au Manitoba.
(Carte 62 G/10 du Système national de référence cartographique; 1985)

gulch (3)

DES	Saltwater channel.	*Chenal d'eau salée.*
OBS	Used in N.S.	*En usage en N.-É.*
EQ		**goulet** (m.)
REL	passage, narrows, channel (1), pass (2), gut	
EX	Camp Island Gulch, N.S./N.-É. 44° 53′ – 62° 09′ (11 D/16)	

gulf

DES	Large inlet of the sea.	*Partie de la mer occupant une large échancrure du littoral.*
OBS	Used on east and north coasts of Canada. The only example in B.C. is Nasoga Gulf, which is a small inlet of the sea.	*En usage sur les côtes est et nord du Canada. En C.-B., ce générique se rencontre dans un seul toponyme, «Nasoga Gulf», où il désigne un bras de mer de petite dimension.*
EQ		**golfe** (m.)
REL	bight, bay, inlet (1), sound (1)	
EX	Amundsen Gulf, N.W.T./T.N.-O. 71° 00′ – 124° 00′ (MCR 125) Gulf of St. Lawrence, 48° 00′ – 62° 00′ (MCR 125)	

gully (1)

DES	Small, deep, steeply graded, V-shaped declivity.	*Entaille étroite et profonde, à pentes raides et en forme de V.*
OBS	Generally smaller than a gulch. Used in Ont. and Man.	*Habituellement plus petite qu'un gulch. En usage en Ont. et au Man.*
EQ		**ravine** (f.)
REL	ravine, gulch (1), valley (1), gorge	
EX	Solomons Gully, Man. 50° 16′ – 101° 04′ (62 K/6)	

gully (2) (Fig. 1)

DES	Narrow saltwater passage between two bodies of water.	*Étroit passage d'eau salée entre deux masses d'eau.*
OBS	Rare; N.B.	*Rare; N.-B.*
EQ		**goulet** (m.)
REL	passage, narrows, channel (1), pass (2), gut	
EX	Old Tracadie Gully, N.B./N.-B. 47° 33′ – 64° 51′ (21 P/10)	

gully (gullies) (3) (Fig. 5)

DES	Small pond(s) and marsh.	*Étang(s) et marche de petites dimensions.*
OBS	Used in Nfld.	*En usage à T.-N.*
EQ		**marais** (m.)
REL	pond (1), marsh, water	
EX	Small Point Gully, Nfld./T.-N. 46° 51′ – 53° 59′ (1 K/13) Wood Chisel Gullies, Nfld./T.-N. 46° 56′ – 53° 54′ (1 K/13)	

gully (gullies) (4) (Fig. 5, 20)

DES	Small watercourse.	*Petit cours d'eau.*
OBS	Rare; Nfld. and N.S.	*Rare; T.-N. et N.-É.*
EQ		[**ruisselet** (m.)]
REL	creek (1), brook, stream	
EX	Long Stone Gully, Nfld./T.-N. 46° 55′ – 53° 55′ (1 K/13) Long Gullies, N.S./N.-É. 44° 49′ – 63° 49′ (11 D/13)	

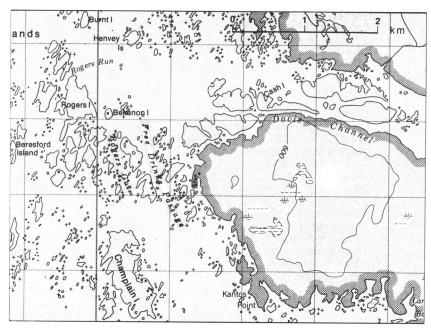

Figure 26. The inshore waters of Georgian Bay, Lake Huron, Ontario, showing Davis Channel, Rogers Gut, Free Drinks Passage, and Rogers Run. (National Topographic System map 41 H/15; 1976)

Figure 26. Eaux intérieures de la baie Georgienne, lac Huron, en Ontario. Entités représentées : Davis Channel, Rogers Gut, Free Drinks Passage et Rogers Run. (Carte 41 H/15 du Système national de référence cartographique; 1976)

gut   (Fig. 20, 26, 62)

DES	Narrow channel, inlet, or cove.	*Chenal, anse ou bras de mer étroit.*
OBS	Used in the Atlantic Provinces and Ont.	*Relevé dans les provinces de l'Atlantique et en Ont.*
EQ		
REL	channel (1), inlet (1), cove, passage, narrows	
EX	Bears Gut (inlet-bras), Nfld./T.-N. 58° 42′ – 63° 00′ (14 L/10)	
	Coys Gut (cove-anse), N.B./N.-B. 45° 51′ – 66° 11′ (21 G/16)	
	Rogers Gut (channel-chenal), Ont. 45° 50′ – 80° 44′ (41 H/15)	

gutter

DES	See **narrows**	*Voir* **narrows**
OBS	Rare; N.S.	*Rare; N.-É.*
EQ		**passage** (m.)
REL	passage, gap (2), gut, channel (1)	
EX	Goose Gutter, N.S./N.-É. 44° 56′ – 62° 05′ (11 D/16)	

gutway

DES	See **channel (2)**	*Voir* **channel (2)**
OBS	Rare; Ont.	*Rare; Ont.*
EQ		**passage** (m.)
REL	pass (2), snye, chokey	
EX	Bull's Gutway, Ont. 51° 14′ – 80° 38′ (42 P/2)	

guzzle

DES	See **brook**	*Voir* **brook**
OBS	Rare; N.B.	*Rare; N.-B.*
EQ		**ruisseau** (m.)
REL	creek (1), stream	
EX	Toby Guzzle, N.B./N.-B. 45° 32′ – 67° 18′ (21 G/11)	

h

handle

DES	See **point (1)**	*Voir* **point (1)**
OBS	Rare; Nfld.	*Rare; T.-N.*
EQ		**pointe** (f.)
REL	spit, peninsula, cape, head (1)	
EX	Handle of the Sug, Nfld./T.-N. 57° 49′ – 61° 48′ (14 F/13)	

harbour(s)   (Fig. 2, 27)

DES	Sheltered water in a shoreline indentation, suitable for mooring or anchoring vessels.	*Étendue d'eau protégée dans un rentrant du littoral, propice au mouillage ou à l'ancrage des navires.*
OBS	Widely used for both a natural sheltered bay and the water area of a port.	*Emploi généralisé. Désigne à la fois une baie servant d'abri naturel et la zone d'eau d'un port.*
EQ		**havre** (m.)
REL	haven, anchorage, bay, cove	
EX	Vancouver Harbour, B.C./C.-B. 49° 18′ – 123° 06′ (92 G/6) Twin Harbours, Ont. 45° 48′ – 82° 19′ (41 G/16)	

North Head   Cuckold Head

Figure 27. Quidi Vidi Harbour,
Newfoundland, looking seaward through
the gut between North Head and Cuckold
Head.
(Ben Hansen)

Figure 27. Quidi Vidi Harbour, à Terre-
Neuve; vue vers la mer montrant
également le passage entre le North Head
et le Cuckold Head.
(Ben Hansen)

hat

DES	Feature with a hat-like appearance.	*Accident géographique en forme de chapeau.*
OBS	Applied to islands, hills, woods, and ridges. Rare; Nfld.	*S'emploie pour des îles, des collines, des bois, et des crêtes. Rare; T.-N.*
EQ		
REL	cap (1)	
EX	Quakers Hat (island-île), Nfld./T.-N. 53° 39′ – 56° 21′ (13 H/9)	
	Carrols Hat (hill-colline), Nfld./T.-N. 47° 51′ – 54° 44′ (1 M/15)	
	Beaver Hat (ridge-chaînon), Nfld./T.-N. 47° 28′ – 52° 56′ (1 N/7)	

haut-fond (m.)

DES	*Elevation of the sea floor or a stream bed, with the top barely submerged and posing a hazard to navigation.*	Élévation du fond de la mer ou d'un cours d'eau, dont le sommet est faiblement immergé et qui présente un danger pour la navigation.
OBS	*Usage has made "haut-fond" and "bas-fond" into synonyms. This is incorrect, since "bas-fond", in its precise but less-known meaning, is the antonym of "haut-fond", and indicates a depression and not an elevation of the seafloor or river bed, where the water is very deep. Underwater feature noted mainly in Que., but also in N.S.*	On relève que l'usage, à tort, a fait de «haut-fond» et de «bas-fond» des synonymes. Cet usage est fautif car «haut-fond» a comme antonyme «bas-fond» qui, dans son sens exact, mais moins connu, représente une dépression et non une élévation du fond de la mer, d'un fleuve ou d'une rivière, où l'eau est très profonde. Entité sous-marine attestée au Qué. surtout mais aussi en N.-É.
EQ	**shoal**	
REL		fond, banc, basse
EX	Haut-fond de Roche, N.-É./N.S. 45° 10′ – 61° 20′ (11 F/3) Haut-fond Collins, Qué./Que. 50° 10′ – 63° 04′ (12 L/3)	

haven

DES	Small harbour.	*Havre de petite dimension.*
OBS	Used in Nfld., Ont., B.C., and N.W.T.	*Relevé à T.-N., en Ont., en C.-B. et dans les T.N.-O.*
EQ		**havre** (m.)
REL	harbour, cove, bay, anchorage	
EX	Milford Haven, Ont. 46° 09′ – 83° 49′ (41 J/4) Gjoa Haven, N.W.T./T.N.-O. 68° 38′ – 95° 53′ (57 B)	

havre (m.)   (Fig. 32)

DES	*Body of water generally protected by natural or artificial barriers, where vessels can berth or anchor.*	Étendue d'eau généralement protégée par des éléments naturels ou artificiels et permettant l'amarrage ou le mouillage des bateaux.
OBS	*The terms "havre" and "port" were interchangeable up to the beginning of the twentieth century. Today, "havre" is generally reserved for the sea, while "port" also applies to rivers and lakes. "Havre" is heard mainly in the Îles-de-la-Madeleine region and the Basse-Côte-Nord (Lower North Shore). In the Maritime Provinces, "havrer" and "se havrer" are used to mean entering a harbour. From the mid-eighteenth century, "havre" also took on the meaning of a small port that is dry at low tide. Used in Que. and the Atlantic Provinces.*	Les termes «havre» et «port» étaient interchangeables jusqu'au début du XXe siècle; aujourd'hui «havre» est généralement réservé à la mer, tandis que «port» s'applique aux cours d'eau et aux lacs, comme à la mer. «Havre» s'entend surtout aux Îles-de-la-Madeleine et sur la Basse-Côte-Nord. Les Acadiens disent «havrer» et «se havrer» au sens d'entrer dans un havre. À partir du milieu du XVIIIe siècle, «havre» prend aussi le sens de petit port qui reste à sec à marée basse. Attesté au Qué. et dans les provinces de l'Atlantique.
EQ	**harbour**	
REL		port
EX	Havre Aubert, Qué./Que. 47° 14′ – 61° 50′ (11 N/4) Havre Boucher, N.-É./N.S. 45° 41′ – 61° 31′ (11 F/12)	

hay

DES	See **meadow (1)**	*Voir* **meadow (1)**
OBS	Rare; Nfld.	*Rare; T.-N.*
EQ		**baissière** (f.)
REL	ground (2), flat (2), intervale	
EX	Long Jims Hay, Nfld./T.-N. 47° 07′ – 54° 03′ (1 M/1)	

haymarsh

DES	See **hay meadow**	*Voir* **hay meadow**
OBS	Rare; N.S.	*Rare; N.-É.*
EQ		**baissière** (f.)
REL	meadow (1), ground (2), flat (2), intervale	
EX	MacAulays Haymarsh, N.S./N.-É. 45° 44′ – 60° 18′ (11 F/9)	

hay meadow

DES	Low-lying area suitable for growing marsh hay.	*Terre basse propice à la croissance du foin de marais.*
OBS	Rare; N.S.	*Rare; N.-É.*
EQ		**baissière** (f.)
REL	meadow (1), ground (2), flat (2), intervale, haymarsh	
EX	Alex Snows Hay Meadow, N.S./N.-É. 43° 55′ – 65° 19′ (20 P/14)	

hazers

DES	Variant of **ears.**	*Variante de* **ears.**
OBS	Literally "hare's ears"; Nfld.	*Déformation de «hare's ears»; T.-N.*
EQ		
REL		
EX	Brigus Hazers (rocks-rochers), Nfld./T.-N. 47° 06′ – 52° 52′ (1 N/2)	

head(s) (1) (Fig. 2, 27, 45)

DES	High, prominent, land feature extending into a sea or lake.	*Saillie de terre élevée qui s'avance dans une mer ou un lac.*
OBS	Widely used. Sand Heads (B.C.) and Sand Head (N.W.T.) are sandy spits.	*Emploi généralisé. Les* Sand Heads *(C.-B.) et* Sand Head *(T.N.-O.) sont des flèches sablonneuses.*
EQ		**cap** (m.)
REL	cape, point (1), headland	
EX	Basin Head, P.E.I./Î.-P.-É. 46° 23′ – 62° 07′ (11 L/8) Easter Head, Sask. 59° 29′ – 109° 04′ (74 N/6) Isaac Heads, Nfld./T.-N. 47° 20′ – 53° 56′ (1 N/5)	

head (2)

DES	Prominent hill or crag-like feature.	*Colline bien démarquée ou relief en forme de pic.*
OBS	Used in Alta. and B.C.	*Relevé en Alb. et en C.-B.*
EQ		**tête** (f.) **(2)**
REL	crag, summit, peak (1), spire, tower	
EX	Diamond Head, B.C./C.-B. 49° 49′ – 123° 00′ (92 G/14) Saracens Head, Alta./Alb. 52° 40′ – 116° 56′ (83 C/10)	

headland

DES	Variant of **head (1)**.	*Variante de* **head (1)**.
OBS	Rare; N.W.T.	*Rare; T.N.-O.*
EQ		**cap** (m.)
REL	cape, point (1)	
EX	Qorbignaluk Headland, N.W.T./T.N.-O. 72° 22′ – 78° 36′ (38 B)	

heath

DES	Flat wet area with low vegetation.	*Terrain plat et humide, occupé par une végétation basse.*
OBS	Used in N.S. and N.B.	*Relevé en N.-É. et au N.-B.*
EQ		**pré** (m.)
REL	bog, barren, marsh	
EX	Goose Heath, N.S./N.-É. 43° 46′ – 65° 43′ (20 P/13)	

heights   (Fig. 28)

DES	Area of high land rising above the adjacent land or water.	*Terre qui, par sa hauteur, domine les terres et les eaux adjacentes.*
OBS	Widely used.	*Emploi généralisé.*
EQ		[**hauteurs** (f.)]
REL	head (2), hills, cape, lookout	
EX	Gladstone Heights, Man. 51° 33′ – 96° 46′ (62 P/10) Queenston Heights, Ont. 43° 09′ – 79° 03′ (30 M)	

highland(s)

DES	Area of elevated relief, not as high or rugged as a range of mountains or as level as a plateau.	*Terrain de relief élevé, moins haut et accidenté qu'une chaîne de montagnes, mais plus irrégulier qu'un plateau.*
OBS	Widely used.	*Emploi généralisé.*
EQ		**massif** (m.)
REL	uplands, hills, heights, range	
EX	Quesnel Highland, B.C./C.-B. 52° 30′ – 121° 00′ (83 D/4) Madawaska Highlands, Ont. 45° 15′ – 77° 35′ (31 F)	

Figure 28. Queenston Heights west of the Niagara River, Ontario, as portrayed by W.H. Bartlett. (Public Archives Canada, C-2316; from N.P. Willis, *Canadian Scenery*, London, 1840, Vol. 1, facing p. 60)

Figure 28. Queenston Heights, à l'ouest de la rivière Niagara, en Ontario. Illustration de W.H. Bartlett. (Archives publiques du Canada, C-2316; tiré de *Canadian Scenery*, N.P. Willis, London, 1840, vol. 1, vis-à-vis p. 60).

hill(s) (Fig. 41, 49)

DES	Elevation of terrain rising prominently above the surrounding land.	*Élévation de terrain se détachant nettement du relief environnant.*
OBS	Generally smaller and with a more rounded profile than a mountain. Widely used.	*«Hill» désigne généralement une élévation de dimension plus petite et de forme plus arrondie que «mountain». Emploi généralisé.*
EQ		**colline** (f.)
REL	highland, mountain, head (2), summit, uplands, heights, knoll (1), tolt, peak (1)	
EX	Antler Hill, Alta./Alb. 52° 04' – 113° 53' (83 A/4) The Cactus Hills, Sask. 50° 06' – 105° 27' (72 I) Cameron Hills, N.W.T./T.N.-O. 60° 06' – 116° 53' (85 C)	

hole (1) (Fig. 20)

DES	Small cove.	*Anse de petite dimension.*
OBS	Used in Nfld., N.B., Ont., and Man.	*Relevé à T.-N., au N.-B., en Ont. et au Man.*
EQ		**anse** (f.)
REL	cove, bay	
EX	Hibbs Hole, Nfld./T.-N. 47° 36′ – 53° 11′ (1 N/11) Hole in the Wall, Man. 53° 01′ – 98° 51′ (63 G/2)	

hole(s) (2)

DES	Small lake or pond.	*Étang ou lac de petite dimension.*
OBS	Used in Nfld., N.B., and Ont.	*Relevé à T.-N., au N.-B. et en Ont.*
EQ		**étang** (m.)
REL	pond (1), puddle	
EX	Garfinkle Hole, Ont. 49° 47′ – 86° 15′ (42 E/16) Seeley Pond Holes, N.B./N.-B. 45° 12′ – 66° 43′ (21 G/2)	

hole (3)

DES	Deep place in a stream.	*Dépression dans le lit d'un cours d'eau.*
OBS	Rare; N.B., Ont., and Man.	*Rare; N.-B., Ont. et Man.*
EQ		**fosse** (f.)
REL	pool (1)	
EX	Five Mile Hole, Man. 56° 32′ – 94° 17′ (54 D/9) Five Fathom Hole, N.B./N.-B. 45° 11′ – 66° 16′ (21 G/1) Tilley's Hole, Ont. 44° 29′ – 78° 07′ (31 D/8)	

hole (4)

DES	Whirlpool.	*Tourbillon.*
OBS	Rare; B.C.	*Rare; C.-B.*
EQ		[**tourbillon** (m.)]
REL	eddy, rip (2), pool (2)	
EX	Devils Hole, B.C./C.-B. 50° 24′ – 125° 12′ (92 K/6)	

hole (5)

DES	Small narrow channel.	*Petit chenal étroit.*
OBS	Used in various provinces, including Nfld., N.S., and Ont.	*Relevé dans plusieurs provinces, dont T.-N., la N.-É. et l'Ont.*
EQ		**passage** (m.)
REL	gut, gully (2), gulch (3), passage, narrows	
EX	Bogus Hole, N.S./N.-É. 45° 54′ – 59° 58′ (11 G/13)	

hollow

DES	Small steep-sided declivity.	*Petite dépression aux parois abruptes.*
OBS	Rare; N.S., N.B., Ont., and Man.	*Rare; N.-É., N.-B., Ont. et Man.*
EQ		[**dépression** (f.)]
REL	ravine, gully (1), gulch (1), valley (1)	
EX	Bear Hollow, Man. 49° 11′ – 99° 09′ (62 G/3) Arthur Jonah Hollow, N.B./N.-B. 45° 49′ – 65° 11′ (21 H/14)	

hook

DES	Feature having the appearance of a hook.	*Accident géographique en forme de crochet.*

| OBS | Applied to curved spits, islands, and river bends. Uncommon; N.S., N.B., Ont., and B.C. | *S'emploie pour désigner des flèches incurvées, des îles et des courbes dans le tracé d'un cours d'eau. Relevé en N.-É., au N.-B., en Ont. et en C.-B. Emploi peu fréquent.* |

EQ

REL

EX   Walker Hook (spit-flèche), B.C./C.-B. 48° 54' – 123° 30' (92 B/13)
Sandy Hook (island-île), Ont. 45° 45' – 80° 03' (41 H/9)
Devils Hook (bend-courbe), N.S./N.-É. 44° 40' – 64° 44' (21 A/10)

horn

DES	Feature having the appearance of the point of a horn.	*Accident géographique rappelant la pointe d'une corne.*

| OBS | Applied to points, rocks, shoals, and peaks. Rare; Nfld., N.S., Ont., and B.C. | *S'emploie pour des pointes, des rochers, des hauts-fonds et des pics. Rare; T.-N., N.-É., Ont. et C.-B.* |

EQ

REL   peak (1), point (2)

EX   Devils Horn (point-pointe), Ont. 45° 58' – 83° 16' (41 G/14)
Squids Horn (rock-rocher), Nfld./T.-N. 49° 39' – 55° 45' (2 E/12)
The Horn (shoal – haut-fond), N.S./N.-É. 44° 37' – 62° 58' (11 D/10)
The Horn (peak-pic), B.C./C.-B. 52° 19' – 126° 14' (93 D/8)

hotspring(s), hot springs

DES	Site of a natural flow of hot or warm water issuing from the ground.	*Point d'apparition, à la surface du sol, d'eaux souterraines chaudes ou tièdes.*
OBS	Used in Alta., B.C., N.W.T., and Y.T.	*Relevé en Alb., en C.-B., dans les T.N.-O. et au Yukon.*
EQ		**[source thermale** (f.)]
REL	spring	
EX	Takhini Hotspring, Y.T./Yuk. 60° 53′ – 135° 22′ (105 D) Rabbitkettle Hotsprings, N.W.T./T.N.-O. 61° 57′ – 127° 11′ (95 E) Ainsworth Hot Springs, B.C./C.-B. 49° 44′ – 116° 55′ (82 F/10)	

hummock(s)

DES	Small rounded hill.	*Petite colline arrondie.*
OBS	Uncommon; Nfld. and N.S. Also used for a similar seafloor feature off Nfld. (Eastern Hummock).	*Peu usité; T.-N. et N.-É. S'emploie aussi pour désigner un relief sous-marin de même nature au large de T.-N. (Eastern Hummock).*
EQ		**buttereau** (m.)
REL	hill, knoll (1), tolt, butte, hump, lump	
EX	Steering Hummock, N.S./N.-É. 46° 00′ – 59° 47′ (11 J/4) Fox Hummocks, Nfld./T.-N. 47° 11′ – 55° 27′ (1 M/3)	

hump

DES	Rounded hill or mountain.	*Colline ou montagne arrondie.*
OBS	Uncommon; Nfld., Ont., Alta., and B.C.	*Emploi peu fréquent; T.-N., Ont., Alb. et C.-B.*
EQ		**bosse** (f.)
REL	hill, knoll (1), mountain, lump	
EX	Camels Hump, B.C./C.-B. 50° 14′ – 118° 50′ (82 L/2)	

i

ice cap(s), icecap (Fig. 29)

DES	Large dome-shaped mass of permanent ice and snow.	*Vaste accumulation de glace et de neige éternelles en forme de dôme.*
OBS	In Canada the use of this generic has in the past been extended to features that would normally be called icefields. The usually accepted form is "ice cap" rather than "icecap". Used in B.C. and N.W.T.	*Au Canada, l'emploi de ce générique a été étendu à des entités qui sont normalement désignées en anglais par le terme «icefield». S'écrit habituellement en deux mots «ice cap». En usage en C.-B. et dans les T.N.-O.*
EQ		[**calotte glaciaire** (f.)]
REL	icefield, glacier, ice shelf	
EX	Barnes Ice Cap, N.W.T./T.N.-O. 70° 00' – 73° 15' (37 E) Pentice Ice Caps, B.C./C.-B. 59° 20' – 137° 23' (114 P) Neil Icecap, N.W.T./T.N.-O. 80° 48' – 82° 43' (340 B)	

icefield

DES	Irregularly shaped mass of permanent snow and ice, generally forming the accumulation area of two or more glaciers.	*Masse de neige et de glace éternelles, de forme irrégulière, qui sert généralement de zone d'accumulation à deux ou plusieurs glaciers.*
OBS	The form and flow of constituent glaciers is controlled by the underlying topography. Used in Alta., B.C., and N.W.T.	*La forme et l'écoulement des glaciers qui en sont issus sont déterminés par la topographie sous-jacente. Relevé en Alb., et C.-B. et dans les T.N.-O.*
EQ		[**champ de glace** (m.)]
REL	ice cap, glacier, ice shelf	
EX	Waputik Icefield, B.C./C.-B. 51° 34' – 116° 27' (82 N/9)	

Figure 29. Neil Icecap, northern Ellesmere Island, Northwest Territories.
(National Air Photo Library, A16785-21; 1959)

Figure 29. Neil Icecap, dans le nord de l'île d'Ellesmere, dans les Territoires du Nord-Ouest.
(Photothèque nationale de l'air, A16785-21; 1959)

ice shelf

DES	Thick and extensive floating sheet of glacier ice attached to the coast.	*Nappe de glace épaisse et très étendue, formée de glaces de glacier et fixée à la côte.*
OBS	Only occurs off the northern coast of Ellesmere Island, N.W.T.	*Ne s'emploie que le long de la côte nord de l'île d'Ellesmere, T.N.-O.*
EQ		**[plate-forme de glace** (f.)]
REL	icefield, ice cap, glacier	
EX	Ward Hunt Ice Shelf, N.W.T./T.N.-O. 83° 07' – 73° 45' (340 H & E)	

île(s) (f.)

DES	*Land surrounded by water.*	Terre entourée d'eau.
OBS	*Used everywhere across the country.*	Attesté partout à travers le pays.
EQ	**island**	
REL		îlet, îlette, îlot
EX	Île aux Trembles, Sask. 55° 26' – 107° 48' (73 O/5) Île d'Orléans, Qué./Que. 46° 55' – 70° 58' (21 L/15) Île au Blé, N.-É./N.S. 43° 41' – 65° 47' (20 P/12) Îles de la Madeleine, Qué./Que. 47° 30' – 61° 45' (11 N)	

îlet (m.)

DES	*See* **îlot**	Voir **îlot**
OBS	*The diminutive of "îlet" is "îlette". Used in Que.*	«Îlet» a pour diminutif «îlette». Attesté au Qué.
EQ	**islet**	
REL		îlette, île
EX	Îlet aux Alouettes, Qué./Que. 48° 06' – 69° 41' (22 C/4)	

îlette (f.)

DES	*See* **îlot**	Voir **îlot**
OBS	*Diminutive of "îlet". Used in N.B.*	Diminutif de «îlet». Attesté au N.-B.
EQ	**islet**	
REL		îlet, île
EX	L'Îlette de Pokesudie, N.-B./N.B. 47° 47′ – 64° 46′ (21 P/15)	

îlot(s) (m.)

DES	*Very small island.*	Très petite île.
OBS	*Used in Que.*	Attesté au Qué.
EQ	**islet**	
REL		îlet, îlette, île
EX	Îlot à Châtigny, Qué./Que. 47° 14′ – 70° 26′ (21 M/1) Îlots Escoumains, Qué./Que. 48° 25′ – 69° 19′ (22 C/6)	

inlet (1)   (Fig. 30, 45)

DES	Elongated body of water extending from a sea or lake.	*Étendue d'eau allongée qui prolonge une mer ou un lac.*
OBS	Widely used.	*Emploi généralisé.*
EQ		**[bras (m.)]**
REL	arm (1), fiord, creek (2), reach, bay, canal (1), channel (1), sound (2)	
EX	Admiralty Inlet, N.W.T./T.N.-O. 72° 30′ – 86° 00′ (48 B) Oxford Inlet, Man. 54° 58′ – 95° 17′ (53 L/14)	

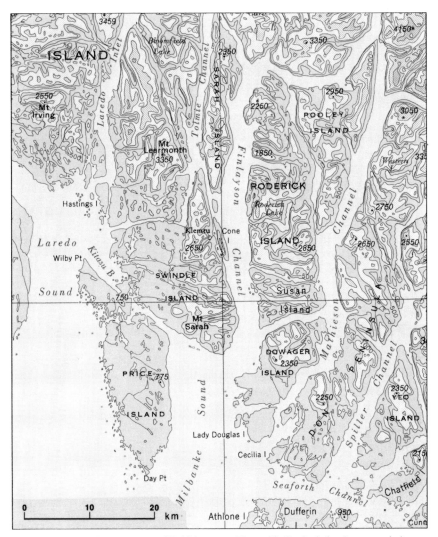

Figure 30. Part of the west coast of British Columbia, showing Laredo Inlet, several channels (e.g. Finlayson Channel), Milbanke Sound and Laredo Sound. (National Topographic System map 103 S.E.; 1977)

Figure 30. Partie de la côte ouest de la Colombie-Britannique. Entités représentées : Laredo Inlet, plusieurs chenaux (dont le Finlayson Channel), Milbanke Sound et Laredo Sound. (Carte 103 S.E. du Système national de référence cartographique; 1977)

inlet (2)

DES	See **pass (2)**	*Voir* **pass (2)**
OBS	Used in N.S., N.W.T., and Y.T.	*Relevé en N.-É., dans les T.N.-O. et au Yukon.*
EQ		**passage** (m.)
REL	passage, narrows, gap (2), pass (2), strait	
EX	Fish Inlet, N.S./N.-É. 43° 25′ – 65° 39′ (20 P/5) Nisutlin Bay Inlet, Y.T./Yuk. 60° 11′ – 132° 40′ (105 C)	

inlet (3)

DES	Watercourse flowing into a sea or lake.	*Cours d'eau se jetant dans une mer ou un lac.*
OBS	Rare; N.B.	*Rare; N.-B.*
EQ		**ruisseau** (m.)
REL	creek (1), brook, stream, outlet (1)	
EX	McDougall Inlet, N.B./N.-B. 45° 19′ – 66° 46′ (21 G/7)	

intervale (Fig. 62)

DES	Low-lying, flat, seasonally-flooded, grassy area adjacent to a watercourse.	*Terre basse, plate et herbeuse, située en bordure d'un cours d'eau qui l'inonde de façon saisonnière.*
OBS	Used only in N.S. and N.B.	*Relevé uniquement en N.-É. et au N.-B.*
EQ		**platin** (m.)
REL	ground (2), meadow (1), glade, flat (2)	
EX	Anderson Intervale, N.S./N.-É. 45° 09′ – 63° 33′ (11 E/2) Meduxnekeag Intervale, N.B./N.-B. 46° 09′ – 67° 35′ (21 J/4)	

island(s)   (Fig. 38, 49)

DES	Land area surrounded by water or marsh.	*Masse de terre entourée d'eau ou de marécages.*
OBS	Widely used.	*Emploi généralisé.*
EQ		**île** (f.)
REL	islet, archipelago, isle	
EX	Cape Breton Island, N.S./N.-É. 46° 00′ – 60° 30′ (11 J) Queen Charlotte Islands, B.C./C.-B. 53° 00′ – 132° 00′ (103 F)	

isle

DES	Variant of **island**.	*Variante de* **island**.
OBS	Widely used.	*Emploi généralisé.*
EQ		**île** (f.)
REL	islet	
EX	Belle Isle, Nfld./T.-N. 51° 57′ – 55° 21′ (3 D) Emerald Isle, N.W.T./T.N.-O. 76° 48′ – 114° 10′ (89 A) Isle of Bays, Sask. 50° 07′ – 105° 55′ (72 I/4)	

islet(s)   (Fig. 45, 49)

DES	Small island.	*Petite île.*
OBS	Widely used.	*Emploi généralisé.*
EQ		**îlot** (m.)
REL	island, rock (1)	
EX	Grassy Islet, Nfld./T.-N. 49° 35′ – 55° 56′ (2 E/12) Rocky Islets, B.C./C.-B. 50° 20′ – 125° 26′ (92 K/6)	

isthmus

DES	Narrow neck of land, bordered on both sides by water, and connecting two larger land areas.	*Étroite langue de terre resserrée entre deux étendues d'eau et reliant deux terrains plus importants.*
OBS	Used in Nfld., N.S., Ont., and N.W.T.	Relevé à T.-N., en N.-É., en Ont. et dans les T.N.-O.
EQ		[**isthme** (m.)]
REL	neck	
EX	Isthmus of Avalon, Nfld./T.-N. 47° 51′ – 53° 58′ (1 N/13) Chignecto Isthmus, N.S./N.-É. 45° 55′ – 64° 10′ (21 H/16)	

j

jaw(s)

DES	Restricted water passage.	*Passage d'eau resserré.*
OBS	Rare; N.S. and N.B.	*Rare; N.-É. et N.-B.*
EQ		**passage** (m.)
REL	narrows, passage, chops (2)	
EX	Devils Jaw, N.S./N.-É. 44° 59′ – 63° 45′ (11 D/13) The Jaws, N.B./N.-B. 45° 26′ – 66° 40′ (21 G/7)	

jugs

DES	Rounded hills close together.	*Groupe de collines arrondies rapprochées.*
OBS	Rare; N.W.T.	*Rare; T.N.-O.*
EQ		**collines** (f.)
REL	hills, paps, nipples	
EX	Twin Jugs, N.W.T./T.N.-O. 65° 56′ – 109° 45′ (76 F)	

k

kap

DES	Variant of **cape**.	*Variante de* **cape**.
OBS	Rare; N.S.	*Rare; N.-É.*
EQ		**cap** (m.)
REL	head (1), point (1), bluff (1)	
EX	Felsen Kap, N.S./N.-É. 44° 16′ – 64° 19′ (21 A/8)	

knap

DES	Bare, raised portion of a hill.	*Partie élevée et dénudée d'une colline.*
OBS	Uncommon; Nfld.	*Peu fréquent; T.-N.*
EQ		**colline** (f.)
REL	hill, knoll (1), tolt, knob, hummock	
EX	Burnt Knap, Nfld./T.-N. 47° 04′ – 53° 33′ (1 N/4)	

knob (Fig. 4, 31)

DES	Rounded usually isolated part of a mountain; a hill.	*Partie d'une montagne aux contours arrondis et habituellement isolée; colline.*
OBS	Widely used.	*Emploi généralisé.*
EQ		**colline** (f.)
REL	hill, knoll (1), tolt, hummock, butte, peak (1), nob	
EX	Stuart Knob, Alta./Alb. 51° 20′ – 115° 27′ (82 O/5) Granite Knob, B.C./C.-B. 49° 48′ – 117° 12′ (82 F/14) East Knob, Ont. 46° 06′ – 81° 56′ (41 I/4)	

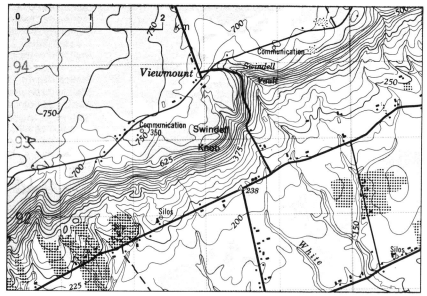

Figure 31. Swindell Knob and Swindell Vault, northwest of the Annapolis Valley, Nova Scotia.
(National Topographic System map 21 H/2; 1984)

Figure 31. Swindell Knob et Swindell Vault, au nord-ouest de la vallée Annapolis, en Nouvelle-Écosse.
(Carte 21 H/2 du Système national de référence cartographique; 1984)

knoll(s) (1)

DES	Small rounded hill.	*Petite colline arrondie.*
OBS	Widely used.	*Emploi généralisé.*
EQ		**buttereau** (m.)
REL	hill, tolt, knob, hummock	
EX	Grant Knoll, B.C./C.-B. 48° 26′ – 123° 26′ (92 B/6) Twin Knolls, N.W.T./T.N.-O. 62° 48′ – 91° 36′ (55 J/13)	

knoll (2)

DES	Small, rounded, isolated elevation of the seabed.	*Petite élévation du fond de la mer, arrondie et isolée.*
OBS	Rare; N.S. and off Nfld.	*Rare. Relevé en N.-É. et au large de T.-N.*
EQ		**dôme** (m.)
REL	peak (2), spur (2), pinnacle (2), shoal	
EX	Ives Knoll, N.S./N.-É. 44° 38′ – 63° 33′ (C.4385) Orphan Knoll, 50° 30′ – 46° 30′ (C.800A)	

kop

DES	Variant of **kopje**.	*Variante de* **kopje**.
OBS	Rare; B.C.	*Rare; C.-B.*
EQ		**colline** (f.)
REL	hill, knoll (1), tolt, knob, butte	
EX	Spion Kop, B.C./C.-B. 49° 06′ – 118° 36′ (82 E/2)	

kopje

DES	Small prominent hill.	*Petite colline proéminente.*
OBS	Afrikaans term. Rare; N.W.T.	*Mot afrikaans. Rare; T.N.-O.*
EQ		**colline** (f.)
REL	hill, knoll (1), tolt, knob, butte, kop	
EX	Hanbury Kopje, N.W.T./T.N.-O. 67° 15′ – 117° 49′ (86 N)	

kwun

DES	See **point (1)**	*Voir* **point (1)**
OBS	Haida Indian term. Rare; B.C.	*Mot haïda. Rare; C.-B.*
EQ		**pointe** (f.)
REL	peninsula, spit, cape, head (1)	
EX	Strathdang Kwun, B.C./C.-B. 53° 40′ – 132° 13′ (103 F/9)	

l

labyrinth

DES	Cluster of islands having a maze of tortuous passages.	*Groupe d'îles formant entre elles un dédale de passages tortueux.*
OBS	Rare; B.C.	*Rare; C.-B.*
EQ		**archipel** (m.)
REL	islands, archipelago	
EX	Murray Labyrinth, B.C./C.-B. 51° 03′ – 127° 32′ (92 M/4)	

lac (m.)   (Fig. 17, 44)

DES	*Body of water surrounded by land and generally having an outlet; or an expansion of a watercourse.*	Nappe d'eau douce entourée de terre, généralement pourvue d'un exutoire, ou élargissement d'un cours d'eau.
OBS	*A lac is larger than an* étang *or a* mare. *Used across the country.*	Le lac est plus grand que l'étang et la mare. Attesté à travers le pays.
EQ	**lake**	
REL		étang, mare
EX	Lac des Deux Montagnes, Qué./Que. 45° 27' – 74° 00' (31 G/8)	
	Lac Grandin, T.N.-O./N.W.T. 63° 59' – 119° 00' (85 M)	
	Lac Arvert, T.-N./Nfld. 52° 18' – 61° 45' (13 C/5)	

lagoon

DES	Body of water, separated from a lake, river, or sea by a narrow land barrier, which may completely enclose it or leave a shallow passageway into it.	*Étendue d'eau complètement ou partiellement isolée d'un lac, d'une rivière ou d'une mer par une étroite barrière de terre.*
OBS	Usually shallow water; some lagoons in B.C. are quite deep.	*Certaines lagunes de la C.-B. sont assez profondes, mais elles constituent l'exception.*
EQ		**lagune** (f.)
REL	lake, pond (1), barachois, basin (2), slough (2)	
EX	Clarence Lagoon, Y.T./Yuk. 69° 37' – 140° 50' (117 C)	
	Esquimalt Lagoon, B.C./C.-B. 48° 26' – 123° 28' (92 B/6)	
	Powers Lagoon, Man. 50° 09' – 101° 04' (62 K/3)	

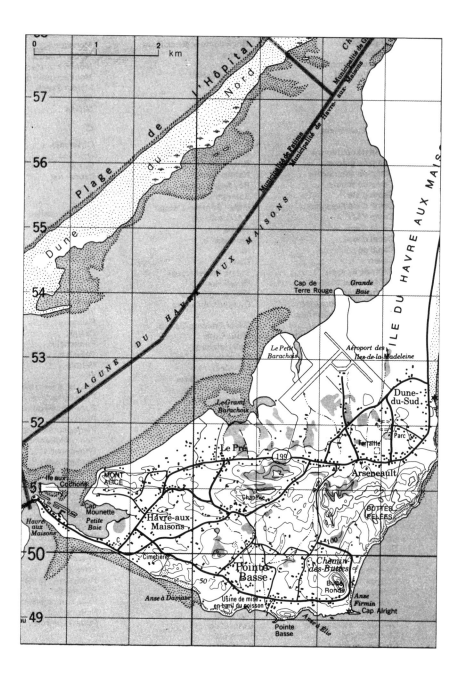

lagune (f.)   (Fig. 32)

DES	*Body of salty or brackish water, separated from the sea or a large lake by a coastal barrier, usually with restricted openings.*	Étendue d'eau salée ou saumâtre, isolée de la mer ou d'un grand lac par une formation littorale généralement percée d'ouvertures.
OBS	*The water is normally shallow, but navigable at high tide. Used in Que.*	Le niveau d'eau est ordinairement peu élevé, mais il permet aux embarcations de circuler à marée haute. Attesté au Qué.
EQ	**lagoon**	
REL		barachois, barasway
EX	Lagune du Havre aux Maisons, Qué./Que. 47° 27′ – 61° 48′ (11 N/5)	

lair

DES	Enclosed valley floor.	*Fond encaissé d'une vallée.*
OBS	Rare; Nfld.	*Rare; T.-N.*
EQ		
REL	valley (1), cirque, basin (3), den	
EX	Torngat Lair, Nfld./T.-N. 59° 09′ – 63° 44′ (14 M/4)	

Figure 32. Part of Île du Havre aux Maisons, Îles de la Madeleine, Quebec, showing Lagune du Havre aux Maisons, Anse à Damase, Le Grand Barachois, Butte Ronde, Cap de Terre Rouge, Dune du Nord, Havre aux Maisons, Mont Alice, and Plage de l'Hôpital.
(National Topographic System map 11 N/5 & 11 M/8; 1974 with additional information to 1982)

Figure 32. Partie de l'île du Havre aux Maisons, îles de la Madeleine, au Québec. Entités représentées : Lagune du Havre aux Maisons, Anse à Damase, Le Grand Barachois, Butte Ronde, Cap de Terre Rouge, Dune du Nord, Havre aux Maisons, Mont Alice et Plage de l'Hôpital.
(Cartes 11 N/5 et 11 M/8 du Système national de référence cartographique; 1974 avec renseignements supplémentaires jusqu'en 1982)

lake(s)

DES	Inland body of standing water.	*Nappe d'eau dormante dans les terres.*
OBS	Lakes may be enlargements of rivers. Widely used.	*Le générique désigne parfois un élargissement d'une rivière. Emploi généralisé.*
EQ		**lac** (m.)
REL	pond (1), lagoon, reservoir, slough (1), tarn, loch, lough	
EX	Lake Winnipeg, Man. 52° 00′ – 97° 00′ (63 A) Okanagan Lake, B.C./C.-B. 49° 45′ – 119° 44′ (82 E/12) Gladstone Lakes, Y.T./Yuk. 61° 22′ – 138° 08′ (115 F & G)	

land(s)

DES	Terrain distinguishable from its surroundings.	*Terrain se distinguant des terres environnantes.*
OBS	Used in the Atlantic Provinces, Ont., and N.W.T.	*Relevé dans les provinces de l'Atlantique, en Ont. et dans les T.N.-O.*
EQ		
REL	country, place, barren	
EX	Musgrave Land, Nfld./T.-N. 53° 33′ – 56° 05′ (13 H/9) The Burnt Lands, Ont. 45° 16′ – 76° 08′ (31 F/8) Loks Land (island-île), N.W.T./T.N.-O. 62° 26′ – 64° 38′ (25 I)	

landing

DES	Place where boats can touch in safety.	*Lieu où les bateaux peuvent accoster en sécurité.*
OBS	Widely used.	*Emploi généralisé.*
EQ		**[débarcadère** (m.)]
REL	ferry, crossing, ford	
EX	Bartlett Landing, Man. 54° 49′ – 99° 58′ (63 J/13) Booth Landing, Ont. 46° 08′ – 79° 13′ (31 L/3)	

154

langue de terre (f.)

DES	*Narrow, elongated strip of land separating two bodies of water.*	Bande de terre étroite et allongée qui sépare deux masses d'eau.
OBS	*Used in Que.*	Attesté au Qué.
EQ	**neck**	
REL		
EX	Langue de terre Chikaskaw, Qué./Que. 55° 43′ – 77° 07′ (33 N/11)	

lead (1)

DES	Channel joined to a larger water feature.	*Chenai relié à une plus grande étendue d'eau.*
OBS	Rare; N.B.	*Rare; N.-B.*
EQ		**passage** (m.)
REL	channel (1), passage, pass (2)	
EX	Coldspring Lead, N.B./N.-B. 45° 55′ – 66° 21′ (21 G/16)	

lead (2)

DES	See **brook**	*Voir* **brook**
OBS	Rare; Nfld.	*Rare; T.-N.*
EQ		**ruisseau** (m.)
REL	creek (1), stream	
EX	Big Rock Lead, Nfld./T.-N. 47° 08′ – 54° 00′ (1 N/4)	

leads (3)

DES	Stretch of open sea characterized by its calmness.	*Étendue de mer libre caractérisée par sa tranquillité.*
OBS	Rare; Nfld.	*Rare; T.-N.*
EQ		
REL		
EX	St. Georges Leads, Nfld./T.-N. 47° 34' – 52° 39' (C.4565)	

ledge(s) (1)

DES	Flat rock area, either projecting from a land mass into the water or rising from the sea floor.	*Terrain rocheux et plat qui peut être soit une saillie de la côte s'avançant dans la mer, soit une élévation du fond de la mer.*
OBS	Common coastal use; may be partly exposed at low water. Sawtooth Ledge (N.W.T.) is a series of small undersea peaks running off islands.	*Générique d'emploi fréquent en milieu côtier. L'accident de terrain peut découvrir en partie à marée basse. Le* Sawtooth Ledge *(T.N.-O.) est une succession de petits pics sous-marins au large des îles.*
EQ		[**chaussée** (f.)]
REL	shelf (1), shoal, rock, point (1)	
EX	Boulder Ledge, B.C./C.-B. 52° 19' – 128° 28' (103 A/8) Peter Ledge, N.W.T./T.N.-O. 63° 27' – 67° 55' (25 O) Lamaline Ledges, Nfld./T.-N. 46° 52' – 55° 55' (1 L/13) Murr Ledges, N.S./N.-É. 44° 30' – 66° 51' (C.4340)	

ledge (2)

DES	Prominent shelf-like platform exposed on the face of a mountain or cliff.	*Plate-forme en saillie sur le versant d'une montagne ou la face d'un escarpement.*
OBS	Few officially named examples; B.C.	*Rare dans les noms approuvés; C.-B.*
EQ		**corniche** (f.)
REL	terrace	
EX	Gates Ledge, B.C./C.-B. 50° 31′ – 118° 11′ (82 L/9)	

ledge (3)   (Fig. 60)

DES	See **ground (1)**	*Voir **ground (1)***
OBS	Used in Nfld.	*En usage à T.-N.*
EQ		
REL	bank (1), shoal	
EX	Mocassin Ledge, Nfld./T.-N. 49° 40′ – 55° 45′ (C.4592)	

leg (1)

DES	See **arm (1)**	*Voir **arm (1)***
OBS	Only in N.B.	*Ne s'emploie qu'au N.-B.*
EQ		[**bras** (m.)]
REL	inlet (1), fiord, reach, bay, cove	
EX	Right Hand Leg, N.B./N.-B. 47° 00′ – 66° 57′ (21 J/15)	

leg (2)

DES	See **arm (2)**	*Voir* **arm (2)**
OBS	Used in Nfld.	*Relevé à T.-N.*
EQ		[**bras** (m.)]
REL	peninsula, point (1)	
EX	Peggys Leg, Nfld./T.-N. 47° 32′ – 52° 41′ (1 N/10)	

limb

DES	See **island**	*Voir* **island**
OBS	Rare; N.S.	*Rare; N.-É.*
EQ		**île** (f.)
REL	islet, rock (1)	
EX	Devils Limb, N.S./N.-É. 43° 24′ – 66° 02′ (20 O/8)	

lip(s)

DES	Top of a steep slope.	*Sommet d'une pente raide.*
OBS	Applied to hills and falls. Rare; Nfld. and N.S.	*S'emploie pour des collines et des chutes. Rare; T.-N. et N.-É.*
EQ		
REL	brow, summit	
EX	Scotchmans Lip (falls-chutes), N.S./N.-É. 44° 46′ – 65° 01′ (21 A/14)	
	Tokems Lips (hills-collines), Nfld./T.-N. 54° 03′ – 59° 07′ (13 J/3)	

loch

DES	Variant of **lake**.	*Variante de **lake**.*
OBS	Gaelic term; generic usually precedes specific. Widely used, but uncommon.	*Mot gaélique. En général, ce générique précède le spécifique. Emploi généralisé mais peu fréquent.*
EQ		**lac** (m.)
REL	pond (1), reservoir, tarn, lochan	
EX	Loch Erne, Ont. 48° 37′ – 90° 21′ (52 G/9) Loch Leven, Sask. 49° 40′ – 109° 30′ (72 F/11) Treasure Loch, Alta./Alb. 59° 56′ – 110° 25′ (74 M/16)	

lochan

DES	Small lake.	*Petit lac.*
OBS	Gaelic term. Uncommon; N.S.	*Mot gaélique. Emploi peu fréquent; N.-É.*
EQ		**étang** (m.)
REL	pond (1), tarn, hole (2), loch	
EX	Lochan Duach, N.S./N.-É. 43° 46′ – 65° 41′ (20 P/13)	

lookoff

DES	Variant of **lookout**.	*Variante de **lookout**.*
OBS	Rare; N.S.	*Rare; N.-É.*
EQ		[**belvédère** (m.)]
REL	summit, hill, head (1)	
EX	Bras d'Or Lookoff, N.S./N.-É. 46° 15′ – 60° 30′ (11 K/2)	

lookout(s)   (Fig. 5)

DES	Elevation from which the surrounding terrain or seascape can be viewed.	*Hauteur d'où il est possible d'observer le terrain ou le paysage marin environnant.*
OBS	Widely used.	*Emploi généralisé.*
EQ		**[belvédère** (m.)]
REL	summit, hill, head (1), lookoff	
EX	Adams Lookout, Alta./Alb. 53° 43′ – 118° 34′ (83 E/10) Nollet Lookout, Sask. 50° 40′ – 107° 53′ (72 J/12) Balaena Lookout, N.W.T./T.N.-O. 69° 44′ – 67° 09′ (27 D) The Lookouts, Nfld./T.-N. 47° 03′ – 53° 32′ (1 N/4)	

loop   (Fig. 33)

DES	See **oxbow**	*Voir* **oxbow**
OBS	Rare; Man.	*Rare; Man.*
EQ		**[boucle** (f.)]
REL	bend, elbow	
EX	Rosedale Loop, Man. 49° 58′ – 97° 41′ (62 H/13)	

lough

DES	Variant of **lake**.	*Variante de* **lake**.
OBS	Gaelic term. Rare; Ont.	*Mot gaélique. Rare; Ont.*
EQ		**lac** (m.)
REL	pond (1), reservoir, tarn	
EX	Lough Garvey, Ont. 45° 40′ – 77° 39′ (31 F/12)	

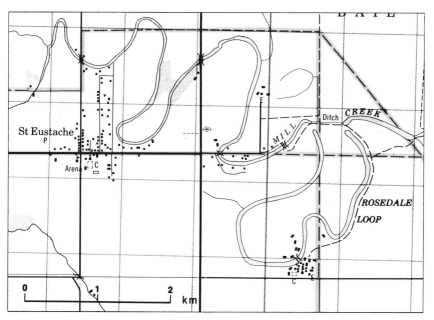

Figure 33. Rosedale Loop, cut off from the drainage of Mill Creek, a tributary of the Assiniboine River, Manitoba. (National Topographic System map 62 H/13; 1975 with added information)

Figure 33. Rosedale Loop, boucle séparée du ruisseau Mill, tributaire de la rivière Assiniboine, au Manitoba. (Carte 62 H/13 du Système national de référence cartographique; 1975 avec renseignements supplémentaires)

lump

DES	Descriptive of the appearance of the feature.	*Relief en forme de protubérance ou de bosse.*
OBS	Widely used.	*Emploi généralisé.*
EQ		**bosse** (f.)
REL	hill, tolt, knob, hump, mountain	
EX	Holms Lump (shoal – haut-fond), N.B./N.-B. 45° 57′ – 65° 59′ (21 H/13) Basil Lump (hill-colline), B.C./C.-B. 54° 29′ – 130° 21′ (103 J/8) Bulleys Lump (mountain-montagne), N.W.T./T.N.-O. 81° 11′ – 69° 15′ (120 C & D)	

lurcher

DES	See **shoal**	*Voir* **shoal**
OBS	Rare; N.S.	*Rare; N.-É.*
EQ		**haut-fond** (m.)
REL	bank (1), ground (1), ledge (1)	
EX	Little Lurcher, N.S./N.-É. 43° 47′ – 66° 26′ (20 O/16)	

m

mal bay   (Fig. 44)

DES	Tidal pond almost completely cut off from the sea by a bar.	*Étang engendré par la marée et presque entièrement isolé de la mer par une barre.*
OBS	Rare; N.B.	*Rare; N.-B.*
EQ		**barachois** (m.)
REL	lagoon, barachois, pond (2)	
EX	Windsors Mal Bay, N.B./N.-B. 47° 57′ – 64° 29′ (21 P/15)	

man

DES	Marker or pile of rocks.	*Repère ou empilement de roches.*
OBS	Possibly a navigation guide. Used in Nfld.	*La structure désignée par ce générique sert parfois de guide aux navigateurs. S'emploie à T.-N.*
EQ		[**cairn** (m.)]
REL	cairn, lookout	
EX	Naked Man, Nfld./T.-N. 47° 38′ – 53° 56′ (1 N/12) American Man, Nfld./T.-N. 47° 21′ – 52° 47′ (1 N/7)	

marais (m.)

DES	*Stagnant body of water of shallow depth, with dense vegetation.*	Nappe d'eau stagnante de faible profondeur, envahie par la végétation.
OBS	*Used in Man., Que., and N.S.*	Attesté au Man., au Qué. et en N.-É.
EQ	**bog**	
REL		bogue, baissière, marche, marécage, mocauque, savane, tourbière
EX	Marais de Guertin, Man. 49° 19′ – 96° 52′ (62 H/7) Marais des Castors, Qué./Que. 46° 16′ – 73° 40′ (31 I/5) Marais des Grosses Coques, N.-É./N.S. 44° 22′ – 66° 05′ (21 B/8)	

marche (f.)

DES	*Low-lying area, frequently flooded and generally covered with grasses and reeds.*	Zone de basses terres aux inondations fréquentes généralement recouverte d'herbages et de roseaux.
OBS	*The generic "marche" is a derivation of the English term "marsh". Used in Que.*	Le générique «marche» est une déformation du terme anglais «marsh». Attesté au Qué.
EQ	**marsh**	
REL		baissière, bogue, marais, marécage, mocauque, savane, tourbière
EX	Marche de l'Ancre, Qué./Que. 47° 12′ – 75° 02′ (31 O/3)	

mare (f.)

DES	*Small body of stagnant, shallow water, which occasionally dries.*	Petite nappe d'eau stagnante et peu profonde, susceptible de s'assécher.
OBS	*A* mare *is smaller than an* étang, *and the water may be salty. Used in Que. and N.B.*	La mare est plus petite que l'étang et peut recueillir de l'eau salée. Attesté au Qué. et au N.-B.
EQ	**pond (1)**	
REL		étang, lac
EX	Mare des Joncs Bleus, Qué./Que. 46° 06′ – 73° 00′ (31 I/3) Mare d'Anguille, N.-B./N.B. 47° 42′ – 64° 44′ (21 P/10)	

marécage (m.)

DES	*Area of terrain saturated or covered by water and supporting mainly bushy vegetation.*	Étendue de terrain imprégnée ou recouverte d'eau, occupée par une végétation surtout arbustive.
OBS	*Used in Que.*	Atteste au Qué.
EQ	**swamp**	
REL		baissière, bogue, marais, marche, mocauque, savane, tourbière
EX	Marécage Scotstown, Qué./Que. 45° 30′ – 71° 13′ (21 E/11)	

mark

DES	See **shoal**	*Voir* **shoal**
OBS	Rare; N.S.	*Rare; N.-É.*
EQ		**haut-fond** (m.)
REL	bank (1), ground (1)	
EX	Georges Mark, N.S./N.-É. 44° 52′ – 62° 08′ (11 D/16)	

marsh(es)   (Fig. 34)

DES	Area of low-lying land, often flooded and usually characterized by growth of grass and reeds.	*Terrain bas, souvent inondé, où croissent habituellement de l'herbe et des roseaux.*
OBS	Widely used.	*Emploi généralisé.*
EQ		**marche** (f.)
REL	swamp, bog, fen, muskeg, mish, mash	
EX	Ladner Marsh, B.C./C.-B. 49° 06' – 123° 04' (92 G/3) Delta Marsh, Man. 50° 12' – 98° 12' (62 J/1) Easter Brook Marshes, Nfld./T.-N. 47° 03' – 54° 03' (1 M/1)	

Figure 34. Corn Creek Marsh, west of Creston, British Columbia.
(Scott Forbes, Canadian Wildlife Service)

Figure 34. Corn Creek Marsh, à l'ouest de Creston, en Colombie-Britannique.
(Scott Forbes, Service canadien de la faune)

mash (Fig. 5)

DES	Variant of **marsh**.	*Variante de* **marsh**.
OBS	Particular to Nfld.	*Propre à T.-N.*
EQ		**marche** (f.)
REL	swamp, bog, fen, muskeg	
EX	Bakeapple Mash, Nfld./T.-N. 47° 33′ – 53° 41′ (1 N/12)	

massif (m.)

DES	*Area of high relief, without apparent orientation.*	Ensemble de reliefs élevés non orientés.
OBS	*Used in Que.*	Attesté au Qué.
EQ	**highlands**	
REL		
EX	Massif Kucyniak, Qué./Que. 60° 51′ – 77° 51′ (35 C/13)	

mead

DES	Variant of **meadow (1)**.	*Variante de* **meadow (1)**.
OBS	Rare; Nfld.	*Rare; T.-N.*
EQ		**baissière** (f.)
REL	swamp, bog, fen, muskeg	
EX	George Mead, Nfld./T.-N. 48° 14′ – 53° 47′ (2 C/4)	

meadow(s) (1)   (Fig. 35, 53)

DES	Low-lying, flat, seasonally wet, grassy area.	*Terrain bas et plat, inondé de façon saisonnière et occupé par une végétation herbeuse.*
OBS	Widely used.	*Emploi généralisé.*
EQ		**baissière** (f.)
REL	ground (2), flat (2), intervale	
EX	Sunpoke Meadow, N.B./N.-B. 45° 47′ – 66° 33′ (21 G/15) Dead Horse Meadows, Alta./Alb. 54° 08′ – 119° 55′ (83 L/4)	

meadow(s) (2)   (Fig. 21)

DES	Alpine or sub-alpine treeless area characterized by seasonal grasses and wild flowers.	*Région sans arbres de type alpin ou subalpin, caractérisée par la présence de fleurs sauvages et d'herbes saisonnières.*
OBS	Used particularly in B.C., Alta., and Y.T.	*Relevé surtout en C.-B., en Alb. et au Yukon.*
EQ		[**alpage** (m.)]
REL		
EX	Fairy Meadow, B.C./C.-B. 51° 47′ – 117° 52′ (82 N/13) Castleguard Meadows, Alta./Alb. 52° 07′ – 117° 12′ (83 C/3)	

mer (f.)

DES	*Immense body of salt water.*	Vaste étendue d'eau salée.
OBS	*A mer differs from an océan in its less considerable abyssal depths. Used off the Nfld. and N.W.T. coasts.*	La mer se distingue de l'océan par la moindre importance des fonds abyssaux. Attesté sur la côte de T.-N. et des T.N.-O.
EQ	**sea (1)**	
REL		océan
EX	Mer du Labrador, 57° 00′ – 54° 00′ (MCR 125 F) Mer de Beaufort, 72° 00′ – 141° 00′ (MCR 125 F)	

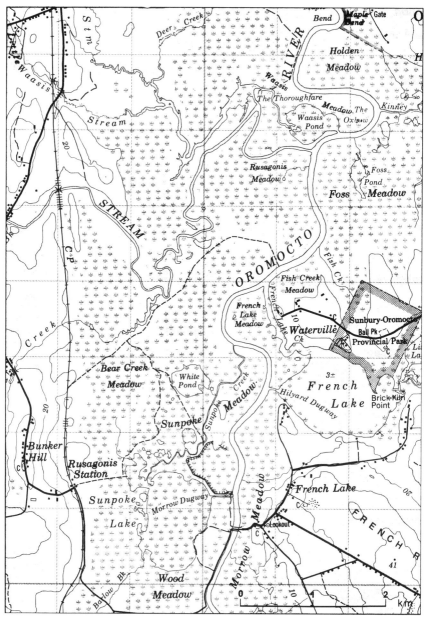

Figure 35. Part of the valley of the Oromocto River, New Brunswick, showing several meadows (e.g. Foss Meadow), Maple Bend, Barlow Brook, Deer Creek, Hilyard Dugway, and Little Waasis Stream. (National Topographic System map 21 G/15; 1986 with added information)

Figure 35. Partie de la vallée de la rivière Oromocto, au Nouveau-Brunswick. Entités représentées : plusieurs baissières (dont la Foss Meadow), Maple Bend, Barlow Brook, Deer Creek, Hilyard Dugway et Little Waasis Stream. (Carte 21 G/15 du Système national de référence cartographique; 1986 avec renseignements supplémentaires)

millpond, mill pond

DES	Water contained behind the dam at a mill site.	*Nappe d'eau retenue par le barrage d'un moulin.*
OBS	Used in N.S., N.B., and Ont.	*En usage en N.-É., au N.-B. et en Ont.*
EQ		**réservoir** (m.)
REL	reservoir, flowage, pond (1), lake	
EX	Chaplin Millpond, N.S./N.-É. 45° 12′ – 62° 50′ (11 E/2) Ameliasburg Mill Pond, Ont. 44° 04′ – 77° 26′ (31 C/3)	

millstream

DES	Small watercourse with a mill site.	*Petit cours d'eau sur le parcours duquel se situe un moulin.*
OBS	Rare; N.S.	*Rare; N.-É.*
EQ		[**bief** (m.)]
REL	creek (1), brook, stream	
EX	Hattie Millstream, N.S./N.-É. 45° 24′ – 61° 57′ (11 F/5)	

mish

DES	Variant of **marsh**.	*Variante de* **marsh**.
OBS	Particular to Nfld.	*Propre à T.-N.*
EQ		**marche** (f.)
REL	swamp, bog, fen, muskeg	
EX	Yellow Mish, Nfld./T.-N. 47° 47′ – 53° 27′ (1 N/14)	

mocauque (m.)

DES	*See* **savane**	Voir **savane**
OBS	*Used in N.B.*	Attesté au N.-B.
EQ	**bog**	
REL		baissière, bogue, marais, marche, marécage, tourbière
EX	Mocauque d'Escuminac, N.-B./N.B. 47° 03′ – 64° 51′ (21 P/2)	

moll

DES	See **rock (1)**	*Voir* **rock (1)**
OBS	Uncommon; Nfld. and N.S.	*Emploi peu fréquent; T.-N. et N.-É.*
EQ		**rocher** (m.)
REL	islet, reef	
EX	The Moll, N.S./N.-É. 44° 55′ – 62° 14′ (11 D/16) Galloping Moll, Nfld./T.-N. 47° 36′ – 57° 41′ (11 P/12) Mad Moll, Nfld./T.-N. 52° 16′ – 55° 35′ (3 D/5)	

mont(s) (m.) (Fig. 32)

DES	*Considerable elevation rising above the surrounding area.*	Importante élévation se détachant du relief environnant.
OBS	*"Mont" is used in toponyms in association with a proper name for reasons of euphony, but is little used in everyday speech. Used across the country.*	Le générique «mont» a très vite disparu du vocabulaire autrement qu'associé à un nom propre pour des raisons d'euphonie. Attesté à travers le pays.
EQ	**mount**	
REL		montagne, bonnet
EX	Mont Farlagne, N.-B./N.B. 47° 24′ – 68° 23′ (21 N/8) Mont des Poilus, C.-B./B.C. 51° 36′ – 116° 36′ (82 N/10) Monts Notre-Dame, Qué./Que. 48° 10′ – 68° 00′ (22 C/1) Monts Chic-Chocs, Qué./Que. 48° 55′ – 66° 00′ (22 B)	

montagne(s) (f.)

DES	*High elevation with steep slopes.*	Relief élevé aux versants raides.
OBS	*A* montagne *is larger than a* colline. *It usually covers a large area and sometimes forms part of a mountain system. Used in a number of provinces including Que., Ont., and N.S.*	La montagne est plus grosse que la colline. Elle occupe habituellement une grande superficie et appartient parfois à un système. Attesté dans plusieurs provinces dont le Qué., l'Ont. et la N.-É.
EQ	**mountain**	
REL		bonnet, mont
EX	Montagne Blanche, Ont. 46° 07' – 80° 35' (41 I/2) Montagne Noire, N.-É./N.S. 46° 37' – 60° 56' (11 K/10) Montagnes Vertes, Qué./Que. 45° 10' – 72° 30' (31 H/2)	

monument

DES	Conspicuous land feature.	*Accident de terrain bien en vue.*
OBS	Applied to rocks, islands, capes, and mountains. Used in Ont. and N.W.T.	S'emploie pour des rochers, des îles, des caps et des montagnes. Relevé en Ont. et dans les T.N.-O.
EQ		
REL	cairn, man	
EX	Gardners Monument (rock-rocher), Ont. 49° 42' – 94° 30' (52 E/9) Agnes Monument (island-île), N.W.T./T.N.-O. 70° 31' – 68° 12' (27 F) Sir John Barrow Monument (mountain-montagne), N.W.T./T.N.-O. 76° 31' – 96° 04' (69 A) Hope Monument (cape-cap), N.W.T./T.N.-O. 74° 37' – 80° 26' (48 E)	

moraine

DES	Long, narrow, steep-sided ridge of unconsolidated material.	*Accumulation de matériaux non consolidés en forme de chaussée longue, étroite et à bords raides.*
OBS	Rare in officially named examples; Ont.	*Rare dans les noms officiels; Ont.*
EQ		[**moraine** (f.)]
REL	ridge (1), esker, back	
EX	Steep Rock Moraine, Ont. 48° 50' – 91° 34' (52 B/13)	

morne(s) (m.)

DES	*Small terrain elevation with gently sloping sides.*	Petite élévation de terrain aux versants en pente douce.
OBS	*Term of Creole origin that means "little mountain" in the Caribbean; apparently an adaptation of the Spanish "morro". Used in Que. and Nfld.*	Terme d'origine créole qui signifie dans les Antilles «petite montagne» et qui serait une modification de «morro» en espagnol. Attesté au Qué. et à T.-N.
EQ	**hill**	
REL		bosse, butte, buttereau, colline, dôme
EX	Gros Morne, T.-N./Nfld. 49° 58' – 55° 51' (2 E/13) Mornes des Caouis, Qué./Que. 49° 50' – 67° 03' (22 G/14)	

motion

DES	Turbulent water at the meeting of strong currents or from ocean swells.	*Eau turbulente causée par la rencontre de forts courants ou par la houle.*
OBS	Rare; Nfld.	*Rare; T.-N.*
EQ		**[ride** (f.)]
REL	rip (2), eddy, pool (2), hole (4), tickle	
EX	North Motion, Nfld./T.-N. 48° 08′ – 52° 53′ (2 C/2)	

mouillage (m.)

DES	*Water area favourable for dropping anchor.*	Emplacement favorable pour jeter l'ancre.
OBS	*The term "mouillage" also means the place of anchorage recommended in sailing instructions or reserved by port authorities. Used in Que.*	Le terme «mouillage» désigne aussi l'emplacement recommandé dans les instructions nautiques ou réservé par les autorités portuaires pour l'ancrage. Attesté au Qué.
EQ		**anchorage**
REL		
EX	Mouillage de la Cage, Qué./Que. 47° 25′ – 70° 28′ (21 M/8)	

mound

DES	Rounded elevation.	*Élévation arrondie.*
OBS	Applied to hills, rocks, and islands. Used in N.B., Ont., Man., and B.C.	*S'emploie pour des collines, des rochers et des îles. Relevé au N.-B., en Ont., au Man. et en C.-B.*
EQ		**butte** (f.)
REL	hill, knob, lump, knoll, tolt, pingo	
EX	Pilot Mound (hill-colline), Man. 49° 13′ – 98° 55′ (62 G/2) East Mound (rock-rocher), Ont. 45° 51′ – 81° 38′ (41 H/13) Pillings Mound (island-île), N.B./N.-B. 45° 37′ – 67° 34′ (21 G/12)	

mount (Fig. 36, 37, 41)

DES	Mass of land prominently elevated above the surrounding terrain, bounded by steep slopes and rising to a summit and/or peaks.	*Élévation de terrain aux versants raides se détachant du relief environnant et se terminant par un sommet ou un ou plusieurs pics.*
OBS	Widely used. "Mount" usually precedes the specific, especially when the specific is a personal name. Never used in the plural.	*Emploi généralisé. Le générique précède généralement le spécifique, en particulier quand celui-ci est un nom de personne. Ne s'emploie jamais au pluriel.*
EQ		**mont** (m.)
REL	mountain, peak (1), dome, tower, hill	
EX	Mount Waddington, B.C./C.-B. 51° 23′ – 125° 16′ (92 N/6) Mount Carmel, Sask. 52° 16′ – 105° 22′ (73 A/6)	

mountain(s) (Fig. 4, 61, 64)

DES	Mass of land prominently elevated above the surrounding terrain, bounded by steep slopes and rising to a summit and/or peaks.	*Élévation de terrain aux versants raides se détachant du relief environnant et se terminant par un sommet ou un ou plusieurs pics.*
OBS	Widely used. "Mountain" always follows the specific. When used in the plural, the application may include a whole region, i.e. peaks, mountains, and intervening valleys.	*Emploi généralisé. Le générique suit invariablement le spécifique. Au pluriel, le mot s'applique parfois à l'ensemble des pics, des montagnes et des vallées intermédiaires d'une région donnée.*
EQ		**montagne** (f.)
REL	mountain, peak (1), dome, tower, hill, range, highlands	
EX	Castle Mountain, Alta./Alb. 51° 19′ – 115° 57′ (82 O/5) St. Elias Mountains, Y.T./Yuk. 60° 33′ – 139° 28′ (115 B & C)	

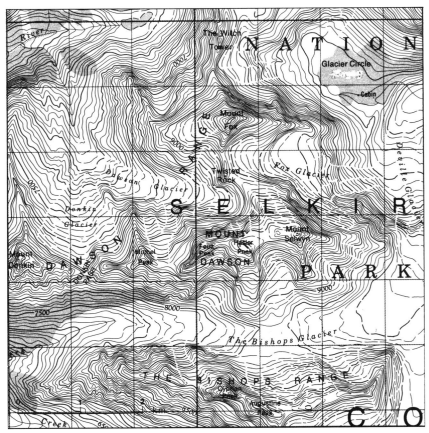

Figure 36. Part of the Selkirk Mountains in Glacier National Park, British Columbia, showing Dawson Range, Mount Dawson with Feuz Peak and Hasler Peak, Glacier Circle, The Bishops Glacier, Donkin Pass, Twisted Rock, and The Witch Tower. (National Topographic System map 82 N/3; 1980)

Figure 36. Partie des monts Selkirk, dans le parc national des Glaciers, en Colombie-Britannique. Entités représentées : Dawson Range, Mount Dawson avec ses Feuz Peak et Hasler Peak, Glacier Circle, The Bishops Glacier, Donkin Pass, Twisted Rock et The Witch Tower. (Carte 82 N/3 du Système national de référence cartographique; 1980)

mouth

DES	See **narrows**	*Voir* **narrows**
OBS	Rare; Nfld. and Ont.	*Rare; T.-N. et Ont.*
EQ		**passage** (m.)
REL	passage, pass (2), gap (2)	
EX	Whale's Mouth, Ont. 45° 58′ – 80° 49′ (41 H/15)	

muskeg

DES	Waterlogged swamp with deep accumulation of organic material.	*Marécage occupé par une épaisse accumulation de matières organiques.*
OBS	Often characterized by growth of black spruce and tamarack. Used in Ont., Man., and Alta.	*On y trouve souvent l'épinette noire et le mélèze. Relevé en Ont., au Man. et en Alb.*
EQ		**fondrière** (f.)
REL	swamp, bog, marsh, fen, barren	
EX	Menigan Muskeg, Ont. 50° 53′ – 80° 48′ (41 I/15) Island Muskeg, Alta./Alb. 51° 45′ – 115° 06′ (82 O/14)	

n

nap (Fig. 20)

DES	Variant of **knap**.	*Variante de* **knap**.
OBS	Rare; Nfld.	*Rare; T.-N.*
EQ		**colline** (f.)
REL	hill, knoll (1), tolt, knob, hummock	
EX	Peters Nap, Nfld./T.-N. 46° 53′ – 53° 58′ (1 K/13)	

narrows

DES	Constricted section of a water body.	*Partie resserrée d'un cours d'eau.*
OBS	Usually having strong tidal currents. Widely used.	*On y trouve habituellement de forts courants de marée. Emploi généralisé.*
EQ		**passage** (m.)
REL	passage, pass (2), gap (2), channel (1)	
EX	Seymour Narrows, B.C./C.-B. 50° 09′ – 125° 21′ (92 K/3) Chesterfield Narrows, N.W.T./T.N.-O. 66° 59′ – 94° 17′ (55 M/16) Peterson Narrows, Man. 57° 53′ – 99° 34′ (64 G/13)	

neck

DES	Narrow strip of land extending into a body of water, sometimes joining two larger land masses.	*Bande de terre étroite s'avançant dans une étendue d'eau et reliant parfois deux masses de terre plus importantes.*
OBS	Used in the Atlantic Provinces, B.C., and N.W.T.	*Relevé dans les provinces de l'Atlantique, en C.-B. et dans les T.N.-O.*
EQ		**langue de terre** (f.)
REL	isthmus, spit	
EX	Digby Neck, N.S./N.-É. 44° 30′ − 66° 05′ (21 A/12) Goose Neck, N.W.T./T.N.-O. 61° 22′ − 116° 00′ (85 F)	

needle(s)

DES	Sharply pointed peak.	*Sommet pointu.*
OBS	Used in Alta. and B.C.	*Relevé en Alb. et en C.-B.*
EQ		[**aiguille** (f.)]
REL	peak (1), spire, pinnacle (1), point (2), mountain	
EX	Kwoiek Needle, B.C./C.-B. 50° 05′ − 121° 48′ (92 I/4) Houdini Needles, B.C./C.-B. 51° 45′ − 117° 51′ (82 N/13)	

ness

DES	See **head (1)** and **point (1)**	*Voir **head (1)** et **point (1)***
OBS	Rare; B.C. and N.W.T.	*Rare; C.-B. et T.N.-O.*
EQ		**cap** (m.)
REL	cape	
EX	Neck Ness, B.C./C.-B. 51° 12′ − 127° 48′ (92 M/4) Fair Ness, N.W.T./T.N.-O. 63° 24′ − 72° 05′ (35 P)	

178

nest (Fig. 5)

DES	See **lookout**	*Voir* **lookout**
OBS	Used in Nfld. and N.S.	*Relevé à T.-N. et en N.-É.*
EQ		[**belvédère** (m.)]
REL	summit, hill, head (1)	
EX	Grepes Nest, Nfld./T.-N. 47° 53′ – 53° 48′ (1 N/13)	
	Crows Nest, N.S./N.-É. 44° 28′ – 63° 42′ (11 D/5)	

névé (Fig. 37)

DES	See **glacier** and **icefield**	*Voir* **glacier** *et* **icefield**
OBS	Historically, "névé" in Canada has been applied to an entire glacier or icefield, rather than to only the area of snow accumulation, which is the usual glaciological application.	*Au Canada, on a l'habitude d'utiliser ce générique pour désigner l'ensemble d'un glacier ou d'un champ de glace, alors que son acception en glaciologie se limite à la zone d'accumulation de la neige.*
EQ		[**névé** (f.)]
REL	ice cap	
EX	Bonney Névé (glacier-glacier), B.C./C.-B. 51° 12′ – 117° 34′ (82 N/4)	
	Illecillewaet Névé (icefield-champ de glace), B.C./C.-B. 51° 13′ – 117° 25′ (82 N/3)	

Figure 37. View of Mount Sir Donald, in the Sir Donald Range, west of Golden, British Columbia, showing Illecillewaet Névé, Asulkan Brook, Glacier Crest, Illecillewaet Glacier and Vaux Glacier, Terminal Peak and Uto Peak.
(C.S.L. Ommanney, National Hydrology Research Institute)

Figure 37. Mount Sir Donald, dans la chaîne Sir Donald, à l'ouest de Golden, en Colombie-Britannique. Entités également représentées : Illecillewaet Névé, Asulkan Brook, Glacier Crest, Illecillewaet Glacier et Vaux Glacier, Terminal Peak et Uto Peak.
(C.S.L. Ommanney, Institut national de recherche en hydrologie)

nez (m.)

DES	*Projection of land jutting out from the shore, or rising prominently from the surrounding terrain.*	Avancée de terre nettement en saillie par rapport au rivage avoisinant ou surplombant le paysage.
OBS	*Applied to various types of geographical features. Descriptive term used in Que., N.B., and N.S.*	Le nez prend diverses formes selon la nature du phénomène géographique. Descriptif attesté au Qué., au N.-B. et en N.-É.
EQ	**nose**	
REL		cap, pointe, promontoire, tête (1)
EX	Le Gros Nez, Qué./Que. 49° 13′ – 66° 01′ (22 G/1) Nez Pointu, N.-B./N.B. 47° 37′ – 65° 10′ (21 P/11) Petit Nez, N.-É./N.S. 43° 34′ – 60° 54′ (11 F/10)	

nipple(s)

DES	See **hill** and **mountain**	*Voir **hill** et **mountain***
OBS	Rare; B.C.	*Rare; C.-B.*
EQ		
REL	peak (1), knoll (1), tolt, pap, jug	
EX	Coast Nipple (hill-colline), B.C./C.-B. 51° 12′ – 127° 40′ (92 M/4) Stone Nipples (mountain-montagne), B.C./C.-B. 49° 59′ – 127° 10′ (92 E/14)	

nob

DES	Variant of **knob**.	*Variante de **knob**.*
OBS	Rare; Nfld. and B.C.	*Rare; T.-N. et C.-B.*
EQ		**colline** (f.)
REL	hill, knoll (1), tolt, hummock, peak (1)	
EX	Fox Nob, Nfld./T.-N. 46° 51′ – 53° 59′ (1 K/13) Robbers Nob, B.C./C.-B. 50° 31′ – 126° 03′ (92 L/9)	

nook

DES	See **cove**	*Voir* **cove**
OBS	Rare; Nfld. and B.C.	*Rare; T.-N. et C.-B.*
EQ		**anse** (f.)
REL	bay, hole (1)	
EX	Boat Nook, B.C./C.-B. 48° 16′ – 123° 18′ (92 B/14)	

nose

DES	Feature having the appearance of a nose.	*Accident géographique dont la forme rappelle un nez.*
OBS	Applied to points, hills, and mountains. Widely used.	*S'emploie pour des pointes, des collines et des montagnes. Emploi généralisé.*
EQ		**nez** (m.)
REL	finger, thumb, point (1)	
EX	Anthonys Nose (point-pointe), N.S./N.-É. 45° 14′ – 63° 26′ (11 E/3) Butchers Nose (hill-colline), Nfld./T.-N. 48° 30′ – 53° 29′ (2 C/11) Fawnie Nose (mountain-montagne), B.C./C.-B. 53° 16′ – 125° 09′ (93 F/6)	

notch

DES	Deep but narrow opening through a ridge or mountain chain.	*Ouverture profonde mais étroite dans une élévation de terrain allongée ou une chaîne de montagnes.*
OBS	Rare; N.S., N.B., and B.C.	*Rare; N.-É, N.-B. et C.-B.*
EQ		[**col** (m.)]
REL	col, gap (1), pass (1)	
EX	Nadir Notch, B.C./C.-B. 51° 43′ – 118° 03′ (82 M/9) Upper Notch, N.B./N.-B. 45° 19′ – 66° 45′ (21 G/7)	

nub

DES	See **islet**	*Voir* **islet**
OBS	Rare; N.B.	*Rare; N.-B.*
EQ		**ilot** (m.)
REL	island, rock (1)	
EX	Hoyt Nub, N.B./N.-B. 45° 03′ – 66° 55′ (21 G/2)	

nubble(s)

DES	See **rock (1)**	*Voir* **rock (1)**
OBS	Uncommon; N.S. and N.B.	*Emploi peu fréquent; N.-É. et N.-B.*
EQ		**rocher** (m.)
REL	reef, islet	
EX	Round Island Nubble, N.S./N.-É. 44° 29′ – 64° 16′ (21 A/8) The Nubbles, N.B./N.-B. 45° 36′ – 67° 32′ (21 G/12)	

nuddick(s)

DES	See **hill**	*Voir* **hill**
OBS	Rare; Nfld.	*Rare; T.-N.*
EQ		**colline** (f.)
REL	knoll (1), tolt, knob	
EX	The Nuddick, Nfld./T.-N. 47° 37′ – 58° 41′ (11 O/10) Bobs Nuddicks, Nfld./T.-N. 47° 38′ – 53° 54′ (1 N/12)	

O

ocean

DES	Large body of salt water, global in scale.	*Vaste étendue d'eau salée couvrant une grande partie du globe terrestre.*
OBS		
EQ		**océan** (m.)
REL	sea (1)	
EX	Atlantic Ocean (MCR 125) Pacific Ocean (MCR 125) Arctic Ocean (MCR 125)	

océan (m.)

DES	*Extensive body of water separating continents.*	Très vaste étendue d'eau séparant les continents.
OBS	*An* océan *differs from a* mer *in its greater abyssal depths.*	L'océan se distingue de la mer par la plus grande importance des fonds abyssaux.
EQ	**ocean**	
REL		mer
EX	Océan Atlantique (MCR 125 F) Océan Pacifique (MCR 125 F) Océan Arctique (MCR 125 F)	

opening   (Fig. 38)

DES	See **gap (2)**	*Voir* **gap (2)**
OBS	Rare; N.W.T.	*Rare; T.N.-O.*
EQ		**passage** (m.)
REL	passage, narrows, pass (2)	
EX	Schooner Opening, N.W.T./T.N.-O. 55° 33′ – 77° 23′ (33 N)	

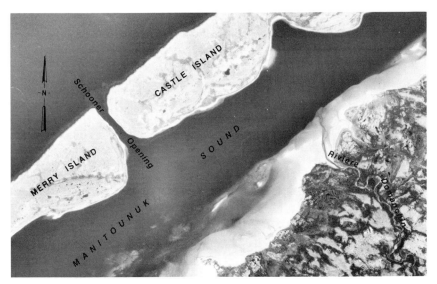

Figure 38. East coast of Hudson Bay, Northwest Territories and Quebec, showing Schooner Opening, Merry Island and Castle Island, Manitounuk Sound, and Rivière Domanchin. (National Air Photo Library, A23865-89; 1974)

Figure 38. Côte est de la baie d'Hudson, dans les Territoires du Nord-Ouest et au Québec. Entités représentées : Schooner Opening, Merry Island et Castle Island, Manitounuk Sound et Rivière Domanchin. (Photothèque nationale de l'air, A23865-89; 1974)

outlet (1)

DES	Watercourse draining from a lake.	*Cours d'eau qui évacue les eaux d'un lac.*
OBS	Rare; N.S. and N.B.	*Rare; N.-É. et N.-B.*
EQ		**décharge** (f.)
REL	creek (1), brook, stream, inlet (3)	
EX	Barren Hill Lake Outlet, N.S./N.-É. 45° 42′ – 60° 38′ (11 F/10) McDougall Outlet, N.B./N.-B. 45° 20′ – 66° 51′ (21 G/7)	

outlet (2)

DES	See **channel (2)**	*Voir* **channel (2)**
OBS	Used in Ont., for the mouths of rivers on the north shore of Georgian Bay.	*Se rencontre en Ont. où il désigne l'embouchure de cours d'eau sur la rive nord de la baie Georgienne.*
EQ		**branche** (f.)
REL	branch, creek (1), brook, stream	
EX	French River Main Outlet, Ont. 45° 56' – 80° 54' (41 H)	

outlet (3)

DES	See **channel (1)**	*Voir* **channel (1)**
OBS	Uncommon; Ont.	*Peu fréquent; Ont.*
EQ		**chenal** (m.)
REL	passage, narrows, pass (2), gut	
EX	Second Island Outlet, Ont. 42° 35' – 80° 16' (40 I/9)	

oven(s)

DES	See **cave**	*Voir* **cave**
OBS	Rare; Atlantic Provinces.	*Rare; provinces de l'Atlantique.*
EQ		**caverne** (f.)
REL	grotto	
EX	Frenchman's Oven, Nfld./T.-N. 47° 39' – 54° 46' (1 M/10) The Bake Ovens, N.S./N.-É. 44° 26' – 64° 10' (21 A/8)	

overfall(s)

DES	See **shoal**	*Voir* **shoal**
OBS	Rare; N.S.	*Rare; N.-É.*
EQ		**haut-fond** (m.)
REL	bank (1), ground (1)	
EX	The Overfall, N.S./N.-É. 45° 04′ – 61° 33′ (11 F/4)	
	Inner Overfalls, N.S./N.-É. 43° 23′ – 65° 42′ (20 P/5)	

overlook

DES	See **lookout**	*Voir* **lookout**
OBS	Rare; B.C.	*Rare; C.-B.*
EQ		[**belvédère** (m.)]
REL	summit, hill, head (1)	
EX	Beaver Overlook, B.C./C.-B. 51° 07′ – 117° 20′ (82 N/3)	

oxbow   (Fig. 39)

DES	A horseshoe-shaped loop, either part of or detached from a meandering watercourse.	*Boucle en forme de fer à cheval qui fait partie d'un cours d'eau à méandres ou qui en est détachée.*
OBS	Uncommon; N.B., Ont., and Man.	*Emploi peu fréquent; N.-B., Ont. et Man.*
EQ		[**boucle** (f.)]
REL	bend, elbow	
EX	Lower Oxbow, N.B./N.-B. 45° 34′ – 65° 01′ (21 H/11) Maxwell Oxbow, Man. 49° 57′ – 97° 38′ (62 H/13)	

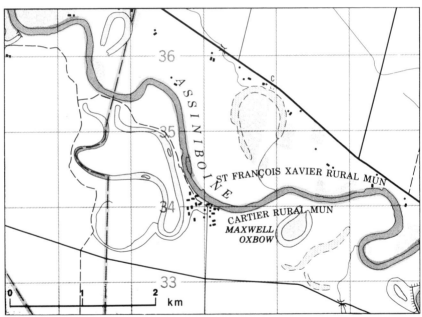

Figure 39. Maxwell Oxbow, beside the Assiniboine River, Manitoba. (National Topographic System map 62 H/13; 1975 with added information)

Figure 39. Maxwell Oxbow, près de la rivière Assiniboine, au Manitoba. (Carte 62 H/13 du Système national de référence cartographique; 1975 avec renseignements supplémentaires)

p

padou (Fig. 62)

DES	Narrow backwater inlet joined to a flowing watercourse.	*Étroit bras de baie relié à un cours d'eau.*
OBS	Used in N.B.	*En usage au N.-B.*
EQ		[**bras** (m.)]
REL	inlet (1), cove, bogan	
EX	Sugar Island Padou, N.B./N.-B. 45° 59′ – 66° 48′ (21 G/15)	

palisade(s)

DES	See **cliff**	*Voir* **cliff**
OBS	Rare; Ont. and Alta.	*Rare; Ont. et Alb.*
EQ		**falaise** (f.)
REL	bluff (1), head (1), wall, ramparts	
EX	The Palisade, Alta./Alb. 52° 59′ – 118° 06′ (83 D/16) Pijitawabik Palisades, Ont. 49° 18′ – 88° 07′ (52 H/8)	

paps

DES	Pair of prominent rounded hills.	*Ensemble formé par deux collines arrondies qui se détachent du relief environnant.*
OBS	Rare; Nfld.	*Rare; T.-N.*
EQ		**collines** (f.)
REL	hills, jugs, nipples, knolls (1)	
EX	Eskimo Paps, Nfld./T.-N. 53° 39′ – 59° 23′ (13 G/11)	

pass (1)   (Fig. 36, 40)

DES	Low opening in a mountain range or hills, offering a route from one side to the other.	*Ouverture basse dans une chaîne de montagnes ou de collines, offrant un passage d'un versant à l'autre.*
OBS	Widely used.	*Emploi généralisé.*
EQ		[**col** (m.)]
REL	col, gap (1), notch, summit	
EX	Rogers Pass, B.C./C.-B. 51° 18' – 117° 31' (82 N/5) Arrowhead Pass, Y.T./Yuk. 63° 38' – 131° 15' (105 O)	

Figure 40. Rogers Pass, southeast British Columbia.
(C.S.L. Ommanney, National Hydrology Research Institute)

Figure 40. Rogers Pass, dans le sud-est de la Colombie-Britannique.
(C.S.L. Ommanney, Institut national de recherche en hydrologie)

pass (2)   (Fig. 41)

DES	Narrow stretch of water connecting two larger water bodies.	*Étroit passage d'eau reliant deux masses d'eau plus importantes.*
OBS	Used in Nfld., Man., B.C., and N.W.T.	*Relevé à T.-N., au Man., en C.-B. et dans les T.N.-O.*
EQ		**passage** (m.)
REL	passage, narrows, pass (2), gap (2), channel (1)	
EX	Active Pass, B.C./C.-B. 48° 52′ – 123° 18′ (92 B/14) Sioux Pass, Man. 50° 15′ – 98° 05′ (62 J/1)	

pass (3)

DES	Narrow strip of land joining larger areas of land in a marsh.	*Étroite bande de terre reliant deux masses de terre plus importantes dans une marche.*
OBS	Rare; Man.	*Rare; Man.*
EQ		[**bras** (m.)]
REL	arm (2), isthmus	
EX	Greys Pass, Man. 50° 12′ – 98° 09′ (62 J/1)	

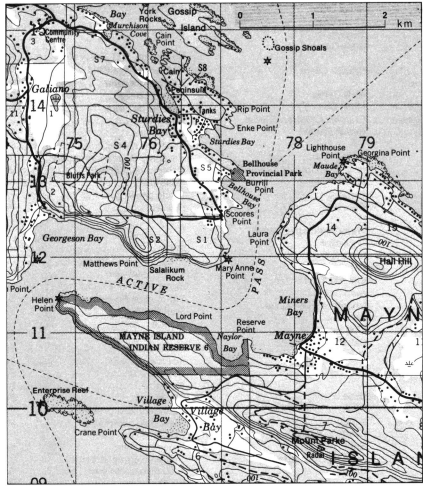

Figure 41. Active Pass, between Galiano Island and Mayne Island, British Columbia, showing Georgeson Bay, Hall Hill, Mount Parke, Cain Peninsula, Helen Point, Enterprise Reef, York Rocks, and Gossip Shoals.
(National Topographic System map 92 B/14; 1980)

Figure 41. Active Pass, entre les îles Galiano et Mayne, en Colombie-Britannique. Entités également représentées : Georgeson Bay, Hall Hill, Mount Parke, Cain Peninsula, Helen Point, Enterprise Reef, York Rocks et Gossip Shoals.
(Carte 92 B/14 du Système national de référence cartographique; 1980)

pass (4)

DES	Low part between elevations on an underwater ridge or between seamounts.	*Dépression entre deux espaces élevés sur une dorsale sous-marine, ou entre deux monts sous-marins.*
OBS	Uncommon; off the Atlantic Provinces.	*Emploi peu fréquent; relevé au large des provinces de l'Atlantique.*
EQ		[**col** (m.)]
REL	saddle (3)	
EX	Flemish Pass, 47° 00′ – 46° 45′ (C.802)	

passage   (Fig. 26, 49)

DES	Narrow stretch of water connecting two larger water bodies.	*Étroite bande d'eau reliant deux masses d'eau plus importantes.*
OBS	Used in the Atlantic Provinces, Ont., B.C., and N.W.T.	*Relevé dans les provinces de l'Atlantique, en Ont., en C.-B. et dans les T.N.-O.*
EQ		**passage** (m.)
REL	narrows, pass (2), gap (2), channel (1), strait	
EX	Abegweit Passage, P.E.I. – N.B./Î.-P.-É. – N.-B. 46° 13′ – 63° 45′ (11 L/4) Tongass Passage, B.C./C.-B. 54° 45′ – 130° 39′ (103 J/10)	

passage (m.)

DES	*Narrow stretch of water between land masses, joining two large bodies of water.*	Étroite nappe d'eau entre des terres, qui réunit deux grandes étendues d'eau.
OBS	*In practice, "passage" and "détroit" were interchangeable. Used in Que.*	Dans la pratique, «passage» et «détroit» peuvent avoir été employés indifféremment l'un pour l'autre. Attesté au Qué.
EQ	**passage**	
REL		chenal, détroit, goulet, passe
EX	Passage de Bougainville, Qué./Que. 51° 17′ – 58° 30′ (12 O/7)	

passe (f.)

DES	*Short and narrow natural waterway, between land areas or shoals.*	Voie naturelle, courte et étroite, entre des terres ou des hauts-fonds.
OBS	*Used in Que. and the Atlantic Provinces.*	Attesté au Qué. et dans les provinces de l'Atlantique.
EQ	**pass (2)**	
REL		chenal, détroit, goulet, passage
EX	Grande passe aux Outardes, T.-N./Nfld. 52° 30′ – 65° 58′ (23 A/12) Passe de l'Est, Qué./Que. 50° 12′ – 60° 00′ (12 K/1) Passe aux Chats, N.-É./N.S. 43° 38′ – 65° 47′ (20 P/12)	

patch(es)

DES	See **shoal**	*Voir* **shoal**
OBS	Used in the Atlantic Provinces, Ont., B.C., and N.W.T. In B.C. a "patch" is covered at low water, but may be identified by kelp on the water surface.	*Relevé dans les provinces de l'Atlantique, en Ont., en C.-B. et dans les T.N.-O. En C.-B., le haut-fond désigné par ce générique est recouvert d'eau à marée basse, mais du kelp flottant à la surface de l'eau en trahit parfois la présence.*
EQ		**haut-fond** (m.)
REL	bank (1), ground (1)	
EX	Kitty Patch, B.C./C.-B. 52° 21' – 128° 26' (103 A/8) Berry Patches, Ont. 46° 17' – 83° 49' (41 J/5)	

paw

DES	Mountain, fancifully shaped like a paw.	*Montagne dont la forme fait penser à une patte d'animal.*
OBS	Rare; B.C.	*Rare; C.-B.*
EQ		**mont** (m.)
REL		
EX	Devils Paw, B.C./C.-B. 58° 44' – 133° 50' (104 K/12)	

peak(s) (1)   (Fig. 36, 37, 45)

DES	Summit of a mountain or hill, or the mountain or hill itself.	*Sommet d'une montagne ou d'une colline, ou la montagne ou la colline proprement dite.*
OBS	Widely used. A mountain may have more than one named peak.	*Emploi généralisé. Sur une montagne donnée, plusieurs pics peuvent avoir reçu un nom.*
EQ		**pic** (m.)
REL	summit, peak (1), point (2), tower, mountain, needle, pinnacle (1)	
EX	Bow Peak, Alta./Alb. 51° 38' – 118° 23' (82 N/9) Dickson Peak, Sask. 49° 00' – 105° 07' (72 H/3) Seven Sisters Peaks, B.C./C.-B. 54° 58' – 128° 12' (103 I/16)	

peak (2)

DES	Prominent seabed elevation, either pointed or of a very limited extent across the summit.	*Élévation du fond de la mer, à sommet pointu ou de très faible extension.*
OBS	Used off Canada's east and west coasts.	*S'emploie au large des côtes est et ouest du Canada.*
EQ		**[pic** (m.)**]**
REL	knoll (2), pinnacle (2), spur (2)	
EX	The Peak, N.S./N.-É. 43° 36' – 65° 50' (C.4216) Eastern Peak, 45° 51' – 63° 06' (C.4023)	

peninsula   (Fig. 2, 41)

DES	Elongated projection of land into a body of water.	*Étendue de terre allongée qui s'avance dans une masse d'eau.*
OBS	Widely used. Usually larger than a point.	*Emploi généralisé. Habituellement de plus grandes dimensions qu'une pointe.*
EQ		**péninsule** (f.)
REL	point (1), spit, cape, head (1)	
EX	Saanich Peninsula, B.C./C.-B. 48° 37′ – 123° 26′ (92 B/11) Boothia Peninsula, N.W.T./T.N.-O. 71° 00′ – 94° 00′ (57 F)	

péninsule   (f.)

DES	*Projection of a land mass into the sea or a large lake.*	Avancée de la masse continentale dans la mer ou dans un très grand lac.
OBS	*A* péninsule *is distinguished from a* presqu'île *by its larger isthmus. Both are usually larger than a* pointe. *Used in Que.*	La péninsule se distingue de la presqu'île par la largeur supérieure de son isthme. La péninsule et la presqu'île sont habituellement plus grosses que la pointe. Attesté au Qué.
EQ	**peninsula**	
REL		presqu'île
EX	Péninsule de la Gaspésie, Qué./Que. 48° 40′ – 66° 00′ (22 A)	

pic (m.)

DES	Elevated relief with a sharply pointed summit.	Relief élevé dont le sommet dessine une pointe aiguë.
OBS	Used in Que. and B.C.	Attesté au Qué. et en C.-B.
EQ	**peak (1)**	
REL		piton, pointu, table
EX	Pic des Érables, Qué./Que. 45° 17′ – 72° 39′ (31 H/7) Pic Tordu, C.-B./B.C. 52° 11′ – 117° 57′ (83 C/4)	

piémont (m.)

DES	Region of rounded slopes at the foot of a mountain area.	Région inclinée aux formes arrondies au pied d'un ensemble montagneux.
OBS	Used in Que.	Attesté au Qué.
EQ	**foothills**	
REL		
EX	Piémont Pattavik, Qué./Que. 62° 16′ – 75° 35′ (35 J/5)	

pikes

DES	Small peaks.	Petits pics.
OBS	Rare; B.C.	Rare; C.-B.
EQ		**pics** (m.)
REL	peaks (1), spires, summits, points (2), pinnacles (1)	
EX	Glacier Pikes, B.C./C.-B. 49° 53′ – 122° 58′ (92 G/15)	

pinacle (m.)

DES	*Massive rocky elevation with irregular sides.*	Élévation de roche massive aux parois irrégulières.
OBS	*Used in Que.*	Descriptif attesté au Qué.
EQ	**pinnacle (1)**	
REL		
EX	Le Petit Pinacle, Qué./Que. 45° 04′ – 72° 45′ (31 H/2)	

pinchgut

DES	Constricted water area.	*Étendue d'eau encaissée.*
OBS	Uncommon; Nfld. and N.S.	*Peu fréquent; T.-N. et N.-É.*
EQ		**anse** (f.)
REL	tickle, gut, run (1), hole (1), cove	
EX	Little Pinchgut, Nfld./T.-N. 47° 35′ – 53° 54′ (1 N/12)	

pingo(s) (Fig. 42)

DES	Isolated, conical, ice-cored mound occuring in areas of permafrost.	*Tertre isolé de forme conique, contenant un noyau de glace et formé en milieu de pergélisol.*
OBS	Limited to N.W.T.; seabed examples in the Beaufort Sea.	*Emploi limité aux T.N.-O. On en trouve au fond de la mer de Beaufort.*
EQ		**[pingo** (m.)]
REL	hill, mound, knoll, cone	
EX	Ibyuk Pingo, N.W.T./T.N.-O. 69° 24' – 133° 05' (107 C) Kugmallit Pingos (undersea – sous-marin), 70° 45' – 132° 40' (C.7651)	

pinnacle(s) (1)

DES	Small pointed peak, or a hill.	*Petit pic pointu, ou colline.*
OBS	Used in Nfld., N.S., N.B., Ont., and B.C.	*S'emploie à T.-N., en N.-É., au N.-B., en Ont. et en C.-B.*
EQ		**pinacle** (m.)
REL	peak (1), spire, needle, point (2)	
EX	Refuse Pinnacle (peak-pic), B.C./C.-B. 50° 01' – 122° 50' (92 J/2) Hayward Pinnacle (hill-colline), N.B./N.-B. 45° 49' – 64° 55' (21 H/15) The Pinnacles (hills-collines), Ont. 43° 58' – 79° 28' (30 M/14)	

pinnacle (2)

DES	Pointed isolated spire or column or rock on the seafloor.	*Flèche, colonne ou rocher pointu et isolé sur le fond de la mer.*
OBS	Uncommon.	*Peu fréquent.*
EQ		**[pinacle** (m.)]
REL	peak (2), spur (2), knoll (2)	
EX	Upper Pinnacle, Nfld./T.-N. 47° 12' – 54° 59' (C.4624) The Pinnacle, Nfld./T.-N. 47° 13' – 54° 59' (C.4624)	

Figure 42. Ibyuk Pingo, near Tuktoyaktuk, Northwest Territories. (H. Kerfoot)

Figure 42. Ibyuk Pingo, près de Tuktoyaktuk, dans les Territoires du Nord-Ouest. (H. Kerfoot)

pitch

DES	See **rapid (1)**	*Voir* **rapid (1)**
OBS	Rare; N.S. and N.B.	*Rare; N.-É. et N.-B.*
EQ		**rapide** (m.)
REL	chute, cataract	
EX	Head Pitch, N.B./N.-B. 45° 29' – 67° 03' (21 G/6) Upper Pitch, N.S./N.-É. 44° 01' – 65° 55' (21 A/4)	

piton (m.)

DES	*See* **pic**	Voir **pic**
OBS	*Descriptive term used in Que.*	Descriptif attesté au Qué.
EQ	**peak (1)**	
REL		pointu, table
EX	Piton Péquin, Qué./Que. 51° 52' – 69° 51' (22 N/13)	

place

DES	Site distinguished from its surroundings.	*Site considéré par rapport à son environnement.*
OBS	Applied to undersea banks, ridges, rapids, coves, and hills, for example. Used in Nfld. and N.S.	*S'emploie, par exemple, pour des bancs sous-marins, des chaînons, des rapides, des anses, et des collines. Relevé à T.-N. et en N.-É.*
EQ		
REL	land, country	
EX	Enoch Place (bank-banc), Nfld./T.-N. 47° 21' – 55° 46' (C.4645) Tims Crossing Place (ridge-chaînon), Nfld/T.-N. 46° 51' – 53° 17' (1 K/14) Pollys Place (rapids-rapide), N.S./N.-É. 43° 42' – 65° 38' (20 P/12) Harbour Place (cove-anse), Nfld./T.-N. 47° 37' – 53° 55' (1 N/12) Devils Dressing Place (hill-colline), Nfld./T.-N. 49° 46C – 56° 56' (12 H/15)	

plage (f.)   (Fig. 32)

DES	*Open portion of a shore, with a gentle slope, made up of sand or pebbles.*	Portion dégagée d'un rivage, de faible pente, constituée de sable ou de galets.
OBS	*A* plage *is normally made up of finer materials than a* grève. *Used in Que. and N.B.*	La plage est habituellement constituée de matériaux plus fins que ceux de la grève. Attesté au Qué. et au N.-B.
EQ	**beach**	
REL		grève
EX	Plage à l'Abattis, Qué./Que. 47° 14' – 70° 37' (21 M/2) Plage Dugas, N.-B./N.B. 47° 47' – 65° 02' (21 P/14)	

plain(s) (Fig. 43)

DES	Area of flat or gently rolling terrain.	*Étendue de terrain à surface plane ou légèrement ondulée.*
OBS	Widely used.	*Emploi généralisé.*
EQ		**plaine** (f.)
REL	plateau, flat (1), flat (2), prairie, meadow (1)	
EX	Abrahams Plain, N.B./N.-B. 44° 52' – 66° 57' (21 B/15) Kootenay Plains, Alta./Alb. 52° 06' – 116° 24' (83 C/1) Plain of the Six Glaciers, Alta./Alb. 51° 24' – 116° 16' (82 N/8)	

Figure 43. View looking southeast across the Kootenay Plains beside the North Saskatchewan River, Alberta.
(Whyte Museum of the Canadian Rockies, Banff, Alberta, # NG9-5; photo taken by Elliott Barnes in 1907)

Figure 43. Kootenay Plains bordant la rivière Saskatchewan Nord, en Alberta, photographiées vers le sud-est.
(Whyte Museum of the Canadian Rockies, Banff, Alberta, photo n° NG9-5; prise par Elliott Barnes en 1907)

plaine (f.)   (Fig. 44)

DES	Extensive surface, generally at low elevation and with little variation in relief.	Surface étendue, généralement de basse altitude, peu accidentée et de faible dénivellation.
OBS	Used in Que. and N.B.	Attesté au Qué. et au N.-B.
EQ	**plain**	
REL		
EX	Plaine de Sangro, Qué./Que. 46° 59′ – 71° 35′ (21 L/13) Plaine à Jérôme, N.-B./N.B. 47° 18′ – 68° 06′ (21 N/8)	

plateau   (Fig. 14)

DES	Extensive, elevated region, with either level terrain, or nearly uniform summit levels.	Région étendue et élevée, à surface plane ou hérissée de sommets de même hauteur.
OBS	Widely used.	Emploi généralisé.
EQ		**plateau** (m.)
REL	plain, highlands, uplands, mountains, coteau	
EX	Old Man On His Back Plateau, Sask. 49° 14′ – 109° 10′ (72 F/3) Nechako Plateau, B.C./C.-B. 54° 30′ – 126° 00′ (93 L/8) Crawford Plateau, Alta./Alb. 51° 10′ – 114° 34′ (82 O/2) Marie Plateau, N.B./N.-B. 47° 21′ – 66° 35′ (21 O/7)	

plateau   (m.)

DES	Large terrain area, high and relatively uniform, bounded by slopes, and having little variation in relief.	Vaste étendue de terrain, élevée et relativement uniforme, délimitée par des versants, peu accidentée et de faible dénivellation.
OBS	Used in Que.	Attesté au Qué.
EQ	**plateau**	
REL		
EX	Plateau Akuliaq, Qué./Que. 59° 57′ – 72° 28′ (34 P/16)	

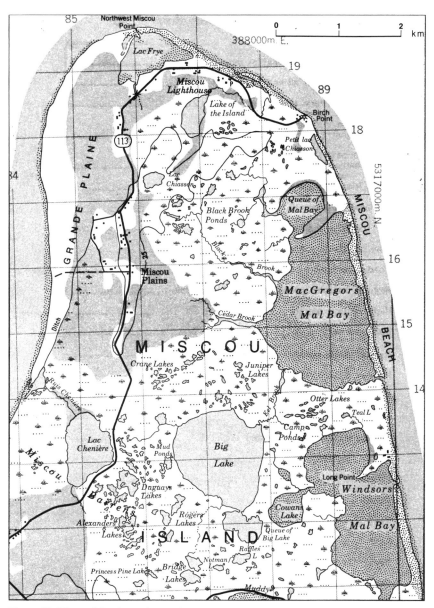

Figure 44. Miscou Island, northeast of Caraquet, New Brunswick, showing Grande Plaine, Miscou Barrens, Miscou Beach, Lac Frye, MacGregors Mal Bay, Camp Ponds, Queue of Mal Bay, and Ruisseau Chenière. (National Topographic System map 21 P/15, 16 & 22 A/1, 2; 1978)

Figure 44. Miscou Island, au nord-est de Caraquet, au Nouveau-Brunswick. Entités représentées : Grande Plaine, Miscou Barrens, Miscou Beach, Lac Frye, MacGregors Mal Bay, Camp Ponds, Queue of Mal Bay et Ruisseau Chenière. (Cartes 21 P/15, 16 et 22 A/1, 2 du Système national de référence cartographique; 1978)

platin (m.)

DES	*Riverside terrain, periodically flooded, and often vegetated.*	Terrain riverain périodiquement submergé où croît souvent de la végétation.
OBS	*Used in N.B.*	Usage local au N.-B.
EQ	**intervale**	
REL		batture
EX	Platin de Saint-Basile, N.-B./N.B. 47° 21′ – 68° 15′ (21 N/8)	

plée (f.)

DES	*Area of land devoid of trees.*	Terrain dépourvu d'arbres.
OBS	*"Plée" would seem to be the noun derived from the adjective "pelé" (devoid of vegetation) or else a phonetic variant of the term "prée" (f.) used in French-speaking areas of the Maritime Provinces for "pré". Used in Que.*	La forme «plée» serait un emploi substantivé de l'adjectif «pelé» (dépourvu de toute végétation) ou encore une variante phonétique du terme «prée» (fém.) utilisé dans les régions francophones des Maritimes au sens de «pré». Attesté au Qué.
EQ	**meadow** (1)	
REL		champ, pré
EX	Grande plée Bleue, Qué./Que. 46° 47′ – 71° 03′ (21 L/14)	

point(s) (1)   (Fig. 41, 49)

DES	Land area jutting into a water feature; also used for a convex change in direction of a shoreline.	*Étendue de terre qui s'avance dans une nappe d'eau. Aussi, inflexion convexe dans le tracé d'un littoral.*
OBS	Widely used. Applied to an extremity of land or more broadly to the land mass itself. The generic may precede or follow the specific. By extension, "point" may be applied to features such as Icefall Point, B.C. (92 N/6), a point of land at a change in direction of a glacier.	*Emploi généralisé. Désigne une extrémité de terre ou, plus largement, la masse de terre proprement dite. Le générique peut précéder ou suivre le spécifique. Par extension, «point» s'emploie parfois pour désigner une pointe de terre à un endroit où un glacier a changé de direction, comme le* Icefall Point, *en C.-B. (92 N/6).*
EQ		**pointe** (f.)
REL	peninsula, spit, cape, head (1)	
EX	Aitken Point, P.E.I./Î.-P.-É. 46° 10′ – 62° 33′ (11 L/2) Calton Point, Y.T./Yuk. 69° 30′ – 139° 09′ (117 D) Point Pelee, Ont. 41° 54′ – 82° 40′ (40 G/15) Point Atkinson, B.C./C.-B. 49° 20′ – 123° 16′ (92 G/6) Clouston Points, N.W.T./T.N.-O. 68° 29′ – 87° 50′ (47 B)	

point (2)

DES	Sharp peak.	*Pic effilé.*
OBS	Rare; Nfld. and B.C.	*Rare; à T.-N. et en C.-B.*
EQ		**pic** (m.)
REL	peak (1), needle, spire, pinnacle (1), head (2)	
EX	Skoatl Point, B.C./C.-B. 51° 09′ – 120° 26′ (92 P/1) Mussel Pond Point, Nfld./T.-N. 47° 04′ – 53° 36′ (1 N/4)	

pointe (f.)   (Fig. 1)

DES	*Elongated projection of land, generally of low elevation, jutting out into a body of water.*	Saillie de terre allongée, généralement peu élevée, qui s'avance dans une étendue d'eau.
OBS	*A* pointe *is very often a change in the shoreline's orientation. It is normally smaller than a* cap. *Used across the country.*	La pointe marque très souvent un changement d'orientation du rivage et est habituellement moins étendue que le cap. Attesté à travers le pays.
EQ	**point (1)**	
REL		cap, nez, promontoire, tête (1)
EX	Pointe du Bout de l'Île, Qué./Que. 46° 51′ – 71° 08′ (21 L/14) Pointe Basse, Alb./Alta. 58° 47′ – 110° 54′ (74 L/15) Pointe d'Herbe, N.-B./N.B. 47° 48′ – 65° 53′ (21 P/15)	

pointers

DES	See **hills**	*Voir* **hills**
OBS	Rare; N.W.T.	*Rare; T.N.-O.*
EQ		**collines** (f.)
REL	peaks (1), summits, mountains	
EX	Sledge Pointers, N.W.T./T.N.-O. 70° 32′ – 69° 05′ (27 F)	

pointu (m.)

DES	*See* **pic**	Voir **pic**
OBS	*Used in N.B.*	Attesté au N.-B.
EQ	**peak (1)**	
REL		piton, table
EX	Pointu de la Rivière Verte, N.-B./N.B. 47° 23′ – 68° 08′ (21 N/8)	

pollack

DES	See **shoal**	*Voir* **shoal**
OBS	Rare; N.S.	*Rare; N.-É.*
EQ		**haut-fond** (m.)
REL	bank (1), ground (1)	
EX	Little Pollack, N.S./N.-É. 44° 27′ – 63° 33′ (11 D/5)	

pond(s) (1) (Fig. 5, 44, 53)

DES	Inland body of standing water, usually smaller than a lake.	*Nappe d'eau dormante entourée de terre, habituellement plus petite qu'un lac.*
OBS	Widely used. In Nfld., "pond" is applied to lakes of all sizes.	*Emploi généralisé. À T.-N., «pond» s'emploie pour des lacs de toutes dimensions.*
EQ		**étang** (m.)
REL	lake, lagoon, hole (2), loch, puddle, tarn, slough (2), water	
EX	Whitney Pond, N.B./N.-B. 47° 00′ – 66° 20′ (21 J/16) Plate Cove Big Pond, Nfld./T.-N. 48° 32′ – 53° 26′ (2 C/11) The Pond that Feeds the Brook, Nfld./T.-N. 47° 31′ – 53° 23′ (1 N/11) Trippers Cove Ponds, Nfld./T.-N. 47° 40′ – 53° 43′ (1 N/12)	

pond (2)

DES	See **barachois** and **cove**	*Voir* **barachois** *et* **cove**
OBS	Used in Nfld. and N.B.	*En usage à T.-N. et au N.-B.*
EQ		**barachois** (m.)
REL	bay, lagoon	
EX	Salt Pond, Nfld./T.-N. 52° 27′ – 55° 41′ (3 D/5) Denton Pond, N.B./N.-B. 45° 55′ – 66° 09′ (21 G/16)	

pool(s) (1)

DES	Deep or still place in a watercourse.	*Partie d'un cours d'eau aux eaux profondes ou tranquilles.*
OBS	Used in the Atlantic Provinces and Ont.	*En usage dans les provinces de l'Atlantique et en Ont.*
EQ		**fosse** (f.)
REL	hole (3), deadwater, steady	
EX	Paradise Pool, N.B./N.-B. 47° 19′ – 66° 28′ (21 O/8) Cameron's Pool, Ont. 49° 09′ – 88° 20′ (52 H/1) Diamond Pools, N.B./N.-B. 45° 18′ – 66° 31′ (21 G/7)	

pool (2)

DES	Whirlpool.	*Tourbillon.*
OBS	Rare; B.C.	*Rare; C.-B.*
EQ		**[tourbillon** (m.)]
REL	eddy, hole (4)	
EX	Slocan Pool, B.C./C.-B. 49° 27′ – 117° 31′ (82 F/5)	

port (1)

DES	See **harbour**	*Voir* **harbour**
OBS	Used for features on the east and west coasts of Canada.	*Relevé sur les côtes est et ouest du Canada.*
EQ		**havre** (m.)
REL	haven, anchorage	
EX	Port Borden, P.E.I./Î.-P.-É. 46° 15′ – 63° 42′ (11 L/4) Port Moody, B.C./C.-B. 49° 18′ – 122° 52′ (92 G/7)	

port (2) (Fig. 45)

DES	Inlet, or part of an inlet, providing shelter to vessels; or a bay.	*Bras de mer ou partie d'un bras de mer pouvant servir d'abri à des bateaux; baie.*
OBS	Used in B.C. and N.W.T.	*En usage en C.-B. et dans les T.N.-O.*
EQ		**[bras** (m.)]
REL	inlet (1), bay, bight	
EX	Port Eliza, B.C./C.-B. 49° 53′ – 127° 01′ (92 E/14) Anna Maria Port, N.W.T./T.N.-O. 63° 44′ – 67° 53′ (25 O) Port Leopold, N.W.T./T.N.-O. 73° 51′ – 90° 20′ (58 D)	

port (m.)

DES	*Natural or man-made shelter for vessels; usually with the necessary equipment for loading and unloading cargoes.*	Abri naturel ou artificiel pour les bateaux; habituellement muni d'installations nécessaires à l'embarquement et au débarquement de leur chargement.
OBS	*The terms "port" and "havre" were interchangeable up to the beginning of the twentieth century; today, "havre" generally refers to the sea, while "port" also applies to rivers and lakes. Used in a number of provinces.*	Les termes «port» et «havre» étaient interchangeables jusqu'au début du XXe siècle; aujourd'hui, «havre» est généralement réservé à la mer tandis que «port» s'applique également aux cours d'eau et aux lacs. Attesté dans plusieurs provinces.
EQ	**port (1)**	
REL		havre
EX	Port Désiré, C.-B./B.C. 48° 50′ – 125° 08′ (92 C/14) Port au Saumon, Qué./Que. 47° 45′ – 69° 57′ (21 N/13) Port de Boucherville, T.N.-O./N.W.T. 63° 12′ – 77° 33′ (35 N/4)	

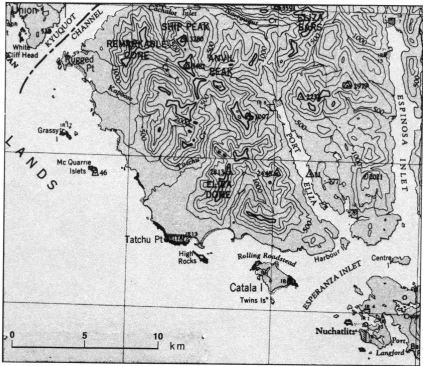

Figure 45. Part of the west coast of Vancouver Island, near Kyuquot, British Columbia, showing Port Eliza, Kyuquot Channel, Remarkable Cone, Eliza Dome, Eliza Ears, White Cliff Head, Esperanza Inlet, McQuarrie Islets, Anvil Peak, Rolling Roadstead, and High Rocks. (National Topographic System map 92 E; 1954)

Figure 45. Partie de la côte ouest de l'île de Vancouver, près de Kyuquot, en Colombie-Britannique. Entités représentées : Port Eliza, Kyuquot Channel, Remarkable Cone, Eliza Dome, Eliza Ears, White Cliff Head, Esperanza Inlet, McQuarrie Islets, Anvil Peak, Rolling Roadstead et High Rocks. (Carte 92 E du Système national de référence cartographique; 1954)

portage

DES	Land route connecting two navigable bodies of water.	*Voie terrestre mettant en communication deux étendues d'eau navigables.*
OBS	Widely used.	*Emploi généralisé.*
EQ		**portage** (m.)
REL	trail	
EX	Faille Portage, N.W.T./T.N.-O. 61° 36' – 125° 45' (95 F) Husky Portage, Man. 59° 50' – 100° 45' (64 N/15) Keskamutinawok Portage, Man. 57° 52' – 98° 33' (64 G/15)	

portage (m.)

DES	*Trail around an obstacle in a watercourse or joining two bodies of water.*	Sentier qui contourne un obstacle dans un cours d'eau ou qui relie deux étendues d'eau.
OBS	*This term also indicates the act of carrying a canoe and goods on one's back to avoid rapids or to pass from one body of water to another. Used in Que.*	Ce terme désigne aussi l'action de transporter sur le dos canot et marchandises afin d'éviter les rapides ou de passer d'une étendue d'eau à une autre. Attesté au Qué.
EQ	**portage**	
REL		
EX	Portage Tasivvik, Qué./Que. 61° 33' – 71° 44' (25 E/12)	

pot(s)

DES	Feature having the shape of a pot.	*Accident géographique en forme de pot.*
OBS	Applied to rocks, pools, springs, and coves. Used in N.S., Ont., and Alta.	*S'emploie pour des rochers, des nappes d'eau, des sources, et des anses. En usage en N.-É., en Ont. et en Alb.*
EQ		
REL	butterpot	
EX	Flower Pot (rock-rocher), N.S./N.-É. 46° 23′ – 60° 23′ (11 K/8) Naustash Eel Pot (stillwater-eau morte), N.S./N.-É. 43° 46′ – 65° 34′ (20 P/13) Ink Pots (springs-sources), Alta./Alb. 51° 17′ – 115° 49′ (82 O/5) The Flower Pot (cove-anse), Ont. 45° 51′ – 80° 39′ (41 H/15)	

pothole(s)

DES	See **slough (1)** and **pond (1)**	*Voir* **slough (1)** *et* **pond (1)**
OBS	Few named examples; N.S., Ont., and Man.	*Rare dans les noms approuvés; N.-É., Ont. et Man.*
EQ		**étang** (m.)
REL	hole (4), lagoon	
EX	Newton's Pothole, Ont. 46° 38′ – 80° 47′ (41 I/10) Hemlock Pothole, N.S./N.-É. 44° 07′ – 65° 21′ (21 A/3) Richardsons Potholes, Man. 50° 09′ – 98° 17′ (62 J/1)	

poulier (m.)

DES	*Curled end of a coastal spit stretching across and tending to block an estuary or bay.*	Extrémité recourbée d'une flèche littorale allongée en travers d'un estuaire ou d'une baie, qu'elle tend à barrer.
OBS	*Used in Que.*	Attesté au Qué.
EQ	**hook**	
REL		
EX	Poulier de Varennes, Qué./Que. 45° 41′ – 73° 27′ (31 H/11)	

prairie

DES	Area of flat or gently rolling grassland; larger than a meadow and often extensive.	*Étendue de terrain herbeux à surface plane ou légèrement ondulée, plus grande qu'une baissière et souvent très vaste.*
OBS	Used in Man., Alta., B.C., and N.W.T.	*En usage au Man., en Alb., en C.-B. et dans les T.N.-O.*
EQ		**[prairie (f.)]**
REL	plain, meadow (1)	
EX	Grande Prairie, Alta./Alb. 55° 12′ – 118° 48′ (83 M/2) Sumas Prairie, B.C./C.-B. 49° 03′ – 122° 08′ (92 G/1)	

pré (m.)   (Fig. 1)

DES	*Flat terrain with low vegetation.*	Terrain plat à végétation courte.
OBS	*Used in N.B. and in N.S.*	Attesté au N.-B. et en N.-É.
EQ	**meadow (1)**	
REL		champ, plée
EX	Pré à Germain, N.-B./N.B. 46° 53′ – 64° 55′ (21 I/15) Le Pré, N.-É./N.S. 45° 15′ – 61° 12′ (11 F/6)	

presqu'île (f.)

DES	*Land almost completely surrounded by water but still connected to the adjacent shore.*	Terre presque entièrement entourée d'eau, reliée au rivage avoisinant.
OBS	*A* presqu'île *is distinguished from a* péninsule *by its narrower isthmus. Both are usually larger than a* pointe. *Used in Que.*	La presqu'île se distingue de la péninsule par la largeur inférieure de son isthme. La presqu'île et la péninsule sont habituellement plus grosses que la pointe. Attesté au Qué.
EQ	**peninsula**	
REL		péninsule
EX	Presqu'île Abatagouche, Qué./Que. 50° 32′ – 73° 52′ (31 I/12)	

profile

DES	See **cliff**	*Voir* **cliff**
OBS	Rare; Ont.	*Rare; Ont.*
EQ		**falaise** (f.)
REL	bluff (1), face, wall	
EX	Duke's Profile, Ont. 44° 25′ – 76° 18′ (31 C/8)	

promontoire (m.)

DES	*Land projection of great size, normally high and massive, jutting into a body of water.*	Saillie de terre de très grande dimension, habituellement élevée et massive, qui s'avance dans une étendue d'eau.
OBS	*Formerly, "promontoire" and "cap" were synonymous. Now "promontoire" indicates an elevated landmass projecting above the water, as opposed to "cap", which identifies either high or low land, jutting into a body of water. A* promontoire *is normally larger than a* cap. *Used in Que.*	Anciennement, «promontoire» et «cap» étaient synonymes. Dans une acception plus restrictive, ce générique indique une masse de terre élevée ou une montagne formant saillie au-dessus des eaux, par opposition au cap qui désigne tout ce qui s'avance dans une étendue d'eau, élevé ou non. Le promontoire est habituellement plus gros que le cap. Attesté au Qué.
EQ	**promontory**	
REL		cap, nez, pointe, tête (1)
EX	Promontoire Colbert, Qué./Que. 62° 32′ – 77° 06′ (35 K/11)	

promontory

DES	See **head (1)**	*Voir* **head (1)**
OBS	Used in Nfld. and N.W.T. The only example in B.C. is Elephant Promontory, which is a mountain peak.	*En usage à T.-N. et dans les T.N.-O. En C.-B., ce générique se rencontre dans un seul toponyme, «Elephant Promontory», où il désigne un pic.*
EQ		**promontoire** (m.)
REL	cape, point (1), peninsula	
EX	Archibald Promontory, N.W.T./T.N.-O. 63° 16′ – 64° 36′ (25 P)	

puddle

DES	Small pond.	*Petit étang.*
OBS	Rare; N.S.	*Rare; N.-É.*
EQ		**mare** (f.)
REL	pond (1), hole (2), tarn, pothole	
EX	Bear Hill Puddle, N.S./N.-É. 44° 38′ – 63° 54′ (11 D/12)	

pughole

DES	Small pond.	*Petit étang.*
OBS	Rare; N.S. and N.B.	*Rare; N.-É. et N.-B.*
EQ		**mare** (f.)
REL	pond (1), hole (2), tarn, pothole	
EX	Hatchet Lake Pughole, N.S./N.-É. 44° 51′ – 62° 50′ (11 D/15)	

punch bowl, punchbowl

DES	Feature having the appearance of a bowl.	*Relief en forme de cuvette.*
OBS	Applied to lakes, ravines, and inlets. Widely used.	*S'applique à des lacs, des ravins et des bras. Emploi généralisé.*
EQ		**[dépression** (f.)**]**
REL	basin (3), cirque, depression	
EX	Committee Punch Bowl (lake-lac), Alta. – B.C./Alb. – C.-B. 52° 24′ – 118° 11′ (83 D/8) Devil's Punch Bowl (ravine-ravin), Ont. 43° 12′ – 79° 45′ (30 M/4) Punchbowl (inlet-bras), Nfld./T.-N. 53° 15′ – 55° 45′ (3 E/4)	

pup   (Fig. 19)

DES	Small watercourse, possibly intermittent; also applied to some valleys.	*Petit cours d'eau, parfois intermittent; s'applique aussi à certaines vallées.*
OBS	Particular to Y.T., where it is used in gold-mining areas of the 1890s.	*Propre au Yukon, où il s'emploie dans les zones d'exploitation aurifère de la fin du XIXᵉ siècle.*
EQ		**[ruisselet** (m.)]
REL	creek (1), brook, stream, gulch (1)	
EX	Six Below Pup, Y.T./Yuk. 63° 57′ – 138° 54′ (115 N & O) Discovery Pup, Y.T./Yuk. 63° 51′ – 138° 52′ (115 N & O)	

q

queue   (Fig. 44)

DES	Tail-shaped extension of a bay or lake.	*Prolongement d'une baie ou d'un lac, en forme de queue.*
OBS	Rare; N.B.	*Rare; N.-B.*
EQ		
REL	arm (1), inlet (1), tail, cove	
EX	Queue of Mal Bay, N.B./N.-B. 48° 00′ – 64° 30′ (21 P/15) Queue of Big Lake, N.B./N.-B. 47° 57′ – 64° 30′ (21 P/15)	

r

race

DES	Swift-flowing part of a watercourse.	*Partie d'un cours d'eau où le courant est rapide.*
OBS	Rare; N.S.	*Rare; N.-É.*
EQ		**rapide** (m.)
REL	rapid (1), chute, flumes, run (2)	
EX	Jerry Race, N.S./N.-É. 44° 43′ – 65° 25′ (21 A/11)	

rade (f.)

DES	*Sheltered expanse of water close to shore, where vessels can anchor in safety.*	Étendue d'eau abritée, située près de la côte, où les navires peuvent mouiller en sécurité.
OBS	*Used in Que.*	Attesté au Qué.
EQ	**road**	
REL		
EX	Rade du Basque, Qué./Que. 48° 02′ – 69° 45′ (22 C/4)	

ramparts (Fig. 46)

DES	Steep rock wall(s).	*Versant(s) rocheux escarpé(s).*
OBS	Used in B.C., Alta., N.W.T., and Y.T. N.W.T. examples refer to rock-walled sections of the Mackenzie River.	*S'emploie en C.-B., en Alb., dans les T.N.-O. et au Yukon. Dans les T.N.-O., désigne des sections du fleuve Mackenzie qui sont bordées de parois rocheuses.*
EQ		[**remparts** (m.)]
REL	wall, bluff (1), cliff	
EX	Monarch Ramparts, B.C. – Alta./C.-B. – Alb. 51° 04′ – 115° 50′ (82 O/4) Lower Ramparts, N.W.T./T.N.-O. 67° 29′ – 133° 36′ (106 N) Ramparts of the Porcupine, Y.T./Yuk. 67° 27′ – 140° 43′ (116 N & O)	

Figure 46. The Ramparts on the Mackenzie River, Northwest Territories, as seen in 1921. (N.W.T. Archives, 86PH 287)

Figure 46. The Ramparts, sur le fleuve Mackenzie, dans les Territoires du Nord-Ouest, tels que vus en 1921. (N.W.T. Archives, 86PH 287)

range(s)   (Fig. 36, 37)

DES	Group or chain of mountains or hills.	*Groupe ou chaîne de montagnes ou de collines.*
OBS	A group of ranges may collectively be identified as either "ranges" or "mountains". Widely used.	*Un groupe de* ranges *peut être appelé «ranges» ou «mountains». Emploi généralisé.*
EQ		**[chaîne** (f.)]
REL	mountains, hills, highlands, uplands	
EX	Dahadinni Range, N.W.T./T.N.-O. 63° 22' – 124° 53' (95 N) Fairholme Range, Alta./Alb. 51° 10' – 115° 18' (82 O/3) Alsek Ranges, Y.T./Yuk. 60° 00' – 137° 30' (115 A) Swannell Ranges, B.C./C.-B. 56° 25' – 126° 10' (94 D/8)	

rapid(s)   (1)   (Fig. 47)

DES	Fast-flowing section of a watercourse, usually with turbulent water or exposed rocks.	*Partie d'un cours d'eau généralement hérissée de rochers, où le courant est rapide et souvent turbulent.*
OBS	Widely used.	*Emploi généralisé.*
EQ		**rapide** (m.)
REL	chute, cataract, run (2), fall	
EX	Five Finger Rapid, Y.T./Yuk. 62° 16' – 136° 21' (115 I) Rapids of the Drowned, N.W.T./T.N.-O. 60° 01' – 111° 52' (75 D)	

Figure 47. Tracking a scow up the Boiler Rapids on the Athabasca River, Alberta, 1914.
(Geological Survey of Canada, Ottawa, 28893)

Figure 47. Halage d'un chaland à contre-courant; Boiler Rapids, rivière Athabasca, en Alberta, 1914.
(Commission géologique du Canada, Ottawa, 28893)

rapids (2)

DES	Constricted passage with strong tidal current.	*Passage resserré traversé par un fort courant de marée.*
OBS	Direction of flow may reverse with tidal changes. Used in B.C.	*La direction de l'écoulement peut s'inverser sous l'effet des variations du niveau de la mer. Relevé en C.-B.*
EQ		[**ride** (m.)]
REL	narrows, rip (2), tickle, eddy	
EX	Yuculta Rapids, B.C./C.-B. 50° 23′ – 125° 09′ (92 K/6)	

rapide(s) (m.)

DES	*Section of a watercourse, often strewn with rocks, where the water becomes rapid and turbulent as a result of an increase in gradient.*	Partie d'un cours d'eau, souvent hérissée de roches, où le courant devient rapide et agité par suite d'une augmentation de la pente.
OBS	*This term is often used in the plural. A* rapide *differs from a* chute, *a* cascade, *and a* sault *in the lack of a distinct break in the watercourse's gradient. Used across the country.*	Ce terme est souvent utilisé au pluriel. Le rapide se différencie de la chute, de la cascade et du sault par son absence de rupture de pente. Attesté à travers le pays.
EQ	**rapids (1)**	
REL		cascades, chute, sault
EX	Rapides du Petit Aigle, Qué./Que. 46° 53′ – 73° 17′ (31 I/14) Rapide Blanc, N.-B./N.B. 47° 26′ – 65° 07′ (21 P/6) Rapides du Joli Fou, Alb./Alta. 56° 04′ – 112° 37′ (84 A/2)	

rattle

DES	Rapids, or a fast-flowing stretch of a watercourse.	*Rapides ou partie d'un cours d'eau où le courant est rapide.*
OBS	"Rattle" describes the sound made by the water. Used in Nfld. and N.S.	*Le mot anglais «rattle» renvoie au bruit que fait l'eau. Utilisé à T.-N. et en N.-É.*
EQ		**rapide** (m.)
REL	rapid (1), chute, brook	
EX	Daniel Rattle, Nfld./T.-N. 55° 55′ – 61° 05′ (13 N/14) Black Rattle, N.S./N.-É. 44° 18′ – 65° 11′ (21 A/6)	

ravin (m.)

DES	*Deep and narrow, V-shaped depression on a slope.*	Entaille profonde et étroite sur un versant, creusée en forme de V.
OBS	*A* ravin *is smaller than a* vallée, *but larger than a* ravine. *The related terms listed all indicate an elongated depression, usually with a stream flowing through. Used in Que.*	Le ravin est plus petit que la vallée, mais plus grand que la ravine. Les termes semblables retenus désignent tous une dépression allongée permettant le passage d'un cours d'eau. Attesté au Qué.
EQ	**ravine**	
REL		canyon, coulée (1), gorge, ravine, rigwash, vallée
EX	Ravin de la Rivière du Loup, Qué./Que. 48° 16′ – 66° 46′ (22 B/7)	

ravine (Fig. 48)

DES	Deep, V-shaped declivity.	*Entaille profonde en V.*
OBS	Usually larger than a gulch, but smaller than a valley. Widely used.	*«Ravine» désigne généralement une entité plus vaste que «gulch» mais plus petite que «valley». Emploi généralisé.*
EQ		**ravin** (m.)
REL	valley, gully (1), gulch (1), coulee, canyon, gorge	
EX	Klockow Ravine, Sask. 50° 48′ – 105° 33′ (72 I/13) Pim Ravine, N.W.T./T.N.-O. 74° 15′ – 117° 38′ (88 F)	

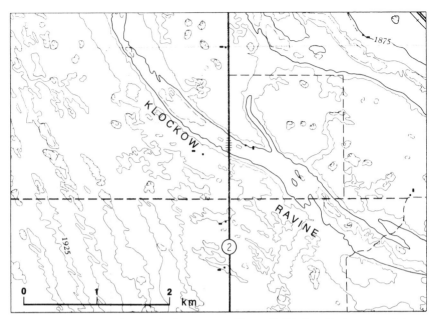

Figure 48. Klockow Ravine, north of
Moose Jaw, Saskatchewan.
(National Topographic System map
72 I/13; 1981)

Figure 48. Klockow Ravine, au nord de
Moose Jaw, en Saskatchewan.
(Carte 72 I/13 du Système national de
référence cartographique; 1981)

ravine (f.)

DES	*Small ravine.*	Petit ravin.
OBS	*The related terms listed all indicate an elongated depression, usually with a stream flowing through. A* ravine *is smaller than both a* ravin *and a* vallée. *Used in Que.*	Les termes semblables retenus désignent tous une dépression allongée permettant le passage d'un cours d'eau. La ravine est plus petite que le ravin et la vallée. Attesté au Qué.
EQ	**gulch (1)**	
REL		canyon, coulée (1), gorge, ravin, rigwash, vallée
EX	La Grande Ravine, Qué./Que. 58° 51′ – 69° 31′ (24 K/13)	

reach

DES	Relatively straight section of a river, lake, or inlet.	*Section relativement droite d'un cours d'eau, d'un lac ou d'un bras.*
OBS	Widely used.	*Emploi généralisé.*
EQ		[**passage** (m.)]
REL	channel (1), inlet (1), sound (2)	
EX	Princess Royal Reach, B.C./C.-B. 50° 02′ – 123° 52′ (92 J/4) Adolphus Reach, Ont. 44° 05′ – 76° 55′ (31 C/2) Meductic Reach, N.B./N.-B. 45° 59′ – 67° 29′ (21 G/14)	

récif(s) (m.)

DES	*Rock or group of rocks at, or just below, the surface of the water, posing a hazard to navigation.*	Rocher ou amoncellement de roches à fleur d'eau ou à très faible profondeur dans la mer, constituant un danger pour la navigation.
OBS	*There is very little distinction between the terms "récif" and "écueil". The generic term "récif" is used by geographers and navigators, whereas "écueil" is used more in the figurative, literary sense. Used in Que.*	La distinction tangible entre les termes «récif» et «écueil» est très mince. Les géographes et les navigateurs emploient le terme générique «récif» tandis que les écrivains utilisent davantage «écueil» au sens figuré. Attesté au Qué.
EQ	**reef**	
REL		caye, roche (1), rocher
EX	Récif du Basque, Qué./Que. 50° 11′ – 66° 22′ (C.1221) Récifs à Loups Marins, Qué./Que. 50° 10′ – 66° 23′ (C.1221)	

reef(s)   (Fig. 41, 49)

DES	Rocks rising to or near the surface of a body of water.	*Rochers à fleur d'eau ou à proximité de la surface d'une étendue d'eau.*
OBS	May be a hazard to surface navigation. Widely used.	*Peut constituer un danger pour la navigation. Emploi généralisé.*
EQ		**récif** (m.)
REL	rock (1), ledge (1), islet	
EX	Escape Reef, Y.T./Yuk. 69° 00' – 137° 15' (117 A) Harbour Reefs, B.C./C.-B. 54° 35' – 130° 27' (103 J/9)	

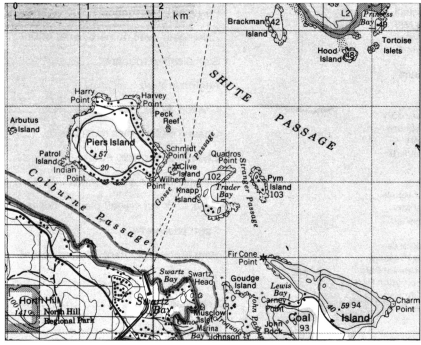

Figure 49. Coast near Swartz Bay, British Columbia, showing Peck Reef, Trader Bay, Horth Hill, Piers Island, Tortoise Islets, Colburne Passage and Stranger Passage, Fir Cone Point, and John Rock. (National Topographic System map 92 B/11; 1981)

Figure 49. Côte avoisinant Swartz Bay, en Colombie-Britannique. Entités représentées : Peck Reef, Trader Bay, Horth Hill, Piers Island, Tortoise Islets, Colburne Passage et Stranger Passage, Fir Cone Point et John Rock. (Carte 92 B/11 du Système national de référence cartographique; 1981)

remous (m.)

DES	*Place in a stream where water swirls in a direction contrary to the current.*	Endroit dans un cours d'eau où l'eau s'agite dans un sens contraire au courant.
OBS	*Used in Que.*	Attesté au Qué.
EQ	**eddy**	
REL		
EX	Le Grand Remous, Qué./Que. 48° 28′ – 71° 18′ (22 D/6)	

reservoir

DES	Inland body of standing water impounded by artificial structures.	*Nappe d'eau retenue par des structures artificielles.*
OBS	Widely used.	*Emploi généralisé.*
EQ		**réservoir** (m.)
REL	lake, flowage, pond (1), millpond	
EX	Spray Lakes Reservoir, Alta./Alb. 50° 54′ – 115° 20′ (82 J/14) Smallwood Reservoir, Nfld./T.-N. 54° 05′ – 64° 30′ (23 I)	

réservoir (m.)

DES	*Body of water maintained at a controlled level.*	Nappe d'eau à niveau contrôlé.
OBS	*Used in Que.*	Attesté au Qué.
EQ	**reservoir**	
REL		
EX	Réservoir Manicouagan, Qué./Que. 51° 05′ – 68° 34′ (22 N/2)	

retreat

DES	See **anchorage**	*Voir* **anchorage**
OBS	Rare; B.C.	*Rare; C.-B.*
EQ		**mouillage** (m.)
REL	harbour, haven, bay	
EX	Schooner Retreat, B.C./C.-B. 51° 28′ – 127° 44′ (92 M/5)	

rib

DES	See **shoal**	*Voir* **shoal**
OBS	Used in Nfld.	*Relevé à T.-N.*
EQ		**haut-fond** (m.)
REL	bank (1), ground (1)	
EX	North Rib, Nfld./T.-N. 52° 18′ – 55° 34′ (3 D/5)	

ridge(s) (1)   (Fig. 4, 21)

DES	Elongated stretch of elevated ground.	*Élévation de terrain allongée.*
OBS	Widely used.	*Emploi généralisé.*
EQ		[**chaînon** (m.)]
REL	hill, escarpment, back, esker, edge	
EX	Parker Ridge, Alta./Alb. 51° 47′ – 115° 05′ (82 O/14) Gesner Ridge, N.B./N.-B. 47° 24′ – 67° 06′ (21 O/6) Jacks Ridges, Nfld./T.-N. 47° 34′ – 53° 53′ (1 N/12)	

ridge (2)

DES	See **shoal**	*Voir* **shoal**
OBS	Used in Nfld., Ont., and B.C.	*S'emploie à T.-N., en Ont. et en C.-B.*
EQ		**haut-fond** (m.)
REL	bank (1), ground (1)	
EX	Deep Ridge, B.C./C.-B. 48° 48′ – 123° 22′ (C.3450) The Ridge, Ont. 44° 31′ – 80° 13′ (41 A/9)	

ridge (3)

DES	Long narrow elevation of the seafloor.	*Élévation étroite et allongée du fond de la mer.*
OBS	Used off east and west coasts of Canada.	*S'emploie au large des côtes est et ouest du Canada.*
EQ		[**dorsale** (f.)]
REL	spur (2), knoll (2)	
EX	Alpha Ridge, 85° 30′ – 110° 00′ (C.800A) Winona Ridge, 50° 17′ – 129° 25′ (C.3001)	

riffle

DES	See **rapid (1)**	*Voir* **rapid (1)**
OBS	May be less turbulent than rapids. Used in B.C. and N.W.T.	*On utilise parfois ce terme au lieu de "rapids" lorsque les eaux sont moins turbulentes. Relevé en C.-B. et dans les T.N.-O.*
EQ		**rapide** (m.)
REL	chute, cataract, run (2)	
EX	Lafferty's Riffle, N.W.T./T.N.-O. 61° 16′ – 124° 05′ (95 F) Hankin Riffle, B.C./C.-B. 54° 44′ – 128° 25′ (103 I/9)	

rift

DES	See **channel (1)**	*Voir* **channel (1)**
OBS	Rare; Ont.	*Rare; Ont.*
EQ		**chenal** (m.)
REL	passage, pass (2), gut, narrows	
EX	Bensons Rift, Ont. 44° 21′ – 75° 59′ (31 B/5)	

rigolet (m.)

DES	*Small natural or man-made watercourse; or a drainage ditch.*	Petit courant naturel ou artificiel; petite rigole d'écoulement.
OBS	*Derived from "rigole" (meaning ditch or channel) and used in Que.*	Dérivé de «rigole» et attesté au Qué.
EQ	**drain**	
REL		
EX	Rigolet de la Baie du Moine, Qué./Que. 46° 06′ – 72° 58′ (31 I/2)	

rigwash (f.)

DES	*See* **ravin**	Voir **ravin**
OBS	*Used in N.S.*	Attesté en N.-É.
EQ	**ravine**	
REL		ravine, canyon, coulée (1), gorge, vault
EX	Rigwash à Bernard, N.-É./N.S. 46° 40′ – 60° 57′ (11 K/10)	

rill

DES	Small watercourse.	*Petit cours d'eau.*
OBS	Rare; B.C.	*Rare; C.-B.*
EQ		[**ruisselet** (m.)]
REL	creek (1), brook, stream, pup	
EX	Park Rill, B.C./C.-B. 49° 12′ – 119° 33′ (82 E/4)	

rim

DES	See **ridge (1)**	*Voir **ridge (1)***
OBS	Rare; N.S. and N.B.	*Rare; N.-É. et N.-B.*
EQ		[**bordure** (f.)]
REL	escarpment, edge	
EX	Ponhook Rim, N.S./N.-É. 44° 18′ – 64° 51′ (21 A/7) Maple Rim, N.B./N.-B. 45° 55′ – 66° 20′ (21 G/16)	

ripple

DES	Area of fast current in narrows of a lake.	*Zone de courant rapide dans une partie resserrée d'un lac.*
OBS	Rare; Ont.	*Rare; Ont.*
EQ		[**ride** (m.)]
REL	eddy, rip (2), rapids (2)	
EX	Perch Ripple, Ont. 50° 41′ – 91° 44′ (52 J/12)	

rips (1)

DES	See **rapid (1)**	*Voir* **rapid (1)**
OBS	Used in N.S. and N.B.	*S'emploie en N.-É. et au N.-B.*
EQ		**rapides** (m.)
REL	chute, cataract, run (2)	
EX	Indian Rips, N.S./N.-É. 45° 10′ – 62° 22′ (11 E/1) Wingdam Rips, N.B./N.-B. 45° 33′ – 67° 25′ (21 G/11)	

rip (2)

DES	Turbulent water where tidal currents meet.	*Zone d'eau turbulente où des courants de marée se rencontrent.*
OBS	Named tidal rips occur in the Bay of Fundy; N.S. and N.B.	*On le trouve dans la toponymie de la baie de Fundy; N.-É. et N.-B.*
EQ		[**ride** (m.)]
REL	eddy, rapid(s), motion, tickle, pool (2)	
EX	Shag Harbour Rip, N.S./N.-É. 43° 25′ – 65° 45′ (C.4216) Bulkhead Rip, N.B./N.-B. 44° 37′ – 66° 39′ (C.4340)	

rise

DES	Broad elevation that rises gently and generally smoothly from the seafloor.	*Vaste élévation du fond marin à pente douce et aux formes généralement unies.*
OBS	Used off east and north coasts of Canada.	*S'emploie au large des côtes est et nord du Canada.*
EQ		[**massif** (m.)]
REL		
EX	Cameron Island Rise, 76° 45′ – 105° 40′ (C.7951) Scotian Rise, 42° 00′ – 60° 00′ (C.1399A)	

rivage (m.)

DES	*Strip of land bordering a body of water: sea, lake, or river.*	Bande de terre qui borde une étendue d'eau plus ou moins considérable : mer, lac, fleuve.
OBS	*When it is beside the sea, this strip of land includes the zone between the high-tide and low-tide marks. When the land is beside fresh water, "rive" may be used. Used in Que.*	Dans le cas où il s'agit de la mer, cette bande de terre comprend notamment la zone entre la laisse de haute mer et la laisse de basse mer. Lorsque cette bordure est adjacente à l'eau douce, on dit aussi «rive». Attesté au Qué.
EQ	**shore**	
REL		côte (2)
EX	Rivage Qainngujuaq, Qué./Que. 60° 02′ – 69° 51′ (25 C/4)	

river (1)   (Fig. 64)

DES	Flowing watercourse.	*Cours d'eau.*
OBS	Widely used. Usually applied to a watercourse larger than a stream, creek, or brook. "River" is also used for a tributary to another river.	*Emploi généralisé. S'emploie habituellement pour un cours d'eau de plus grande dimension que celui que désignent les génériques «stream», «creek» et «brook». «River» s'emploie aussi pour un affluent d'une autre rivière.*
EQ		**rivière** (f.) **fleuve** (m.) (Churchill (T.-N.), Columbia, Fraser, Mackenzie, Nelson, Saint-Laurent)
REL	creek (1), brook, stream, channel (2)	
EX	Nelson River, Man. 57° 04′ – 92° 30′ (54 F/2) Athabasca River, Alta./Alb. 58° 40′ – 110° 50′ (74 L) River Don, N.B./N.-B. 47° 08′ – 67° 00′ (21 O/2) River of Rum, Nfld./T.-N. 47° 00′ – 54° 09′ (1 L/16)	

river (2)

DES	Tidal flow between offshore islands.	*Courant de marée entre des îles en milieu marin.*
OBS	Rare; N.B.	*Rare; N.-B.*
EQ		**passage** (m.)
REL	gut, narrows, tickle	
EX	Indian River, N.B./N.-B. 44° 56' – 66° 59' (21 B/15)	

rivière (f.)   (Fig. 38)

DES	*Watercourse of variable importance having tributaries and flowing into another body of water.*	Cours d'eau d'importance variable recevant des tributaires et se déversant dans une nappe d'eau ou un cours d'eau plus important.
OBS	*The flow of a* rivière *is less than that of a* fleuve*, but more than that of a* ruisseau. *During the eighteenth and nineteenth centuries the distinction was established between "rivière" and "fleuve"; the "fleuve Saint-Laurent" (St. Lawrence River) had been called the "rivière (de) Saint-Laurent" until the eighteenth century. Used across the country.*	Le débit de la rivière est inférieur à celui du fleuve, mais supérieur à celui du ruisseau. Cependant, c'est au cours des XVIIIe et XIXe que la distinction s'est établie entre «rivière» et «fleuve»; ainsi, le Saint-Laurent s'est appelé rivière (de) Saint-Laurent jusqu'au XVIIIe siècle. Attesté à travers le pays.
EQ	**river (1)**	
REL		fleuve
EX	Rivière Richelieu, Qué./Que. 46° 03' – 73° 07' (31 I/3) Rivière Grosses Coques, N.-É./N.S. 44° 23' – 66° 04' (21 B/8) La Petite Rivière Jaillante, Alb./Alta. 55° 13' – 112° 49' (83 P/2)	

road(s)

DES	Sheltered body of water.	*Étendue d'eau abritée.*
OBS	Used in Nfld., P.E.I., B.C., and N.W.T.	*S'emploie à T.-N., à l'Î.-P.-É., en C.-B., et dans les T.N.-O.*
EQ		**rade** (f.)
REL	bay, harbour, bight, roadstead, anchorage	
EX	St. Peters Road, P.E.I./Î.-P.-É. 46° 09′ – 63° 10′ (11 L/3) Totnes Road, N.W.T./T.N.-O. 66° 22′ – 62° 20′ (16 L & K) Royal Roads, B.C./C.-B. 48° 25′ – 123° 27′ (92 B/6)	

roadstead   (Fig. 45)

DES	See **channel (1)**	*Voir* **channel (1)**
OBS	Rare; B.C.	*Rare; C.-B.*
EQ		**chenal** (m.)
REL	anchorage, passage, gut, inlet (1), road	
EX	Rolling Roadstead, B.C./C.-B. 49° 51′ – 127° 03′ (92 E/14)	

roche   (f.) (1)

DES	*See* **rocher**	Voir **rocher**
OBS	*Used in Que.*	Attesté au Qué.
EQ	**rock (1)**	
REL		caye, récif
EX	Roche à Veillon, Qué./Que. 47° 12′ – 70° 22′ (C.1233)	

DES	*Rocky hill, mountain, or escarpment.*	Colline, montagne ou escarpement rocheux.
OBS	*Used in Alta. and in N.W.T.*	Attesté en Alb. et dans les T.N.-O.
EQ	**rock (2)**	
REL		cran
EX	Roche à Bosche, Alb./Alta. 53° 12′ – 118° 02′ (83 E/1) Roche-qui-trempe-à-l'eau, T.N.-O./N.W.T. 63° 18′ – 123° 38′ (95 0/5)	

Figure 50. Sir Sandford Fleming Expedition at Jasper House, Alberta, 1872, with Roche Miette in the background.
(Public Archives Canada, PA 9147)

Figure 50. Expéditon de Sir Sandford Fleming à Jasper House, en Alberta, en 1872, avec la Roche Miette en arrière-plan.
(Archives publiques du Canada, PA 9147)

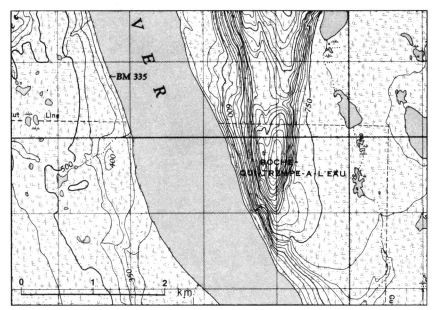

Figure 51. Roche-qui-trempe-à-l'eau, rising above the Mackenzie River, north of Wrigley, Northwest Territories. (National Topographic System map 95 O/5; 1961)	Figure 51. Roche-qui-trempe-à-l'eau, rocher qui émerge du fleuve Mackenzie, au nord de Wrigley, dans les Territoires du Nord-Ouest. (Carte 95 O/5 du Système national de référence cartographique; 1961)

rocher (m.)

DES	*Solid isolated mass rising from the bed of the sea, a lake, or stream.*	Masse solide isolée, s'élevant du fond de la mer, d'un lac ou d'un cours d'eau.
OBS	*Used in Que. and Nfld.*	Attesté au Qué. et à T.-N.
EQ	**rock (1)**	
REL		roche (1), caye, récif
EX	Rocher Percé, Qué./Que. 48° 31' – 64° 12' (22 A/9) Petit Rocher, T.-N./Nfld. 51° 03' – 55° 46' (C.4583)	

rock(s) (1)   (Fig. 41, 49)

DES	Small mass of rock usually projecting above the water surface.	*Petite masse rocheuse qui affleure habituellement à la surface de l'eau.*
OBS	Usually smaller than an island. Widely used.	*Ce générique désigne généralement une entité de plus petite dimension que «island». Emploi généralisé.*
EQ		**rocher** (m.)
REL	reef, islet, brandies, sunker	
EX	Puffin Rock, Nfld./T.-N. 49° 04′ – 53° 33′ (2 F/4) Lynch Rocks, N.S./N.-É. 44° 29′ – 63° 52′ (11 D/5)	

rock(s) (2)   (Fig. 36)

DES	Rocky hill, mountain, or cliff; or a large boulder.	*Colline, montagne ou falaise rocheuse; rocher de grande dimension.*
OBS	Widely used.	*Emploi généralisé.*
EQ		[**rocher** (m.)]
REL	mountain, crag, shoulder	
EX	Bailey Rock (hill-colline), N.B./N.-B. 45° 34′ – 66° 36′ (21 G/10) Brewster Rock (mountain-montagne), Alta./Alb. 51° 05′ – 115° 45′ (82 O/4) Gibraltar Rock (cliff-falaise), B.C./C.-B. 50° 20′ – 115° 39′ (82 J/5) Barrel Rock (boulder-rocher), Man. 52° 23′ – 97° 07′ (63 A/6) Gull Rocks (cliff-falaise), Y.T./Yuk. 62° 50′ – 136° 46′ (115 I/15)	

rock pile

DES	See **islet**	*Voir* **islet**
OBS	Rare; Man.	*Rare; Man.*
EQ		**îlot** (m.)
REL	island, rock (1)	
EX	Weasel Island Rock Pile, Man. 51° 41′ – 99° 43′ (62 O/13)	

roost

DES	See **rock (2)**	*Voir* **rock (2)**
OBS	Rare; Nfld., N.S., and Ont.	*Rare; T.-N., N.-É. et Ont.*
EQ		[**rocher** (m.)]
REL	mountain, crag, shoulder	
EX	Shag Roost, Nfld./T.-N. 47° 37′ – 54° 04′ (1 M/9) Crows Roost, N.S./N.-É. 45° 54′ – 59° 57′ (11 G/13) Gull Roost, Ont. 45° 58′ – 81° 32′ (41 H/13)	

roundabout

DES	See **pond (1)**	*Voir* **pond (1)**
OBS	Rare; Nfld.	*Rare; T.-N.*
EQ		**étang** (m.)
REL	lake, hole (2), puddle	
EX	Big Roundabout, Nfld./T.-N. 47° 29′ – 52° 44′ (1 N/7)	

route

DES	See **portage**	*Voir* **portage**
OBS	Rare; Ont. and N.W.T. Historical trails.	*Rare; Ont. et T.N.-O. Sentier d'importance historique.*
EQ		**portage** (m.)
REL	trail	
EX	Little Lakes Route, Ont. 49° 51′ – 81° 31′ (41 H/13) Pikes Portage Route, N.W.T./T.N.-O. 62° 45′ – 108° 40′ (75 K)	

rub   (Fig. 5)

DES	Smooth sloping ground on a bank, headland, or point.	*Terrain en pente douce sur une rive, un cap ou une pointe.*
OBS	Used in Nfld., commonly as "Otter Rub".	*Utilisé à T.-N., fréquemment sous la forme composée «Otter Rub».*
EQ		[**pente** (f.)]
REL	bank (2), scrape, slide (1), cape, head (1), cliff	
EX	Black Otter Rub, Nfld./T.-N. 47° 41′ – 56° 19′ (11 P/9)	

ruisseau   (m.)   (Fig. 44)

DES	*Small, natural watercourse receiving its water from a small-sized catchment basin.*	Petit cours d'eau naturel qui reçoit les eaux d'un bassin versant de petite dimension.
OBS	*Used in several provinces.*	Attesté dans plusieurs provinces.
EQ	**stream**	
REL		coulée (2), crique (1)
EX	Ruisseau Pierrot, T.N.-O./N.W.T. 61° 07′ – 112° 37′ (85 H/2) Ruisseau Daoust, Qué./Que. 45° 37′ – 74° 12′ (31 G/9) Ruisseau Jourdain, T.-N./Nfld. 52° 54′ – 66° 12′ (23 B/16)	

run   (1)   (Fig. 26, 52)

DES	Narrow water passage.	*Étroit passage d'eau.*
OBS	Used in the Atlantic Provinces and Ont.	*S'emploie dans les provinces de l'Atlantique et en Ont.*
EQ		**passage** (m.)
REL	narrows, passage, gap (2)	
EX	Frenchmans Run, Nfld./T.-N. 53° 13′ – 55° 45′ (3 E/4) Tignish Run, P.E.I./Î.-P.-É. 46° 57′ – 64° 00′ (21 I/16) Deer Island Run, Ont. 44° 51′ – 79° 42′ (31 D/13)	

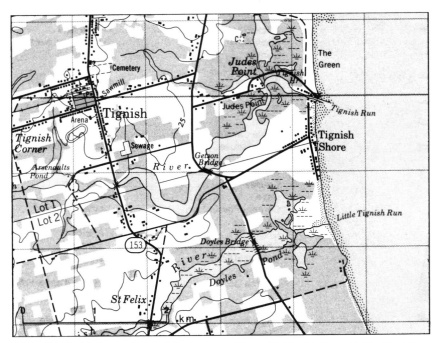

Figure 52. Tignish Run and Little Tignish Run, near Tignish, Prince Edward Island. (National Topographic System map 21 I/16 & 11 L/13; 1978)

Figure 52. Tignish Run et Little Tignish Run, près de Tignish, à l'Île-du-Prince-Édouard. (Cartes 21 I/16 et 11 L/13 du Système national de référence cartographique; 1978)

run(s) (2)   (Fig. 59)

DES	Fast-flowing section of a watercourse.	*Partie d'un cours d'eau où le courant devient plus rapide.*
OBS	Used in N.S.	*S'emploie en N.-É.*
EQ		**rapide** (m.)
REL	rapid (1), chute, race	
EX	Drawknife Run, N.S./N.-É. 44° 03′ – 65° 17′ (21 A/3)	
	Gull Lake Runs, N.S./N.-É. 44° 34′ – 65° 17′ (21 A/11)	

run (3)

DES	Small watercourse.	*Petit cours d'eau.*
OBS	Rare; N.S.	*Rare; N.-É.*
EQ		[**ruisselet** (m.)]
REL	creek (1), brook, stream	
EX	Fox Point Lake Run, N.S./N.-É. 44° 36′ – 64° 04′ (21 A/9)	

run (4)

DES	See **ridge (1)**	*Voir* **ridge (1)**
OBS	Rare; Nfld.	*Rare; T.-N.*
EQ		[**chaînon** (m.)]
REL	hill, back, edge	
EX	Long Run, Nfld./T.-N. 47° 28′ – 52° 44′ (1 N/7)	

runoff

DES	Watercourse draining from a lake.	*Cours d'eau ayant sa source dans un lac.*
OBS	Rare; N.S.	Rare; N.-É.
EQ		**décharge** (f.)
REL	outlet (1), brook	
EX	Runoff of Jordan, N.S./N.-É. 44° 05′ – 65° 18′ (21 A/3)	

runround

DES	Subsidiary channel to the main channel of watercourse.	*Ramification du chenal principal d'un cours d'eau.*
OBS	Rare; N.B.	*Rare; N.-B.*
EQ		**faux chenal** (m.)
REL	channel (2), branch, snye	
EX	Clarence Stream Runround, N.B./N.-B. 45° 20′ – 66° 59′ (21 G/7)	

S

saddle (1)

DES	See **pass (1)**	*Voir* **pass (1)**
OBS	Rare; B.C.	*Rare; C.-B.*
EQ		[**col** (m.)]
REL	col, gap (1), notch	
EX	Symphony Saddle, B.C./C.-B. 52° 06′ – 126° 09′ (93 D/1)	

saddle (2)

DES	Water passage between an island and the shore.	*Passage d'eau entre une île et la terre ferme.*
OBS	Rare; B.C.	*Rare; C.-B.*
EQ		**passage** (m.)
REL	passage, pass (2), gap (2), river (2)	
EX	Magin Saddle, B.C./C.-B. 50° 53′ – 127° 49′ (92 L/13)	

saddle (3)

DES	See **pass (4)**	*Voir* **pass (4)**
OBS	Seafloor feature. Uncommon; off the Atlantic Provinces.	*Relief sous-marin. Peu fréquent, se rencontre au large des provinces de l'Atlantique.*
EQ		[**col** (m.)]
REL		
EX	Cartwright Saddle, 54° 40′ – 55° 55′ (C.813)	

salt lake

DES	Inland body of standing water that dries in summer, leaving salt crusts.	*Nappe d'eau stagnante à l'intérieur des terres, qui s'assèche en été en laissant une croûte de sel.*
OBS	Rare; Sask.	*Rare; Sask.*
EQ		[**lac salé** (m.)]
REL	lake, slough, pothole	
EX	Dana Salt Lake, Sask. 52° 14′ – 105° 42′ (73 A/5)	

sand(s) (1)

DES	See **shoal**	*Voir* **shoal**
OBS	Rare in official names; P.E.I., Ont., B.C., and N.W.T.	*Rare dans les noms approuvés; Î.-P.-É., Ont., C.-B. et T.N.-O.*
EQ		**haut-fond** (m.)
REL	bank (1), ground (1)	
EX	Base Sand, B.C./C.-B. 54° 05′ – 130° 14′ (103 J/1) Mosquito Sands, P.E.I./Î.-P.-É. 46° 12′ – 62° 28′ (11 L/1)	

sand(s) (2)

DES	See **beach**	*Voir* **beach**
OBS	Used in Nfld. and N.S.	*En usage à T.-N. et en N.-É.*
EQ		**plage** (f.)
REL	shore	
EX	The Big Sand, N.S./N.-É. 45° 02′ – 61° 56′ (11 F/4) Salmon Cove Sands, Nfld./T.-N. 47° 47′ – 53° 10′ (1 N/14)	

sandbank(s)

DES	See **bank (2)**	*Voir* **bank (2)**
OBS	Rare in official names; Nfld. and Ont.	*Rare dans les noms approuvés; T.-N. et Ont.*
EQ		**[banc de sable** (m.)]
REL	hill, cliff, sand hills	
EX	Henry Island Sandbank, Ont. 45° 54′ – 82° 47′ (41 G/15) The Sandbanks, Nfld./T.-N. 47° 36′ – 57° 39′ (11 P/12)	

sand hills

DES	Hills rising steeply from the shoreline or from the surrounding terrain.	*Collines aux versants raides s'élevant au-dessus du littoral ou du terrain environnant.*
OBS	Used in P.E.I., Ont., Man., Sask., and Alta.	*En usage à l'Î.-P.-É., en Ont., au Man., en Sask. et en Alb.*
EQ		**dunes** (f.)
REL	hills, sandbanks, dune, beach	
EX	Cascumpec Sand Hills, P.E.I./Î.-P.-É. 46° 47′ – 64° 01′ (21 I/16) Great Sand Hills, Sask. 50° 30′ – 109° 00′ (72 K/11) Brightstone Sand Hills, Man. 50° 22′ – 96° 12′ (62 I/8)	

sault (m.)

DES	*Break in the descent of a watercourse.*	Rupture de pente d'un cours d'eau.
OBS	*In the eighteenth century, "sault", "chute d'eau", and "rapide" were used on maps to indicate similar features. Since then "sault" has been gradually replaced in everyday language by "chute". Used in Que. and N.B.*	Au XVIIIe siècle, ce générique était utilisé sur les cartes aussi bien que «chute d'eau» et «rapide». À partir du XVIIIe siècle, «sault» est progressivement remplacé par «chute» dans la langue parlée. Attesté au Qué. et au N.-B.
EQ	**falls**	
REL		cascades, chute, rapide
EX	Sault Blanc, Qué./Que. 50° 18′ – 65° 20′ (22 I/6) Deuxième Sault, N.-B./N.B. 47° 28′ – 68° 14′ (21 N/8)	

savane(s) (f.)

DES	*Low, sometimes swampy ground, characterized by abundant moss and few trees.*	Terrain bas, parfois marécageux, caractérisé par l'abondance des mousses et la rareté des arbres.
OBS	*This term of Spanish origin (sabana) is itself borrowed from the Arawak (Haiti). The definition provided here describes usage in French-speaking Canada. It differs from the general geographical meaning of a dry vegetation complex. Widely used in Que. and also noted in the Maritime Provinces.*	Ce terme d'origine espagnole (sabana) est lui-même emprunté à l'arawak (Haïti). La définition ci-dessus est le sens qu'on lui donne au Canada français. Dans le jargon des géographes, toutefois, il s'entend d'une association végétale sèche. Très répandu au Qué. et attesté aussi dans les Maritimes.
EQ	**bog**	
REL		mocauque, baissière, bogue, marais, marche, marécage, tourbière
EX	Savane du Lac aux Rats, Qué./Que. 46° 42′ – 72° 50′ (31 I/10) Les Grandes Savanes, Qué./Que. 48° 36′ – 69° 09′ (22 C/11)	

248

savannah (Fig. 53)

DES	See **meadow (1)**	*Voir* **meadow (1)**
OBS	Rare; N.S. Not a savannah in the conventional sense.	*Rare; N.-É. À ne pas confondre avec l'acception habituelle de ce mot.*
EQ		**baissière** (f.)
REL	ground (2), intervale, glade, prairie, barren, marsh	
EX	Black Georges Savannah, N.S./N.-É. 43° 41' – 65° 42' (20 P/12)	

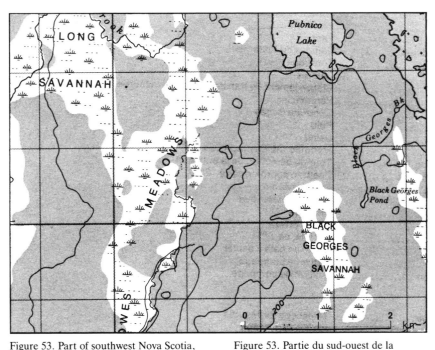

Figure 53. Part of southwest Nova Scotia, showing Long Savannah and Black Georges Savannah, Lowes Meadows, Black Georges Pond, and Black Georges Brook.
(National Topographic System map 20 P/12; 1976)

Figure 53. Partie du sud-ouest de la Nouvelle-Écosse. Entités représentées : Long Savannah et Black Georges Savannah, Lowes Meadows, Black Georges Pond et Black Georges Brook.
(Carte 20 P/12 du Système national de référence cartographique; 1976)

scarp

DES	Variant of **escarpment**.	*Variante de* **escarpment**.
OBS	Rare; Ont. and N.W.T.	*Rare; Ont. et T.N.-O.*
EQ		**escarpement** (m.)
REL	bank (2), coteau, hill, ridge (1), cliff	
EX	Kee Scarp, N.W.T./T.N.-O. 65° 19′ – 126° 43′ (96 E) Cuesta Scarp, Ont. 47° 45′ – 85° 45′ (41 N/13)	

scrape

DES	Bare place on a steep hillside.	*Zone dénudée sur le versant escarpé d'une colline.*
OBS	Only used in Nfld., where it refers to a slope usually worn by wood being slid down to the shore.	*Ne s'emploie qu'à T.-N., où il désigne habituellement une pente dénudée par le frottement des billes que l'on fait glisser jusqu'au rivage.*
EQ		[**pente dénudée** (f.)]
REL	rub, slide (1), cliff	
EX	Inside Scrape, Nfld./T.-N. 46° 50′ – 54° 11′ (1 L/16)	

sea (1)

DES	Large body of salt water.	*Vaste étendue d'eau salée.*
OBS	Used off the east and north coasts of Canada.	*S'emploie au large des côtes est et nord du Canada.*
EQ		**mer** (f.)
REL	ocean	
EX	Beaufort Sea, 72° 00′ – 141° 00′ (MCR 125) Labrador Sea, 57° 00′ – 54° 00′ (MCR 125)	

sea (2)

DES	See **pond (1)**	*Voir* **pond (1)**
OBS	Rare; Nfld.	*Rare; T.-N.*
EQ		**étang** (m.)
REL	lake, lagoon, puddle, hole (1)	
EX	Old Sea, Nfld./T.-N. 47° 17′ – 53° 13′ (1 N/6)	

seaside

DES	Narrow stretch of land bordering the sea.	*Étroite bande de terre confinant à la mer.*
OBS	Rare in official names; N.S.	*Rare dans les noms approuvés; N.-É.*
EQ		**rivage** (m.)
REL	shore, beach	
EX	Atlantic Seaside, N.S./N.-É. 44° 19′ – 64° 18′ (21 A/8)	

seat

DES	Feature fancifully shaped like a chair or stool.	*Relief dont la forme fait penser à une chaise ou à un tabouret.*
OBS	Applied to mountains and rocks. Rare; N.S., B.C., and N.W.T. Arthur Seat (B.C.) is probably a transfer name from Scotland.	*S'emploie pour des montagnes et des rochers. Rare; N.-É., C.-B. et T.N.-O. Le nom «Arthur Seat» qui fait partie de la toponymie de la C.-B. est probablement emprunté tel quel à l'Écosse.*
EQ		
REL	chair, couch	
EX	President's Seat (mountain-montagne), N.W.T./T.N.-O. 62° 39′ – 66° 46′ (25 J & G) Devils Seat (rock-rocher), N.S./N.-É. 44° 30′ – 63° 55′ (11 D/5)	

sentier (m.)

DES	*Path used for travel on foot.*	Chemin réservé pour la marche.
OBS	*Used in Que.*	Attesté au Qué.
EQ	**trail**	
REL		
EX	Sentier John-Carmen-McCallum, Qué./Que. 45° 36′ – 76° 40′ (31 F/10)	

sgurra

DES	See **hill**	*Voir* **hill**
OBS	From Gaelic term for hill. Rare; N.S.	*Du mot gaélique signifiant «colline». Rare; N.-É.*
EQ		**colline** (f.)
REL	summit, peak (1), knob	
EX	Sgurra Bhreac, N.S./N.-É. 45° 56′ – 60° 26′ (11 F/16)	

shelf (1)

DES	Feature having the appearance of a shelf.	*Accident géographique ayant l'aspect d'une plate-forme.*
OBS	Applied to shoals and glaciers. Rare; Ont. and Y.T.	*S'emploie pour des hauts-fonds et des glaciers. Rare; Ont. et Yukon.*
EQ		**[plate-forme** (f.)]
REL	ledge (1)	
EX	Middle Shelf (shoal – haut-fond), Ont. 44° 47′ – 79° 56′ (31 D/13) The Great Shelf (glacier-glacier), Y.T./Yuk. 60° 22′ – 139° 01′ (115 B & C)	

shelf (2)

DES	Seafloor zone adjacent to the continent and extending from the low-water line to a depth at which there is usually a marked increase of slope towards oceanic depths.	*Zone du fond marin adjacente au continent et s'étendant du niveau des basses mers jusqu'à la profondeur à laquelle on note habituellement une nette augmentation de la pente vers les grands fonds.*
OBS	Used off the east, west, and north coasts of Canada.	*S'emploie au large des côtes est, ouest et nord du Canada.*
EQ		**[plate-forme** (f.)**]**
REL		
EX	Scotian Shelf, 44° 00′ – 62° 30′ (C.1339A) Queen Elizabeth Shelf, 80° 30′ – 100° 00′ (C.7000)	

shingle (Fig. 54)

DES	Offshore bar of pebbles and coarse gravel.	*Barre constituée de galets et de gros graviers.*
OBS	Uncommon; Ont.	*Peu fréquent; Ont.*
EQ		**barre** (f.)
REL	bar, shoal, bank (1), ground (1), islet	
EX	Kokanongwi Shingle, Ont. 45° 56′ – 81° 33′ (C.2286)	

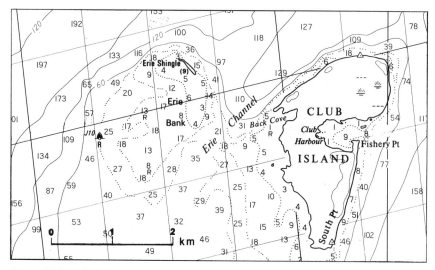

Figure 54. Erie Shingle, Erie Bank, and Erie Channel, in Georgian Bay, east of Manitoulin Island, Lake Huron, Ontario. (Canadian Hydrographic Service chart 2245; 1986)

Figure 54. Erie Shingle, Erie Bank et Erie Channel, dans la baie Georgienne, à l'est de l'île Manitoulin, lac Huron, en Ontario. (Carte 2245 du Service hydrographique du Canada; 1986)

shoal(s) (Fig. 41)

DES	Elevation of the bed of a body of water; composed of unconsolidated material and posing a hazard to surface navigation.	*Élévation du lit d'une étendue d'eau constituée de matériaux non consolidés et présentant un risque pour la navigation de surface.*
OBS	May be exposed at low water; usually applied to fishing areas. Widely used.	*Cette élévation peut découvrir à marée basse. Le générique désigne habituellement des zones de pêche. Emploi généralisé.*
EQ		**haut-fond** (m.)
REL	bank (1), ground (1)	
EX	Alexander Shoal, Nfld./T.-N. 59° 31′ – 63° 16′ (C.5450) Churchill Shoals, N.W.T./T.N.-O. 58° 52′ – 93° 45′ (C.5408)	

shore

DES	Narrow stretch of land bordering a body of water.	*Étroite bande de terre confinant à une étendue d'eau.*
OBS	Used in the Atlantic Provinces.	*En usage dans les provinces de l'Atlantique.*
EQ		**rivage** (m.)
REL	beach, seaside	
EX	Shea Shore, P.E.I./Î.-P.-É. 46° 59′ – 63° 59′ (21 I/16) Highland Shore, Nfld./T.-N. 47° 41′ – 53° 43′ (1 N/12)	

shoulder

DES	Ridge on a mountain, commonly having the appearance of a shoulder.	*Sur une montagne, élévation ayant généralement la forme d'une épaule.*
OBS	Rare; Alta.	*Rare; Alb.*
EQ		**[épaulement** (m.)]
REL	ridge (1), lump, summit, spur (1)	
EX	Woolley Shoulder, Alta./Alb. 52° 17′ – 117° 24′ (83 C/6)	

sinker

DES	Variant of **sunker**.	*Variante de **sunker**.*
OBS	Rare; N.S.	*Rare; N.-É.*
EQ		**rocher** (m.)
REL	reef, islet, sunker	
EX	Outside Sinker, N.S./N.-É. 45° 09′ – 61° 39′ (11 F/4)	

skerries

DES	Group of small rocky islands and shoals.	*Groupe d'îles rocheuses et de hauts-fonds de petites dimensions.*
OBS	Rare; Nfld. and N.W.T.	*Rare; T.-N. et T.N.-O.*
EQ		**îles** (f.)
REL	archipelago, islands, labyrinth	
EX	South Skerries, N.W.T./T.N.-O. 62° 23′ – 78° 12′ (35 K & L) Northeast Skerries, Nfld./T.-N. 49° 24′ – 53° 37′ (2 F/5)	

slide (1)   (Fig. 55)

DES	Scar and/or material from landslide or debris flow.	*Niches d'arrachement formées et (ou) matériaux transportés par des glissements de terrain, des éboulements ou des coulées.*
OBS	Uncommon in official names; Nfld., Alta., and B.C.	*Peu fréquent dans les noms approuvés; T.-N., Alb. et C.-B.*
EQ		**[glissement** (m.)]
REL	scrape, rub, bank (2), cliff	
EX	Frank Slide, Alta./Alb. 49° 35′ – 114° 24′ (82 G/9) Jeopardy Slide, B.C./C.-B. 51° 07′ – 117° 37′ (82 N/4) Redland Slide, Nfld./T.-N. 47° 24′ – 54° 15′ (1 M/8)	

slide (2)

DES	See **chute**	*Voir **chute***
OBS	Rare; Ont.	*Rare; Ont.*
EQ		**chute** (f.)
REL	run (2), rapid (1), cataract	
EX	Long Slide, Ont. 45° 52′ – 79° 58′ (31 E/13)	

Figure 55. Frank Slide, Crowsnest Pass, Alberta.
(Alberta Culture – Historic Sites Service, All Sites Brochure)

Figure 55. Frank Slide, col Crowsnest, en Alberta.
(Alberta Culture – Historic Sites Service, All Sites Brochure)

slope

DES	Gradient at the seaward edge of the continental shelf.	*Déclivité vers le large à partir de la bordure de la plate-forme continentale.*
OBS	Used for seafloor features off the east and north coasts of Canada.	*S'emploie pour des entités sousmarines au large des côtes est et nord du Canada.*
EQ		**[pente** (f.)]
REL		
EX	Scotian Slope, 43° 00′ – 61° 00′ (C.1399A) Queen Elizabeth Slope, 80° 15′ – 105° 00′ (C.7000)	

257

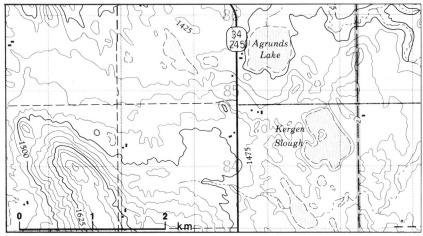

Figure 56. Kergen Slough, southwest of Portage la Prairie, Manitoba. (National Topographic System map 62 G/10; 1985)

Figure 56. Kergen Slough, au sud-ouest de Portage la Prairie, au Manitoba. (Carte 62 G/10 du Système national de référence cartographique; 1985)

slough(s) (1) (Fig. 56)

DES	Shallow water-filled or marshy depression with no external drainage.	*Dépression peu profonde remplie d'eau ou marécageuse, sans écoulement vers l'aval.*
OBS	Widely used. In the Prairies, sloughs may dry out completely during the summer.	*Emploi généralisé. Dans les Prairies, les terrains désignés par ce générique peuvent s'assécher complètement durant l'été.*
EQ		**marécage** (m.)
REL	lake, pond (1), marsh, fen, lagoon, barachois	
EX	Ardens Slough, Alta./Alb. 58° 53′ − 111° 27′ (74 L/14) Slough of Despond, Ont. 44° 46′ − 80° 58′ (41 A/15) Sheppard Sloughs, Sask. 52° 14′ − 109° 43′ (73 C/4)	

slough (2) (Fig. 57)

DES	Backwater area, usually marshy; or a meander channel cut off from the main drainage.	*Eau de retenue habituellement dans une région marécageuse; ou un chenal à méandres détaché du cours d'eau principal.*
OBS	Widely used.	*Emploi généralisé.*
EQ		**faux chenal** (m.)
REL	channel (2), snye, oxbow, pond (1), lake	
EX	Deas Slough, B.C./C.-B. 49° 07′ – 123° 04′ (92 G/3) ` Big Rat Slough, N.W.T./T.N.-O. 61° 04′ – 112° 54′ (85 H) Gwachoo Slough, Y.T./Yuk. 66° 37′ – 134° 23′ (106 L/9)	

Figure 57. A view across Six Mile Slough, at the south end of Kootenay Lake, near Creston, British Columbia. (Scott Forbes, Canadian Wildlife Service)

Figure 57. Vue du Six Mile Slough, à l'extrémité sud du lac Kootenay, près de Creston, en Colombie-Britannique. (Scott Forbes, Service canadien de la faune)

sluice

DES	Shallow, constricted, saltwater passage.	*Passage d'eau salée peu profond et resserré.*
OBS	Rare in official names; N.S.	*Rare dans les noms approuvés; N.-É.*
EQ		**passage** (m.)
REL	passage, pass (2), gap (2), narrows	
EX	Indian Sluice, N.S./N.-É. 43° 47′ – 65° 56′ (20 P/13)	

snout

DES	See **hill**	*Voir* **hill**
OBS	Rare; Nfld.	*Rare; T.-N.*
EQ		**colline** (f.)
REL	knoll (1), tolt	
EX	Peter Snout, Nfld./T.-N. 47° 54′ – 57° 56′ (11 P/13)	

snye

DES	Subsidiary channel to the main channel of a watercourse.	*Ramification secondaire du chenal principal d'un cours d'eau.*
OBS	Usually a channel with less water than the main stream. Uncommon; Ont., Alta., and N.W.T.	*Désigne habituellement une branche transportant moins d'eau que la branche principale. Peu fréquent; Ont., Alb. et T.N.-O.*
EQ		**faux chenal** (m.)
REL	channel (2), slough (2)	
EX	Back Snye, Ont. 45° 59′ – 80° 09′ (41 H/16) The Big Snye, N.W.T./T.N.-O. 61° 18′ – 117° 40′ (85 F)	

soi

DES	Saltwater basin connected to the sea.	*Bassin d'eau salée communiquant avec la mer.*
OBS	Rare; N.S.	*Rare; N.-É.*
EQ		**barachois** (m.)
REL	barachois, lagoon, pond (2)	
EX	Dover Soi, N.S./N.-É. 44° 30' – 63° 52' (11 D/5)	

sommet (m.)

DES	*The highest part of a mountain or hill.*	Partie la plus élevée d'une montagne ou d'une colline.
OBS	*General term describing features such as* pic, piton, pointu, *and* table. *Used in Que.*	Terme général qui sert à définir partiellement des phénomènes géographiques tels que «pic», «piton», «pointu» et «table». Attesté au Qué.
EQ	**summit**	
REL		tête (2)
EX	Sommet Albert Sud, Qué./Que. 48° 54' – 66° 12' (22 B/16)	

sound (1)   (Fig. 30, 38)

DES	Large body of water from which two or more inlets, arms, or channels branch off.	*Grande étendue d'eau qui se ramifie en deux ou plusieurs passages, bras ou branches.*
OBS	Used in B.C. and N.W.T.	*S'emploie en C.-B. et dans les T.N.-O.*
EQ		**détroit** (m.)
REL	strait, basin (2), channel (1)	
EX	Lancaster Sound, N.W.T./T.N.-O. 74° 13' – 84° 00' (48 E & 38 F) Milbanke Sound, B.C./C.-B. 52° 19' – 128° 33' (103 A)	

sound (2)

DES	Arm of the sea or of a lake; inlet.	*Bras d'une mer ou d'un lac; parfois synonyme de «inlet».*
OBS	Widely used.	*Emploi généralisé.*
EQ		[**bras** (m.)]
REL	arm (1), inlet (1), fiord, reach	
EX	Cumberland Sound, N.W.T./T.N.-O. 65° 10′ – 65° 30′ (26 H) Parry Sound, Ont. 45° 22′ – 80° 08′ (41 H/8) Howe Sound, B.C./C.-B. 49° 25′ – 123° 23′ (92 G/6)	

sound (3)

DES	See **deadwater**	*Voir* **deadwater**
OBS	Rare; N.S.	*Rare; N.-É.*
EQ		
REL	steady (1)	
EX	Chalk Line Sound, N.S./N.-É. 43° 39′ – 65° 35′ (20 P/12)	

spindle

DES	See **spit**	*Voir* **spit**
OBS	Rare; N.S.	*Rare; N.-É.*
EQ		**flèche** (f.)
REL	point (1), peninsula	
EX	Johns Island Spindle, N.S./N.-É. 43° 33′ – 65° 47′ (20 P/12)	

spire(s) (Fig. 58)

DES	Tall, slender, sharp-pointed peak; or a mountain.	*Pic effilé; montagne.*
OBS	Used in B.C. and Y.T.	*S'emploie en C.-B. et au Yukon.*
EQ		**[flèche** (f.)]
REL	needle, peak (1), point (2), pinnacle (1)	
EX	Drury Spire, Y.T./Yuk. 62° 20′ – 134° 26′ (105 L) Fire Spires, B.C./C.-B. 49° 46′ – 122° 26′ (92 G/16)	

spit

DES	Long, low, narrow projection of unconsolidated material extending into a body of water.	*Accumulation de matériaux non consolidés, de forme allongée, basse et étroite, qui s'avance en saillie dans une étendue d'eau.*
OBS	Deposition feature; subject to modification by water action. Widely used.	*Forme de dépôt pouvant être modifiée par l'action des vagues. Emploi généralisé.*
EQ		**flèche** (f.)
REL	point (1), peninsula, bar, hook	
EX	Avadlek Spit, Y.T./Yuk. 69° 34′ – 139° 17′ (117 D) Boughton Spit, P.E.I./Î.-P.-É. 46° 12′ – 62° 27′ (11 L/1)	

spot

DES	Small shoal.	*Petit haut-fond.*
OBS	Generally refers to a small fishing ground; Nfld. and N.S.	*Désigne généralement une petite zone de pêche; T.-N. et N.-É.*
EQ		**haut-fond** (m.)
REL	bank (1), ground (1), patch	
EX	Paddy Outside Spot, Nfld./T.-N. 49° 33′ – 55° 20′ (2 E/11) Georges Spot, N.S./N.-É. 44° 44′ – 62° 38′ (11 D/10)	

Figure 58. Snowpatch Spire, in the Purcell Mountains, west of Radium Hot Springs, British Columbia.
(Glen Boles)

Figure 58. Snowpatch Spire, dans les monts Purcell, à l'ouest de Radium Hot Springs, en Colombie-Britannique.
(Glen Boles)

spout

DES	Fast-flowing watercourse, rapids, or falls.	*Cours d'eau au courant rapide, rapides ou chutes.*
OBS	Uncommon; Nfld. and N.S.	*Peu fréquent; T.-N. et N.-É.*
EQ		
REL	chute, race, rapid (1), slide (2)	
EX	Zinck Spout, N.S./N.-É. 44° 38′ – 64° 48′ (21 A/10) The Spout, Nfld./T.-N. 47° 33′ – 52° 41′ (1 N/10)	

spring(s)

DES	Site of a natural flow of water issuing from the ground.	*Issue naturelle par laquelle une eau souterraine s'écoule à la surface du sol.*
OBS	Widely used.	*Emploi généralisé.*
EQ		[**source** (f.)]
REL	hotspring	
EX	Bratton Spring, Alta./Alb. 49° 44′ – 113° 51′ (82 H/12) Calder Springs, Sask. 51° 42′ – 105° 22′ (72 P/11)	

spur (1)

DES	Subsidiary ridge extending laterally from a mountain or ridge.	*Ramification latérale d'un ensemble montagneux ou rocheux.*
OBS	Rare in official names; Ont. and B.C.	*Rare dans les noms approuvés; Ont. et C.-B.*
EQ		[**éperon** (m.)]
REL	ridge (1), shoulder	
EX	Entiako Spur, B.C./C.-B. 53° 13′ – 125° 17′ (93 F/3)	

spur (2)

DES	Subordinate elevation, ridge, or rise projecting outward from a larger undersea feature.	*Élévation dorsale ou massif qui est le prolongement d'un ensemble sous-marin plus vaste.*
OBS	Used for seafloor features off the east coast of Canada.	*S'emploie pour des reliefs sousmarins au large de la côte est du Canada.*
EQ		**éperon** (m.)
REL	peak (2), pinnacle (2)	
EX	Sackville Spur, 48° 15′ – 46° 30′ (C.802)	

steady (steadies) (1)

DES	Still water of a brook or river, not apparently affected by stream flow.	*Partie calme d'un ruisseau ou d'une rivière, où l'eau ne semble pas troublée par le courant.*
OBS	Used in Nfld.	*Utilisé à T.-N.*
EQ		**fosse** (f.)
REL	deadwater	
EX	Alder Steady, Nfld./T.-N. 49° 13′ – 57° 47′ (12 H/4) Big Steadies, Nfld./T.-N. 48° 01′ – 53° 13′ (2 C/3)	

steady (steadies) (2)

DES	See **gully (3)**	*Voir* **gully (3)**
OBS	Used in Nfld.	*Utilisé à T.-N.*
EQ		**marais** (m.)
REL	pond (1), marsh, water	
EX	Indian Steady, Nfld./T.-N. 50° 41′ – 57° 14′ (12 I/11) Goose Steadies, Nfld./T.-N. 47° 18′ – 53° 17′ (1 N/6)	

steps

DES	Feature having the appearance of steps.	*Accident géographique ayant la forme d'un escalier.*
OBS	Applied to slopes and falls. Used in N.B. and Alta. as "Giant(s) Steps".	*S'emploie pour des talus et des chutes. Relevé en N.-B. et en Alb. dans le toponyme «Giant(s) Steps».*
EQ		
REL		
EX	Giant Steps (falls-chutes), Alta./Alb. 51° 21' – 116° 14' (82 N/8) Giants Steps (hill-colline), N.B./N.-B. 45° 09' – 66° 13' (21 G/1)	

still

DES	See **pond (1)**	*Voir* **pond (1)**
OBS	Rare; N.S.	*Rare; N.-É.*
EQ		**étang** (m.)
REL	puddle, hole (2)	
EX	Long Still, N.S./N.-É. 45° 12' – 62° 45' (11 E/2)	

stillwater(s) (Fig. 59)

DES   See **deadwater**   *Voir* **deadwater**

OBS   Used in N.S. and N.B.   *S'emploie en N.-É. et au N.-B.*

EQ

REL   steady

EX   Ponwauk Stillwater, N.B./N.-B. 45° 19′ – 67° 27′ (21 G/6)
       Costley Stillwaters, N.S./N.-É. 45° 19′ – 61° 44′ (11 F/5)

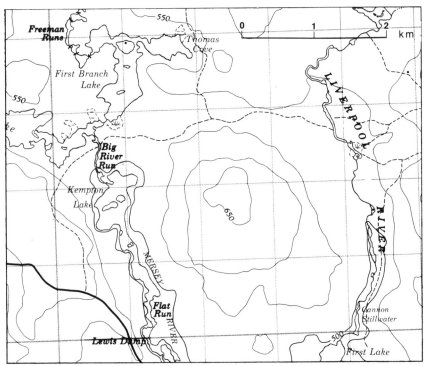

Figure 59. Mersey River and Liverpool River, south of Bridgetown, Nova Scotia, showing Cannon Stillwater, Lewis Dump, Freeman Runs, Big River Run and Flat Run.
(National Topographic System map 21 A/11; 1976 with added information)

Figure 59. Rivières Mersey et Liverpool, au sud de Bridgetown, en Nouvelle-Écosse. Entités représentées : Cannon Stillwater, Lewis Dump, Freeman Runs, Big River Run et Flat Run.
(Carte 21 A/11 du Système national de référence cartographique; 1976 avec renseignements supplémentaires)

stone(s)

DES	Small rock in water or on land.	*Masse rocheuse de petite taille dans l'eau ou sur terre.*
OBS	Uncommon; Nfld., N.S., N.B., Ont., and B.C.	*Peu fréquent, se rencontre à T.-N., en N.-É., en N.-B., en Ont. et en C.-B.*
EQ		**rocher** (m.)
REL	rock (1), reef	
EX	The Rocking Stone, N.S./N.-É. 44° 36' – 63° 37' (11 D/12) Plum Stone, Ont. 44° 33' – 78° 09' (31 D/9) Cook Stone, Nfld./T.-N. 47° 41' – 59° 17' (11 O/11) Dog Stones, Nfld./T.-N. 49° 36' – 55° 56' (2 E/12)	

strait(s)

DES	Passage, usually navigable, connecting two larger bodies of water.	*Passage, généralement navigable, reliant deux masses d'eau plus importantes.*
OBS	Widely used.	*Emploi généralisé.*
EQ		**détroit** (m.)
REL	passage, pass (2), narrows, channel (1), sound (1)	
EX	Cabot Strait, N.S./N.-É. 47° 30' – 59° 45' (11 O) Hudson Strait, N.W.T./T.N.-O. 62° 00' – 70° 00' (25 L) Juan de Fuca Strait, B.C./C.-B. 48° 15' – 124° 00' (92 B/5) Loon Straits, Man. 51° 32' – 96° 36' (62 P/10)	

strand

DES	See **shore**	*Voir* **shore**
OBS	Rare; Nfld.	*Rare; T.-N.*
EQ		**riage** (m.)
REL	beach, seaside	
EX	Porcupine Strand, Nfld./T.-N. 53° 53' – 57° 14' (13 H/14)	

stream   (Fig. 35)

DES	Watercourse, smaller than a river.	*Cours d'eau de plus petite dimension qu'une rivière.*
OBS	Common in the Atlantic Provinces; also isolated examples in Ont., Man., and B.C.	*Commun dans les provinces de l'Atlantique; se trouve aussi dans quelques toponymes de l'Ont., du Man. et de la C.-B.*
EQ		**ruisseau** (m.)
REL	creek (1), brook, river	
EX	Baltimore Stream, N.B./N.-B. 45° 57' – 66° 09' (21 G/16) Kemp Stream, B.C./C.-B. 48° 22' – 123° 46' (92 B/5)	

stretch

DES	See **reach**	*Voir* **reach**
OBS	Uncommon; N.B. and Ont.	*Peu fréquent; N.-B. et Ont.*
EQ		[**passage** (m.)]
REL	channel (1)	
EX	Long Lookum Stretch, N.B./N.-B. 47° 43' – 66° 47' (21 O/10) Manitou Stretch, Ont. 49° 09' – 93° 07' (52 F/3)	

sugarloaf, sugar loaf (sugar loaves)

DES	Conical hill with rounded top.	*Colline de forme conique et au sommet arrondi.*
OBS	Used in Nfld., N.S., and Ont.	*S'emploie à T.-N., en N.-É. et en Ont.*
EQ		**[pain de sucre** (m.)]
REL	hill, cone, pingo, mound, knoll (1)	
EX	St. Mary's Sugarloaf, Nfld./T.-N. 47° 03' – 53° 55' (1 N/4) Little Sugar Loaf, Nfld./T.-N. 50° 52' – 56° 59' (12 I/15) Sugar Loaves, Nfld./T.-N. 49° 38' – 56° 00' (12 H/9)	

summit

DES	High point of a mountain or hill.	*Point culminant d'une montagne ou d'une colline.*
OBS	Widely used.	*Emploi généralisé.*
EQ		**sommet** (m.)
REL	peak (1), brow, mountain, hill, col	
EX	Keno Summit, Y.T./Yuk. 63° 57' – 135° 13' (105 M) Arbutus Summit, B.C./C.-B. 49° 13' – 124° 53' (92 F/2)	

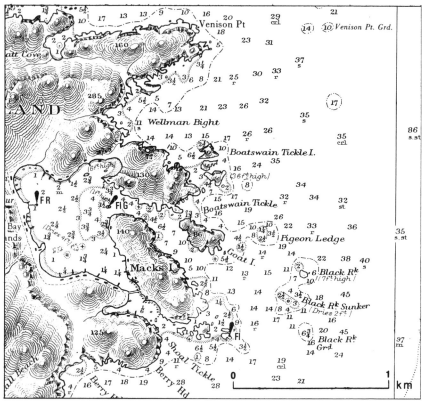

Figure 60. West coast of Notre Dame Bay, Newfoundland, showing Black Rock Sunker, Wellman Bight, Boatswain Tickle and Shoal Tickle, Black Rock Ground, and Pigeon Ledge. (Canadian Hydrographic Service chart 4592; 1983)

Figure 60. Côte ouest de la baie Notre Dame, à Terre-Neuve. Entités représentées : Black Rock Sunker, Wellman Bight, Boatswain Tickle et Shoal Tickle, Black Rock Ground et Pigeon Ledge. (Carte 4592 du Service hydrographique du Canada; 1983)

sunker (Fig. 60)

DES	Submerged rock over which the sea breaks.	*Rocher submergé sur lequel les vagues déferlent.*
OBS	Used in Nfld. and N.S.	*Utilisé à T.-N. et en N.-É.*
EQ		**rocher** (m.)
REL	reef, islet, sinker	
EX	Kelpy Sunker, Nfld./T.-N. 47° 11′ – 54° 51′ (1 M/2) Anchor Cove Sunkers, Nfld./T.-N. 47° 23′ – 54° 30′ (1 M/7)	

swale(s)

DES	Shallow marshy depression.	*Dépression marécageuse peu profonde.*
OBS	Rare; N.S., Ont., and Man.	*Rare; N.-É., Ont. et Man.*
EQ		**baissière** (f.)
REL	marsh, swamp, fen, bog, barren	
EX	Willow Swale, Man. 49° 01′ – 99° 56′ (62 G/4) Big Swales, N.S./N.-É. 45° 32′ – 63° 38′ (11 E/12)	

swamp

DES	Low-lying land, permanently saturated with water and usually having trees and shrubs.	*Terre basse, constamment imprégnée d'eau et généralement parsemée d'arbres et d'arbustes.*
OBS	Used in the Maritime Provinces, Ont., Man., and B.C.	*S'emploie dans les Maritimes, en Ont., au Man. et en C.-B.*
EQ		**marécage** (m.)
REL	marsh, bog, fen, muskeg	
EX	Long Swamp, P.E.I./Î.-P.-É. 46° 27′ – 63° 56′ (11 L/5) Brokenhead Swamp, Man. 49° 44′ – 96° 20′ (62 H/9)	

t

table

DES	A flat-topped area of land.	*Étendue de terrain à surface plane.*
OBS	Rare in official names; Nfld.	*Rare dans les noms approuvés; T.-N.*
EQ		**table** (f.)
REL	plateau	
EX	Devils Dancing Table, Nfld./T.-N. 47° 46′ – 56° 09′ (11 P/16)	

table (f.)

DES	*Mountain top with a flat surface.*	Sommet de montagne à surface plane.
OBS	*Descriptive term used in Que.*	Descriptif attesté au Qué.
EQ	**table**	
REL		pic, piton, pointu
EX	Table à Roland, Qué./Que. 48° 31′ – 64° 14′ (22 A/9)	

tail

DES	A tail-shaped feature.	*Relief en forme de queue.*
OBS	Applied to rocks, reefs, and points. Uncommon; Atlantic Provinces and Ont.	*S'emploie pour des rochers, des récifs et des pointes. Peu usité; provinces de l'Atlantique et Ont.*
EQ		
REL	queue	
EX	Swallow Tail (point-pointe), N.B./N.-B. 44° 46′ – 66° 44′ (21 B/15) Tail of the Wolf (reef-récif), Nfld./T.-N. 50° 51′ – 57° 11′ (C.4680) Serpent Tail (rock-rocher), Nfld./T.-N. 49° 41′ – 54° 49′ (C.4548)	

tarn(s)   (Fig. 61)

DES	Small mountain lake.	*Petit lac de montagne.*
OBS	Used in Nfld. and B.C.	*S'emploie à T.-N. et en C.-B.*
EQ		**lac** (m.)
REL	lake, pond (1), puddle, hole (2)	
EX	Grapeblue Tarn, Nfld./T.-N. 58° 55′ – 63° 45′ (14 L/13)	
	Crystal Tarns, B.C./C.-B. 50° 07′ – 122° 21′ (92 J/1)	

Figure 61. Torngat Mountains, Newfoundland (Labrador), showing several tarns (e.g. Grapeblue Tarn), Western Glacier, Snowbridge Gorge, and Selamiut Tower.
(National Air Photo Library, A25268-69; 1979)

Figure 61. Monts Torngat, Terre-Neuve (Labrador). Entités représentées : plusieurs lacs de montagne (dont le Grapeblue Tarn), Western Glacier, Snowbridge Gorge et Selamiut Tower.
(Photothèque nationale de l'air, A25268-69; 1979)

275

tavern

DES	See **pond (1)**	*Voir* **pond (1)**
OBS	Rare; Nfld.	*Rare; T.-N.*
EQ		**étang** (m.)
REL	lake, hole (2)	
EX	North Shoe Tavern, Nfld./T.-N. 47° 02′ – 53° 08′ (1 N/3)	

terrace

DES	Relatively flat, horizontal, or gently inclined surface, sometimes long and narrow; bounded by a steeper ascending slope on one side and by a steeper descending slope on the opposite side.	*Surface relativement plane, horizontale ou à pente douce, parfois allongée et étroite, bordée de part et d'autre par des talus plus inclinés, respectivement ascendant et descendant.*
OBS	Rare; N.W.T.	*Rare; T.N.-O.*
EQ		**terrasse** (f.)
RL	bench, ledge (2)	
EX	Hottes Terrace, N.W.T./T.N.-O. 80° 57′ – 78° 40′ (340 A)	

terrasse (f.)

DES	*Shelf-like platform.*	Plate-forme surélevée.
OBS	*Used in Que.*	Attesté au Qué.
EQ	**terrace**	
REL		
EX	Terrasse Katjik, Qué./Que. 58° 04′ – 68° 21′ (24 K/1)	

tête (f.) (1)

DES	*See* **cap**	Voir **cap**
OBS	*Used in Que.*	Attesté au Qué.
EQ	**head (1)**	
REL		nez, pointe, promontoire
EX	Tête Sheldrake, Qué./Que. 50° 16′ – 64° 55′ (22 I/7)	

tête (f.) (2)

DES	*See* **sommet**	Voir **sommet**
OBS	*Used in Alta. and N.W.T.*	Attesté en Alb. et dans les T.N.-O.
EQ	**head (2)**	
REL		sommet
EX	Tête Roche, Alb./Alta. 52° 53′ – 118° 34′ (83 D/5) Tête Blanche, T.N.-O./N.W.T. 66° 46′ – 65° 09′ (26 I)	

thoroughfare (Fig. 62)

DES	Narrow channel joining two water bodies.	*Chenal étroit mettant en communication deux étendues d'eau.*
OBS	Used in Nfld. and N.B.	*S'emploie à T.-N. et au N.-B.*
EQ		**chenal** (m.)
REL	channel (2), passage, pass (2), tickle, gut, fare, chokey	
EX	Sugar Island Thoroughfare, N.B./N.-B. 45° 59′ – 66° 48′ (21 G/15)	

Figure 62. Part of the Saint John River valley above Fredericton, New Brunswick, showing Keswick Island Thoroughfare and Sugar Island Thoroughfare, Burpee Bar, The Gut, Pickards Intervale, Sugar Island Padou and Pickards Padou.
(Department of Natural Resources and Energy, New Brunswick, 6305-54; 1963)

Figure 62. Partie de la vallée de la rivière Saint-Jean, en amont de Fredericton, au Nouveau-Brunswick. Entités représentées : Keswick Island Thoroughfare et Sugar Island Thoroughfare, Burpee Bar, The Gut, Pickards Intervale, Sugar Island Padou et Pickards Padou.
(Ministère des Ressources naturelles et de l'Énergie, Nouveau-Brunswick, 6305-54; 1963)

278

throughlet

DES	See **channel (1)**	*Voir* **channel (1)**
OBS	Rare; N.W.T.	*Rare; T.N.-O.*
EQ		**chenal** (m.)
REL	passage, pass (2), tickle, gut	
EX	Hurin Throughlet, N.W.T./T.N.-O. 63° 58′ – 78° 00′ (35 N & M)	

thrum(s)

DES	Rock or small island.	*Rocher ou petite île.*
OBS	Uncommon; N.S.	*Peu fréquent; N.-É.*
EQ		**rocher** (m.)
REL	rock (1), islet, island, thrumcap	
EX	Bald Thrum, N.S./N.-É. 43° 32′ – 65° 36′ (20 P/12) Bear Point Thrums, N.S./N.-É. 43° 28′ – 65° 40′ (20 P/5)	

thrumcap, thrum cap

DES	Variant of **thrum**.	*Variante de* **thrum**.
OBS	Uncommon; N.S.	*Peu fréquent; N.-É.*
EQ		**rocher** (m.)
REL	rock (1), islet	
EX	Big Thrumcap, N.S./N.-É. 45° 35′ – 63° 30′ (11 D/12) Little Thrum Cap, N.S./N.-É. 43° 49′ – 66° 08′ (20 O/16)	

thumb

DES	Feature having the appearance of a thumb.	*Relief dont la forme rappelle un pouce.*
OBS	Applied to mountains, hills, and points. Rare; N.S., Alta., B.C., and N.W.T.	*S'emploie pour des montagnes, des collines et des pointes. Rare; N.-É., Alb., C.-B. et T.N.-O.*
EQ		
REL	finger	
EX	Devils Thumb (mountain-montagne), Alta./Alb. 51° 25′ – 116° 15′ (82 N/8) Churchill's Thumb (hill-colline), N.W.T./T.N.-O. 63° 30′ – 67° 53′ (25 O) Teachers Thumb (point-pointe), N.S./N.-É. 43° 30′ – 65° 34′ (20 P/12)	

tickle(s)   (Fig. 60)

DES	Narrow stretch of saltwater; usually with hazardous tides, currents, and rocks.	*Étroite bande d'eau salée, où les marées, les courants et les rochers rendent la navigation périlleuse.*
OBS	Used in Nfld; rare in N.S. and N.W.T.	*S'emploie à T.-N.; se rencontre aussi, mais plus rarement, en N.-É. et dans les T.N.-O.*
EQ		**passage** (m.)
REL	channel (1), narrows, rip (2), thoroughfare, inlet (1)	
EX	Cut Throat Tickle, Nfld./T.-N. 54° 29′ – 57° 06′ (13 I/6) Leading Tickles, Nfld./T.-N. 49° 30′ – 55° 26′ (2 E/11)	

tilt

DES	Variant of **tolt**.	*Variante de **tolt**.*
OBS	Rare; Nfld.	*Rare; T.-N.*
EQ		**buttereau** (m.)
REL	knoll (1), hill, knob, hummock	
EX	Fosses Tilt, Nfld./T.-N. 47° 51′ – 53° 24′ (1 N/14)	

tolt

DES	Prominent rounded summit rising above the surrounding country.	*Sommet de forme arrondie qui s'élève au-dessus du relief environnant.*
OBS	Used in Nfld.	*S'emploie à T.-N.*
EQ		**buttereau** (m.)
REL	knoll (1), hill, knob, hummock, tilt	
EX	Snooks Tolt, Nfld./T.-N. 47° 44′ – 54° 58′ (1 M/10)	

tongue

DES	See **spit**	*Voir* **spit**
OBS	Rare; B.C.	*Rare; C.-B.*
EQ		**flèche** (f.)
REL	point (1), peninsula	
EX	Ripple Tongue, B.C./C.-B. 54° 58′ – 129° 56′ (103 I/13)	

tooth (teeth)

DES	Feature having the appearance of a tooth.	*Relief dont la forme rappelle une dent.*
OBS	Applied to rocks, islands, and reefs. Rare; Nfld., Ont., and N.W.T.	*S'emploie pour des rochers, des îles et des récifs. Rare; T.-N., Ont. et T.N.-O.*
EQ		
REL	fang, point (2)	
EX	Parker Tooth (rock-rocher), Nfld./T.-N. 49° 40′ – 55° 46′ (2 E/12) The Tooth (island-île), Ont. 45° 56′ – 82° 13′ (41 G/16) Alligators Teeth (reef-récif), N.W.T./T.N.-O. 63° 27′ – 68° 02′ (C.7127)	

topsail (Fig. 63)

DES	See **hill**	*Voir* **hill**
OBS	Uncommon; Nfld.	*Peu fréquent; T.-N.*
EQ		**colline** (f.)
REL	knoll, tolt, summit, uplands	
EX	Mizzen Topsail, Nfld./T.-N. 49° 06′ – 56° 37′ (12 H/2) Gaff Topsail, Nfld./T.-N. 49° 08′ – 56° 38′ (12 H/2)	

tourbière (f.)

DES	*Moist environment characterized by partial decomposition of plant matter that leads to the formation of peat.*	Milieu humide caractérisé par une décomposition partielle des végétaux qui amène la formation de tourbe.
OBS	*Used in Que.*	Attesté au Qué.
EQ	[peat bog]	
REL		baissière, bogue, marais, marche, marécage, mocauque, savane
EX	Tourbière Smith, Qué./Que. 46° 45′ – 70° 59′ (21 L/15)	

tower(s) (Fig. 36, 61)

DES	Feature having the appearance of a tower.	*Relief ayant la forme d'une tour.*
OBS	Applied to mountains, peaks, hills, and sea stacks. Used in Alta., B.C., N.W.T., and Y.T.	*S'emploie pour des montagnes, des pics, des collines et d'autres hauteurs sous-marines. Relevé en Alb., en C.-B., dans les T.N.-O. et au Yukon.*
EQ		
REL	crag, point (2), castle, ramparts, fortress	
EX	Caswall Tower, N.W.T./T.N.-O. 74° 42′ – 91° 12′ (58 E) Tower of Babel, Alta./Alb. 51° 19′ – 116° 10′ (82 N/8) Leaning Towers, B.C./C.-B. 49° 58′ – 116° 35′ (82 F/15)	

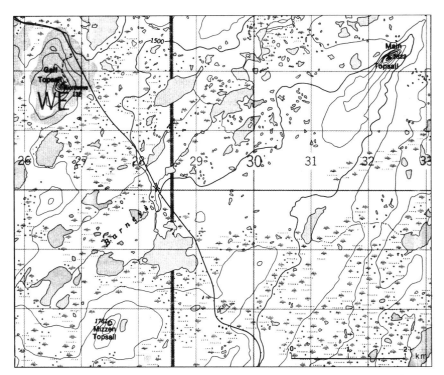

Figure 63. Gaff Topsail, Main Topsail, and
Mizzen Topsail, east of Deer Lake,
Newfoundland.
(National Topographic System map
12 H/2; 1973)

Figure 63. Gaff Topsail, Main Topsail et
Mizzen Topsail, à l'est de Deer Lake, à
Terre-Neuve.
(Carte 12 H/2 du Système national de
référence cartographique; 1973)

trail

DES	Footpath or track.	*Piste ou sentier.*
OBS	Officially named examples in Sask., Alta., and Y.T.	*Se rencontre dans des noms officiels en Sask., en Alb. et au Yukon.*
EQ		**sentier** (m.)
REL	portage, route	
EX	Conservative Trail, Y.T./Yuk. 63° 40′ – 136° 25′ (115 P) 56 Trail, Sask. 53° 52′ – 106° 26′ (73 G/16)	

trap

DES	See **pond (1)**	*Voir* **pond (1)**
OBS	Rare; N.S.	*Rare; N.-É.*
EQ		**mare** (f.)
REL	hole (2), puddle, lake	
EX	Cooper Trap, N.S./N.-É. 43° 57′ – 65° 08′ (20 P/14)	

trench

DES	Large-scale elongated depression between mountain ranges.	*Vaste dépression de forme allongée entre des chaînes de montagnes.*
OBS	Few officially named examples; B.C. and Y.T.	*Rare dans les noms approuvés; C.-B. et Yukon.*
EQ		[**fossé** (m.)]
REL	valley (1), canyon	
EX	Rocky Mountain Trench, B.C./C.-B. 54° 30′ – 122° 30′ (93 NE) Shakwak Trench, Y.T./Yuk. 61° 15′ – 138° 40′ (115 G & F)	

trou (m.) (1)

DES	*Small cove.*	Petite anse.
OBS	*Used in Que.*	Attesté au Qué.
EQ	**hole (1)**	
REL		anse, baie, crique (2)
EX	Trou Saint-Patrice, Qué./Que. 46° 51′ – 71° 02′ (21 L/14)	

trou (m.) (2)

DES	*Deep opening in the ground.*	Ouverture profonde à la surface du sol.
OBS	*Used in Que.*	Attesté au Qué.
EQ	[**hole**]	
REL		
EX	Trou des Guillemots, Qué./Que. 48° 29′ – 64° 09′ (22 A/8)	

trough

DES	Long depression of the seafloor, characteristically flat-bottomed and steep-sided.	*Dépression allongée du fond de la mer, habituellement caractérisée par un fond plat et des versants abrupts.*
OBS	Uncommon; B.C. and N.W.T.	*Peu fréquent; C.-B. et T.N.-O.*
EQ		[**dépression** (f.)]
REL	deeps	
EX	Berkeley Trough, N.W.T./T.N.-O. 76° 57′ – 99° 40′ (C.7078) Ballenas Trough, B.C./C.-B. 49° 15′ – 123° 43′ (C.3577)	

tuck

DES	Clump of stunted trees or scrub.	*Groupe d'arbres rabougris ou broussailles.*
OBS	Used in Nfld.	*S'emploie à T.-N.*
EQ		**bosquet** (m.)
REL	woods, bluff (2), grove	
EX	Doyles Tuck, Nfld./T.-N. 47° 05′ – 54° 03′ (1 M/1)	

turn(s)

DES	See **bend**	*Voir* **bend**
OBS	Uncommon; N.B. and Man. Turn of the Bald Head (Nfld.) is a cove.	*Peu fréquent; N.-B. et Man. Le Turn of the Bald Head (T.-N.) est en fait une anse.*
EQ		**courbe** (f.)
REL	elbow, oxbow	
EX	Davis Turn, N.B./N.-B. 46° 10′ – 65° 54′ (21 I/4) Crooked Turn, Man. 53° 57′ – 97° 51′ (63 H/13) Round Turns, N.B./N.-B. 46° 11′ – 65° 41′ (21 I/4)	

tusk(s)   (Fig. 21)

DES	Steep-sided peak.	*Pic aux versants abrupts.*
OBS	Uncommon; B.C.	*Peu fréquent; C.-B.*
EQ		**pic** (m.)
REL	peak (1), spire, fang, tower	
EX	The Black Tusk, B.C./C.-B. 49° 58′ – 123° 03′ (92 G/14) Walrus Tusks, B.C./C.-B. 52° 14′ – 126° 11′ (93 D/1)	

U

uplands

DES	Area of elevated terrain.	*Étendue de terrain élevée.*
OBS	Few officially named examples; Sask. and Y.T.	*Rare dans les noms approuvés; Sask. et Yukon.*
EQ		[**hautes-terres** (f.)]
REL	mountains, hills, highlands, plateau, range	
EX	Touchwood Uplands, Sask. 51° 15′ – 103° 45′ (62 M/5) Burwash Uplands, Y.T./Yuk. 61° 20′ – 139° 20′ (115 G & F)	

V

vale

DES	Variant of **valley (1)**.	*Variante de* **valley (1)**.
OBS	Rare; Nfld. and N.W.T.	*Rare; T.-N. et T.N.-O.*
EQ		**vallée** (f.)
REL	ravine, gully (1), hollow	
EX	Black Rock Vale, N.W.T./T.N.-O. 81° 48′ – 67° 20′ (120 C & D) Vale of Cirques, Nfld./T.-N. 58° 57′ – 63° 35′ (14 L/13)	

vallée (f.)

DES	*Elongated depression bounded by slopes and generally occupied by a watercourse or other body of water.*	Dépression allongée délimitée par deux versants et généralement occupée par un cours d'eau ou une nappe d'eau.
OBS	*A* vallée *is much larger than a* ravin, *and is not necessarily V-shaped. The related terms listed all indicate an elongated depression usually with a stream flowing through. Used in Que.*	La vallée est beaucoup plus grande que le ravin et n'est pas forcément en forme de V. Les termes semblables retenus désignent tous une dépression allongée permettant le passage d'un cours d'eau. Attesté au Qué.
EQ	**valley (1)**	
REL		canyon, coulée (1), gorge, ravin, ravine, rigwash
EX	Vallée des Castors, Qué./Que. 46° 11′ – 74° 34′ (31 J/2)	

Figure 64. Pemberton Valley and Lillooet River, British Columbia, with Coast Mountains beyond. (Glenn Woodsworth)

Figure 64. Pemberton Valley et Lillooet River, en Colombie-Britannique, avec la chaîne Côtière en arrière-plan. (Glenn Woodsworth)

valley (1)   (Fig. 64)

DES	Long relatively narrow depression, commonly containing a river or other water feature.	*Dépression de forme allongée et relativement étroite, souvent parcourue par un cours d'eau.*
OBS	Widely used, but not common in official names. Name usually taken from the watercourse in the valley. Particularly in B.C., named valleys are usually associated with settlement.	*Emploi généralisé; peu fréquent, cependant, dans les noms approuvés. En règle générale, la vallée prend le nom du cours d'eau qui l'arrose. En C.-B., en particulier, les vallées ayant un nom sont généralement associées à l'habitat humain.*
EQ		**vallée** (f.)
REL	ravine, gully (1), gulch (1), hollow, coulee, canyon, gorge, vale	
EX	Big Muddy Valley, Sask. 49° 03′ – 104° 51′ (72 H/2) Pemberton Valley, B.C./C.-B. 50° 30′ – 123° 00′ (92 J) Valley of Diamonds, N.B./N.-B. 45° 17′ – 66° 24′ (21 G/8)	

valley (2)

DES	Relatively shallow wide depression of the seafloor, usually with a bottom having a continuous gradient.	*Dépression large et relativement peu profonde du fond de la mer, dont le thalweg présente habituellement une pente continue.*
OBS	Used off east, west, and north coasts of Canada.	*S'emploie au large des côtes est, ouest et nord du Canada.*
EQ		[**vallée** (f.)]
REL	basin (1)	
EX	Shediac Valley, 47° 20′ – 64° 25′ (C.801)	

vault (Fig. 6, 31)

DES	See **ravine**	*Voir* **ravine**
OBS	Used in N.S.	*S'emploie en N.-É.*
EQ		**ravin** (m.)
REL	valley (1), gully (1), gulch (1)	
EX	Church Vault, N.S./N.-É. 45° 09′ – 64° 44′ (21 H/2)	

view

DES	See **lookout**	*Voir* **lookout**
OBS	Rare; N.W.T.	*Rare; T.N.-O.*
EQ		[**belvédère** (m.)]
REL	summit, brow, head (1)	
EX	The Grand View, N.W.T./T.N.-O. 66° 48′ – 130° 10′ (106 J)	

volcanoes (Fig. 65)

DES Hills related to volcanic activity. *Collines associées à une activité volcanique.*

OBS Rare; B.C. *Rare; C.-B.*

EQ **[volcans** (m.)]

REL cone, hill, crater

EX Flourmill Volcanoes, B.C./C.-B. 52° 04′ – 120° 18′ (93 A/1)

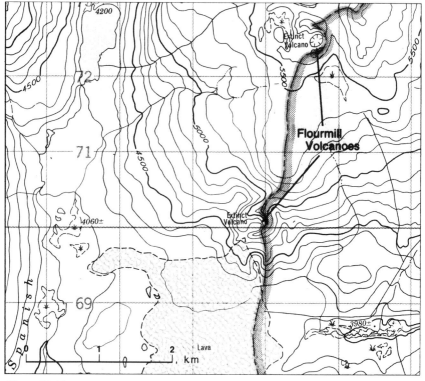

Figure 65. Flourmill Volcanoes, in the Quesnel Highland, east of Williams Lake, British Columbia.
(National Topographic System map 93 A/1; 1973)

Figure 65. Flourmill Volcanoes, dans le massif Quesnel, à l'est de Williams Lake, en Colombie-Britannique.
(Carte 93 A/1 du Système national de référence cartographique; 1973)

W

wall (Fig. 66)

DES	Steep rock face.	*Façade rocheuse à pente raide.*
OBS	Used in Alta. and B.C.	*S'emploie en Alb. et en C.-B.*
EQ		[**muraille** (f.)]
REL	bluff (1), cliff, ramparts	
EX	Weeping Wall, Alta./Alb. 52° 10′ – 117° 00′ (83 C/3) The Chinese Wall, B.C./C.-B. 50° 54′ – 117° 25′ (82 K/14) Wall of Jericho, Alta./Alb. 51° 30′ – 116° 06′ (82 N/9)	

wash

DES	See **breaker**	*Voir* **breaker**
OBS	Rare; N.S.	*Rare; N.-É.*
EQ		**brisants** (m.)
REL	reef, islet, ledge (1)	
EX	Sallys Wash, N.S./N.-É. 45° 21′ – 60° 59′ (11 F/7)	

Figure 66. Weeping Wall, overlooking the North Saskatchewan River, northwest of Lake Louise, Alberta.
(Alberta Culture – Historic Sites Service, RG 80-5-12)

Figure 66. Weeping Wall, muraille surplombant la rivière Saskatchewan Nord, au nord-ouest de Lake Louise, en Alberta.
(Alberta Culture – Historic Sites Service, RG 80-5-12)

water(s)

DES	A natural body of flowing or standing water.	*Étendue d'eau courante ou dormante naturelle.*
OBS	Applied to a variety of fresh and saltwater features, including bays, inlets, rivers, and chains of lakes. Used in Nfld., P.E.I., Ont., and B.C.	*S'emploie pour diverses étendues d'eau douce et salée, notamment des baies, des bras, des rivières et des chaînes de lacs. Relevé à T.-N., à l'Î.-P.-É., en Ont. et en C.-B.*
EQ		
REL	pond (1), marsh, gully (3), inlet (1), river	
EX	March Water (bay-baie), P.E.I./Î.-P.-É. 46° 31′ – 63° 43′ (11 L/12) Allan Water (river-rivière), Ont. 50° 33′ – 89° 45′ (52 I/12) Selkirk Water (inlet-bras), B.C./C.-B. 48° 26′ – 123° 23′ (92 B/6) Lockyers Waters (lakes-lacs), Nfld./T.-N. 47° 21′ – 53° 17′ (1 N/6)	

waterfall

DES	Variant of **fall**.	*Variante de **fall**.*
OBS	Rare in official names; B.C.	*Rare dans les noms approuvés; C.-B.*
EQ		**chute** (f.)
REL	cascade	
EX	Lord Waterfall, B.C./C.-B. 49° 53′ – 126° 46′ (92 E/15)	

way

DES	Narrow navigable stretch of water, giving access to a harbour.	*Voie d'eau étroite et navigable, débouchant sur un havre ou un port.*
OBS	Rare; N.S.	*Rare; N.-É.*
EQ		**passage** (m.)
REL	narrows, passage, inlet (1), channel (1)	
EX	Lockeport Western Way, N.S./N.-É. 43° 38′ – 65° 06′ (20 P/11)	

wedge

DES	Feature having the shape of a wedge.	*Accident géographique en forme de coin.*
OBS	Applied to mountains and peninsulas. Rare; N.S. and Alta.	*S'emploie pour des montagnes et des péninsules. Rare; N.-É. et Alb.*
EQ		
REL	peninsula	
EX	Tusket Wedge (peninsula-péninsule), N.S./N.-É. 43° 43' – 65° 59' (20 P/12) The Wedge (mountain-montagne), Alta./Alb. 50° 51' – 115° 07' (82 J/14)	

weir

DES	See **rapid (1)**	*Voir* **rapid (1)**
OBS	Rare in official names; N.S.	*Rare dans les noms officiels; N.-É.*
EQ		**rapide** (m.)
REL		
EX	Eel Weir, N.S./N.-É. 44° 20' – 65° 12' (21 A/6)	

woods

DES	Tract of treed land.	*Étendue de terrain peuplée d'arbres.*
OBS	Few officially named examples; Nfld., N.S., and Man.	*Rare dans les noms approuvés; T.-N., N.-É. et Man.*
EQ		**bois** (m.)
REL	bluff (2), tuck, grove	
EX	Black Rock Woods, N.S./N.-É. 45° 23' – 64° 23' (21 H/8) Oxbow Woods, Man. 50° 09' – 98° 22' (62 J/1) St. Shores Woods, Nfld./T.-N. 46° 40' – 53° 37' (1 K/12)	

xyz

Figures

Figures

299

Abbreviations of Generic Terms

Some generic terms, such as "archipelago", "glacier" and "mountain", are fairly long words which often require abbreviation to meet space limitations or to avoid their repetition in a series of names.

As no one standard exists for Canadian use, different publishers use their own abbreviations. Neither the ACGAN, nor its parent body, the CPCGN, has a mandate to standardize abbreviations. Therefore, some short forms used by national mapping and charting organizations are listed below for the information of users of this glossary. The first column lists the generic; the second column shows the abbreviations found on past or present Canadian nautical charts produced by the Canadian Hydrographic Service; the third column shows those abbreviations accepted for use on maps of the National Topographic System which are produced by the Surveys and Mapping Branch, Energy, Mines and Resources Canada.

Abréviations des génériques

Certains génériques, comme «archipel», «glacier» et «montagne», sont des mots assez longs qu'il est souvent nécessaire d'abréger pour les faire entrer dans un espace déterminé, ou pour masquer une répétition.

La façon d'abréger les génériques varie d'un éditeur à l'autre, car il n'existe pas au Canada de norme en ce domaine. Or, il n'appartient pas au Comité consultatif de la nomenclature glaciologique et alpine ni au CPCNG de normaliser les abréviations. Aussi, nous énumérons ci-dessous, à titre d'information, quelques abréviations d'emploi courant dans les organismes nationaux de cartographie. La première colonne contient les génériques, la deuxième les abréviations utilisées jusqu'à maintenant sur les cartes nautiques produites par le Service hydrographique du Canada et la troisième, les abréviations qu'il est convenu d'employer sur les cartes du Système national de référence cartographique que produit la Direction des levés et de la cartographie, au ministère de l'Énergie, des Mines et des Ressources.

Generic/ générique	C.H.S./ S.H.C.	S. & M./ L. et C.
Anchorage	Anch, Anche	Anch
Archipel	Arch	Arch
Archipelago	Arch	Arch
Baie	B	B
Bank	Bk	
Banks	Bks	
Bay	B	B

Generic/ générique	C.H.S./ S.H.C.	S. & M./ L. et C.
Branch		Br
Brook	Bk, Br	Bk
Canal (E) (F)		Can
Cap	C	C
Cape	C	C
Channel	Ch, Chan	Chan
Chenal	Ch	Chen
Cours d'eau		C d'eau
Cove	C	C
Creek	Cr	Ck
Crique	Cr	Cr
Détroit		Dt
Dome	Dm	
Dôme	Dm	
Entrance	Ent	
Estuaire	Est	
Étang		Étg
Fiord	Fd	Fd
Fjord	Fd	Fd
Fleuve		Fl
Glacier (E)	Gl	Gla
Glacier (F)	Gl	Glac
Golfe	G	G
Goulet		Goul
Ground	Gd, Gr, Grd	
Gulf	G	G
Harbour	Harb, Hbr, Hr	Hr
Haut-fond		Ht-fond
Haven	Hn	
Head	Hd	Hd
Headland	Hd	
Île	I	Î
Îles	Is	
Îlet	It	
Îlets	Its	

Generic/générique	C.H.S./S.H.C.	S. & M./L. et C.
Îlot	It	
Îlots	Its	
Inlet	Int	In
Island	I	I
Islands	Is	
Islet	It	It
Islets	Its	
Isthmus		Isth
Lac	L	L
Lagoon	Lag	Lag
Lagune	Lag	Lag
Lake	L	L
Landing	Ldg, Lndg	Ldg
Ledge	Le	
Ledges	Les	
Loch	L	
Lough	L	
Mont	Mt	Mt
Montagne	Mtn	Mgne
Montagnes	Mtns	
Mouillage	Mouil	Mouill
Mount	Mt	Mt
Mountain	Mtn	Mtn
Mountains	Mtns	
Narrows	Nars, Nrs	Nrs
Passage (E)	Pass	Pass
Passage (F)	Pass	Pge
Peak	Pk	Pk
Peninsula	Pen	Pen
Péninsule	Pen	Pénins
Point	Pt	Pt
Pointe	Pte	Pte
Pond	P	Pd
Presqu'île		Presq'Î
Promontoire	Prom	Promt
Promontory	Prom	Prom

Generic/ générique	C.H.S./ S.H.C.	S. & M./ L. et C.
Rade	Rd	
Range		Rge
Rapides	R	
Rapids	R	
Récif	Rf	Rf
Récifs	Rfs	
Reef	Rf	Rf
Reefs	Rfs	
Reservoir		Res
Réservoir		Rvoir
River	R	R
Rivière	R	Riv
Roadstead	Rd	
Roche	R	
Rocher	R	Roch
Rock	R, Rk	Rk
Rocks	Rks	
Ruisseau	Ruis	Ruiss
Shoal	Sh, Shl	Sh
Sound	Sd	Sd
Strait	Str	Str
Stream	Str	Stm
Vallée		Vall
Valley		Val

Bibliography

Bibliographie

This short, annotated bibliography cites some works that were useful in the preparation of this glossary. It is not a comprehensive or complete listing of works consulted, but should prove useful for anyone wishing to explore generic terminology and definitions in more detail.

Cette courte bibliographie analytique cite certains ouvrages qui ont servi à la préparation de ce glossaire. Elle ne représente pas une liste détaillée et complète de tous les ouvrages consultés, mais elle sera utile pour quiconque désire étudier en détail les définitions et la terminologie des génériques.

Baker, B.B., Jr., W.R. Deebel and R.D. Geisenderfer, ed. *Glossary of Oceanographic Terms*. 2nd ed. Washington: United States Naval Oceanographic Office, 1966, vi, 204 p. (Special Publication, SP-35)

A good, comprehensive glossary, although now a little dated. It includes descriptive definitions for most marine and shoreline generics.

Ce glossaire est utile et complet, mais quelque peu désuet. Il comprend des définitions descriptives de la plupart des termes génériques relatifs à l'océan et au littoral.

Bates, Robert L. and Julia A. Jackson, ed. *Glossary of Geology*. 2nd ed. Falls Creek, Va.: American Geological Institute, 1980, x, 751 p.

The standard geological dictionary, including many generics defined from a geological viewpoint.

Le dictionnaire géologique par excellence, qui comprend des définitions géologiques de bon nombre de termes génériques.

Blackshaw, Alan. *Mountaineering: From Hill Walking to Alpine Climbing.* Harmondsworth, GB: Penguin, 1970, 552 p. (Penguin Handbook, PH103)

This contains a glossary of Gaelic, Norse, and Welsh words contained in British place names; some of these terms have been transferred to Canada.

Cet ouvrage contient un glossaire des mots gaéliques, norses et gallois utilisés dans les toponymes britanniques; certains de ces mots sont également utilisés au Canada.

Blais, Suzelle. *Apport de la toponymie ancienne aux études sur le français québécois et nord-américain : documents cartographiques du régime français.* Québec: Gouvernement du Québec, Commission de toponymie, 1983, ix, 105 p. (Études et recherches toponymiques, 6)

This recent and highly informative publication is particularly useful for geographers, linguists, and philologists. It emphasizes place names that are directly related to everyday language, but with particular reference to New France.

Ce récent ouvrage a une grande portée documentaire. Il est d'un intérêt particulier non seulement pour le géographe, mais aussi pour le linguiste et le philologue. L'accent est mis sur les toponymes directement reliés au vocabulaire commun, mais propres à la Nouvelle-France.

Canadian Permanent Committee on Geographical Names. *Gazetteer of Canada/ Répertoire géographique du Canada.* Ottawa: Dept. of Energy, Mines and Resources, Surveys and Mapping Branch, 1972-

This is the current series of gazetteers, published for the two territories and for each province, except Quebec. Most volumes have a glossary of generic terms as used in the particular jurisdiction.

Il s'agit de la série courante des répertoires géographiques publiés pour les deux territoires et pour chaque province sauf le Québec. La plupart des volumes contiennent un glossaire des termes génériques utilisés dans chaque juridiction.

Canadian Permanent Committee on Geographical Names. Advisory Committee on Undersea Feature Names. *Gazetteer of Undersea Feature Names, 1983/ Répertoire des noms d'entités sous-marines, 1983.* Ottawa: Dept. of Fisheries and Oceans, 1983, vi, 191 p.

This contains an excellent glossary of terms and definitions in French and English; several are used verbatim in the present work.

Cet ouvrage contient un excellent glossaire, en anglais et en français, de termes et définitions, dont plusieurs sont utilisés textuellement dans le présent volume.

Conseil international de la langue française. *Vocabulaire de la géomorphologie et index allemand et anglais.* Paris: Hachette; La maison du dictionnaire, c1979, 218 p.

This French-language publication contains terms and definitions, along with synonyms, related terms, and whenever possible, English and German equivalents. However, the CILF recommends that these equivalents be used with care. This book is well structured and easy to use.

Cet ouvrage français offre des génériques avec définitions, synonymes, termes reliés et équivalents en langue anglaise et allemande (aussi souvent que possible): cependant, le CILF recommande d'utiliser ces équivalents avec précaution. Ce vocabulaire est un ouvrage bien structuré et facile de consultation.

Conseil international de la langue française. *Vocabulaire de l'océanologie.* Paris: C.I.L.F.; Hachette, c1976, 431 p.

This publication reflects new ideas in oceanography. Prepared by experts in a variety of fields, it offers a comprehensive and specialized collection of oceanographic terms.

Cette publication est le reflet direct des conceptions nouvelles de l'Homme vis-à-vis de l'océan et regroupe en un tout cohérent des notions de l'océanologie souvent dispersées. Il s'agit d'un lexique spécialisé car le choix des termes est strictement océanologique et est le fruit d'un travail de spécialistes de disciplines variées.

A Dictionary of Geography. By Francis John Monkhouse. 2nd ed. London, GB: Edward Arnold, 1970, vi, 378 p.

One of the best general dictionaries of geographical terms.

Cet ouvrage est un des meilleurs dictionnaires généraux des termes géographiques.

Dictionary of Geography. Ed. by Sir Laurence Dudley Stamp. New York: Wiley, 1966, xv, 492 p.

Strong British emphasis and rather dated, but it contains many historical references along the lines of the *Oxford English Dictionary.*

Cet ouvrage un peu désuet est doté d'un accent britannique marqué; il contient de nombreuses références historiques qui rappellent l'*Oxford English Dictionary.*

Dictionary of Newfoundland English. Ed. by G.M. Story, W.J. Kirwin and J.D.A. Widdowson. Toronto: University of Toronto Press, c1982, lxxvii, 625 p.

A fascinating and scholarly book, including over 100 generic terms found in the toponymy of Newfoundland.

Cet ouvrage captivant et érudit comprend plus d'une centaine de termes génériques retrouvés dans la toponymie de Terre-Neuve.

Dictionnaire de la géographie. Sous la dir. de Pierre George. 2e éd. rev. et augm. Paris: Presses universitaires de France, 1974, c1970, 451 p.

This unilingual French publication presents an image of the world from a geographical point of view. It gives an alphabetical listing of terms and definitions used in both earth and human sciences, and comments on them. The book is both reliable and easy to use.

Cet ouvrage unilingue français offre une image géographique du monde en définissant et commentant le vocabulaire des Sciences de la Terre et de l'Homme. Les termes sont présentés par ordre alphabétique. Ce volume est fiable et agréable à consulter.

Dictionnaire de l'eau. Par l'Association québécoise des techniques de l'eau, Comité d'étude des termes de l'eau et l'Office de la langue française. Québec: OLF, 1981, xiv, 544 p.

This dictionary, prepared by engineers from the Association québécoise des techniques de l'eau and terminologists from the Office de la langue française, is the first book published by the Office that was produced entirely by computer. Reliable and easy to use, it contains terms and definitions, as well as English equivalents.

Ce dictionnaire est le premier ouvrage de l'Office entièrement réalisé avec l'aide de l'ordinateur. Facile de consultation, cette publication fiable offre des termes avec définitions et des équivalents anglais. Ont collaboré à cet ouvrage, les ingénieurs de l'Association québécoise des techniques de l'eau ainsi que les terminologues de l'Office.

Dictionnaire nord-américain de la langue française. Par Louis-Alexandre Bélisle; dir. du projet, Hervé Jolin; correct.-rev. Geneviève Pommaret Borrel, Monique Patris Jolin. Éd. ent. ref. comprenant: suppléments de biographies, histoire, géographie et des plus importantes villes du monde avec leur population. Montréal: Beauchemin, c1979, 1196 p.

This general modern language dictionary contains terms and expressions used by authors from Acadia, Quebec, Louisiana, and New England. It is both reliable and easy to use, and is a reflection of the French language spoken in North America.

Il s'agit d'un dictionnaire général de la langue vivante dans lequel l'usager retrouve des termes et des expressions relevés dans des écrits d'auteurs originaires de l'Acadie, du Québec, de la Louisiane et de la Nouvelle-Angleterre. Cette source fiable et de consultation facile, est un reflet du français parlé en Amérique du Nord.

Hydrographic Dictionary, Pt. 1/Dictionnaire hydrographique, part. 1. By International Hydrographic Bureau. 3rd ed. Monaco: IHB, 1974, 370 p. (Special Publication, 32)

This dictionary covers all fields in the science of hydrography. The English terms and expressions are presented alphabetically, and they and their definitions are also given in French. The book includes an index of French terms. It is one of the most reliable books of its kind.

Ce dictionnaire touche à toutes les disciplines qu'englobe l'hydrographie. Les termes et expressions ainsi que leurs définitions sont bilingues et présentés par ordre alphabétique anglais. L'usager y retrouve à la fin un index français de toute la terminologie répertoriée. Cette publication compte parmi les plus fiables.

Sealock, Richard Burl, Margaret M. Sealock, and Margaret S. Powell. *Bibliography of Place-Name Literature: United States and Canada.* 3rd ed. Chicago: American Library Association, 1982, xii, 435 p.

A good starting point for general research on toponymy.

Cet ouvrage représente un bon point de départ pour la recherche en toponymie.

Vocabulaire de terminologie géographique. Préparé sous la dir. de Jean-Claude Fortin, collab. Réal Dumoulin. Éd. provisoire. Québec: Gouvernement du Québec, Commission de toponymie, 1985, 47 p.

This unilingual French publication reflects the character of the Quebec landscape. The 185 generics that have been standardized or recommended in the *Gazette officielle du Québec* are defined according to the geographical features found in Quebec. This highly useful book is the result of serious and competent work.

Cette publication unilingue française reflète les réalités du paysage québécois; en effet, les 185 génériques normalisés ou recommandés dans la *Gazette officielle du Québec* au moment de la parution de cette publication, sont définis conformément aux réalités géographiques du Québec. Cet ouvrage fort utile est le résultat d'un travail effectué avec sérieux et compétence.

Webster's New Geographical Dictionary. Springfield, Mass.: Merriam-Webster, c1984, xxix, 1376 p.

Based largely on the *Webster's Third International Dictionary.*

Cet ouvrage se fonde largement sur le *Webster's Third International Dictionary*.

Wheeler, Arthur O. *The Selkirk Mountains: A Guide for Mountain Climbers and Pilgrims.* Winnipeg: Stovel Co., c1912, various pagings.

This contains an appendix on mountain terminology. The book and its author were influential in the development of mountain terminology in British Columbia and Alberta.

Cet ouvrage contient une annexe sur la terminologie des montagnes. L'ouvrage et son auteur ont grandement influencé l'utilisation de la terminologie alpine dans les montagnes en Colombie-Britannique et en Alberta.